T0365100

Women and False Choice
The Truth about Sexism

How to Fight Sexism in the Workplace

Muna Jawhary (PhD)

BALBOA.
PRESS
A DIVISION OF HAY HOUSE

Copyright © 2014 Muna Jawhary.

All rights reserved. No part of this book may be used or reproduced by any means, graphic, electronic, or mechanical, including photocopying, recording, taping or by any information storage retrieval system without the written permission of the publisher except in the case of brief quotations embodied in critical articles and reviews.

Balboa Press books may be ordered through booksellers or by contacting:

Balboa Press
A Division of Hay House
1663 Liberty Drive
Bloomington, IN 47403
www.balboapress.com
1 (877) 407-4847

Because of the dynamic nature of the Internet, any web addresses or links contained in this book may have changed since publication and may no longer be valid. The views expressed in this work are solely those of the author and do not necessarily reflect the views of the publisher, and the publisher hereby disclaims any responsibility for them.

The author of this book does not dispense medical advice or prescribe the use of any technique as a form of treatment for physical, emotional, or medical problems without the advice of a physician, either directly or indirectly. The intent of the author is only to offer information of a general nature to help you in your quest for emotional and spiritual well-being. In the event you use any of the information in this book for yourself, which is your constitutional right, the author and the publisher assume no responsibility for your actions.

Any people depicted in stock imagery provided by Thinkstock are models, and such images are being used for illustrative purposes only. Certain stock imagery © Thinkstock.

Printed in the United States of America.

ISBN: 978-1-4525-2074-2 (sc)
ISBN: 978-1-4525-2075-9 (e)

Balboa Press rev. date: 10/14/2014

To all the women past, present and future:
May you always speak your truth.

"Read about the women in the bible, Esther, Ruth, Martha, Mary, these women changed the world forever"
http://www.youtube.com/watch?v=uWi5iXnguTU)

"The emotional, sexual, and psychological stereotyping of females begins when the doctor says, 'it's a girl'."
Republican Shirley Chisholm (The first African-American woman elected to congress, 1972 presidential candidate)

CONTENTS

Acknowledgements

For my mother
who is behind all this ....

For Farrah and Emry
who light up my world every waking moment.....

and

For Mark
whose care and support made it all possible

WHY THIS BOOK?

I was attending a corporate dinner one evening, sitting next to a hedge fund owner and having a conversation about life, work and childcare. I asked him about their family situation and whether his wife works or not. He responded *automatically*: "we have two boys and my wife stopped working to look after them." Perhaps reading the question still hanging in my mind "why did she, and not him, stop working to look after the children?" he added quickly and emphatically: "she made a choice, it was *her* choice".

It was one of those light bulb moments, when something that was lingering at the back of one's mind suddenly clicks in place: society claims that women are free to make their own life-career choices, when in fact women have little or no choice in the matter. In male dominated societies, the choices that women make when they have children are severely constrained by men's unwillingness to share care, and by outdated work norms that are designed for those who are 'care free'.[1]

In the fast moving, cutthroat, globalised capitalist markets of today, working full time and all hours god sent is seen as a badge of honour; flexibility, particularly part time, is seen as the kiss of death to one's career. Those who ask for flexibility are seen as uncommitted and are passed on for pay, promotion and career development. Very few employers offer genuinely flexible work and almost none is offered at management or executive levels. Furthermore, women are still seen as the ones who '*should*' care for children and the elderly in society. Given that, flexible work is synonymous with 'caring women' and works as a

---

[1]   A term coined by Hanlon, 2012.

vehicle to putting their careers on permanently lower trajectories than those of 'care free men'. Since women themselves believe they are the ones who should care, they believe that working full time and long hours, which is the only route to success in capitalist economies, will lose them not only a good quality family life but also their own peace of mind in fulfilling their destiny as women.

I was quite taken by my interlocutor's archetypal alpha male confidence regarding his status in society, in the workplace and in his own home. There was no questioning on his part of all the social layers that led his wife to this 'choice': of putting men's careers first; of masculinising the workplace to such an extent that success is all or nothing; of women still assuming all of the care responsibilities in the twenty first century; of society's inauthentic approach to women's work, asking them to work on the one hand, but refusing to offer genuine enough support to keep them on similar career tracks to men. I turned to my interlocutor and said that I don't believe that his wife had a real choice; I believe instead that she had a "false" choice. I still remember the discomfort with which my statement was received by my dinner companion, since I seemed to question the *raison d'être* of his social identity.

This was the spark for writing this book.

The interest in the subject of sex equality, however, has been a lifelong obsession. Why women and men exist in a hierarchy in society, rather than have the same status and start from a level playing field, and why women and men have a different sense of entitlement in life have been a source of endless fascination to me. From a very young age, I was aware of my mother's frustration for not being allowed to further her education beyond high school, while her brothers were encouraged to do so. Like many other parts of the world, the Middle East where my mother grew up viewed young men's education as 'useful' but young women's education as an obstacle to finding husbands, getting married and having children. My mother was super intelligent, with a curiosity about the physical world in which we lived and how everything in it worked that was matched only by the most illustrious of scientists. Her family's decision to deprive her of understanding the nuts and bolts of science, through higher education, was therefore a stab in the heart. With this going on in my immediate background, I was highly sensitised to the frustration of women's ambitions by society's rigid rules that still differ for girls from boys and for women from men.

I did my absolute best to make my life different from my mother's, to avoid repeating her fate. I moved away from the Middle East, acquired not one or two but four university degrees, managed to have a high flying career and staved off marriage till I was nearly forty. And yet, once my first child was born, a spanner was thrown in the wheel that was my career. A high flying career and looking after children are not compatible. So I slowed down, came back to earth and got myself a modest research job. And yet, every evening there was this unspoken struggle between myself and my boss, who knew I had an infant, about the appropriate time to leave work. I needed to sneak in half an hour to see her before she went to bed. On the occasions that I managed to do that, which was never before 6:30 p.m., I was met with disapproval and reprimand next day. Had I stayed the extra half hour, the argument went, my research product would have been infinitely better. After two years of these machinations and of having missed two years of my daughter's life (since half an hour in the morning and half in the evening don't really count as knowing your child), I threw in the towel and resigned from work. Sitting at home without a job and looking after an infant struck me as not significantly different from my mother's fate. It hit me very hard. I needed to know what is it about contemporary societies that even in Europe women do not advance in life and in their careers as much as men do. It felt like a real calling for me to find ways and means to push the frontiers for women's accomplishments in life. My own way of pushing the frontiers has always been in 'questioning' the *status quo*, and on this occasion I did it through writing.

My curiosity about why do men *still* have more success and a higher status in society than women was piqued by the comments of the hedge fund owner. I was intrigued to say the least why in the 21st century Western societies still have the conditions that allow men to believe that they are more entitled to success than women. Things have changed considerably in the last fifty years, and women's position in society is not as inferior to men's as it was before the second wave of feminism. But nor is it equal. Why is that?

INTRODUCTION

"It ain't what you know that gets you in trouble.
It's what you know for sure that just ain't so."
Mark Twain *(Author and humorist)*

The two waves of feminism vocalised an objection to women's subordinate position in society and mobilised significant social forces toward equalising women's status with that of men. Countless campaigns, laws, riots, books, workshops, seminars etc. have addressed the issue of sex inequality since then, but have they made a difference? Without a doubt: a good number of us watching an episode of Mad Men could be looking at our mothers, rather than our grandmothers, serving coffee in the office and being sexually harassed by male executives. A more relevant question therefore is why does sex inequality persist despite these monumental efforts? Why do women still have a lower status in society than men?

With the momentum of the second wave all but dissipated, sex equality does not look achievable in our life time, or even in our children's life time; the methods used so far have made a significant difference but have not been effective in eradicating sexism. What I believe is missing is that we haven't yet fully unmasked gender for what it is: a thick and needless layer of social conditioning. Instead, we are still attempting to eradicate sexism by making 'gender beliefs' more equal. This stance implicitly accepts gender as a template for who women and men are, for organising the relationship between them and for organising their relationship with society. But like a class system, gender is an artificial social system that has built in division and difference. It is designed in the first place to differentiate between people using artificial criteria, allowing one group of people to have privilege that is denied to other groups in order to maintain their higher status in society. And just as it is not enough to say that all individuals within a class system are equal to bring about social equality, since the very existence of such a system has inequality built rigidly into it, it is not enough to say that women should have equal rights to men, while maintaining their gender identity in place. The gender system is predicated on difference and division between women and men, granting men the higher status and women the subordinate in society, because men are perceived to have superior qualities that enable them to amass resources, power and prestige. Gender, in other words, has sexism built into it and to eradicate sex inequality from the gender system is an oxymoron. What is needed instead is the eradication of the gender system itself. And yet, our blind spot to what gender really is can be gleaned from the interchangeable use in common language of 'sex', indicating whether we are female or male, and 'gender'.

So what is gender?

Gender is the collection of ideas about who we are as women and men; the agreements we reach in society about the rules of engagement governing women's and men's actions; and the practices we put in place to allow women and men to fulfil their gender roles. The women and men conceived by the gender system are socially constructed; their traits, attributes, dispositions and behaviours are construed in a way that meets gender prescriptions for each sex. Society creates an extensive array of institutions, structures and social patterns to help boys and girls and men and women internalise these attributes and behaviours, in order for gender to be created and recreated. Gender identity becomes a straight jacket that is difficult for most of us to escape, given the high agreement in society regarding gender rules of engagement. Furthermore, as we act and re-enact gender over the millennia, our gender identity becomes indistinguishable from who we truly are. Inevitably, whenever the real self is not honoured but replaced by a socially constructed identity, alienation and unhappiness set in. It is perhaps not an exaggeration to say that the alienation created by gender is a major contributor to the currently high levels of human unhappiness.

The thrust of the gender system is that women are more suited for childcare and men are more suited for work outside the home. Implicitly, the gender system assumes that women have the innate qualities of emotional connection, nurturance and empathy and men the innate qualities of rationality, decision making and leadership. The least benign aspect of gender as a social system is the qualities that it leaves out from men's and women's personalities, namely emotional competence in men and professional competence in women. With men seen as emotionally incompetent and women as professionally incompetent, gender ends are served as women continue to be assigned care, even when they work, and men continue to be assigned work, even when they care. As men thrive in public life, amassing resources, power and prestige in the process, and women thrive in the home, caring not only for their young ones but also for their male partners, the gender hierarchy is held firmly in place.

The implications of this gender dogma on women's and men's lives are profound.

Seeing women in society primarily as providers of care and service robs them of full self-expression; of creating a self that goes well beyond being of service to others to include what each individual woman might find fulfilling. Furthermore, service in the way society constructs women as providers of, is one of subservience rather than one of privilege, which is evident from its elimination from men's socially constructed self. Many women are gripped by depression when their children leave home, because their self-concept does not go beyond serving their loved ones. Similarly, many men suffer debilitating self-doubt on retirement, because the male self-concept does not go far beyond economic provision. When the socially constructed *raison d'être* for women and men is no longer present, they construe themselves as 'useless' to society and their self-worth suffers accordingly.

But is it possible to change a dogma that has been with us for millennia? This book argues that it is. Ideas are just that, ideas! They change over time, and there is nothing new in that. The earth was flat one day, and now it is spherical. All planets revolved around the earth one day, and now they together with the earth revolve around the sun. Genes were immutable one day, and now they interact with the environment in a two way dance. And these are scientific ideas, subject to overly rigorous tests and proofs. Social ideas that attempt to understand and explain the human condition are far more elusive and difficult to prove. We can and we have changed them as suited as over the centuries. Slavery was once the norm, now the mere thought that it was practiced at some point in time is abhorrent to us. The same is true of apartheid. And these are two good examples of an imbalance in the rights and privileges given to different social groups. As far as social concepts relating to women and men go, while it was acceptable that women didn't vote at the turn of the twentieth century, or that married women couldn't join the civil service or women in general were not allowed to participate in sports, it is now considered anomalous. These ideas were not arbitrary, but arose from assumptions held about women's minds and bodies, in the form of commonsense beliefs that were seen as truths - in the case of banning women from sports, the issue received emphatic backing from the medical profession at the time.[2] More recently, attitudes and behaviour toward women that were prevalent in the fifties and sixties are now considered highly sexist.

What is evident therefore is that at any given point in time we live our life within a framework of ideas that seem to us like the truth. But when a challenge is posed to these ideas, and sometimes this is all it takes for social change to happen, we move away from that framework toward a new set of ideas to which we assign the 'truth', and so on.

---

[2]   Archer and Lloyd, 2002: 4.

By the same token, ideas governing sex roles and sex relations are constantly changing and yet, at any given point in time, they seem appropriate and 'normal'; until a challenge is posed that is. A challenge to the idea of men being the sole bread winners has gathered such momentum that the majority of women in the OECD countries nowadays engage in paid work. However, sex roles and sex relations within the home have only been challenged slightly, and are therefore still largely based on gender precepts. In the workplace too, the original template for work design and organisation has not changed commensurately with the dramatic rise in women's participation in paid work, but still rather resemble the template that accommodated a predominantly male labour force all those decades ago. These aspects reflect more accurately that at a societal level, conceptions of men's masculinity and women's femininity, which are at the heart of designing gender roles and therefore sex inequality, of assigning care to women and work to men, have only undergone cosmetic change and that there is considerable work to be done still.

In this book I will open up the question of what is masculinity and what is femininity and are men masculine only and women feminine only, to uncover the reasons for our resistance to changing sex roles which is the key to unlocking sex equality. I will show our fundamental errors, misunderstandings and misconceptions about those aspects of our humanity and offer an alternative way of embracing masculinity and femininity, not only in our self-concept as women and men, but also in our organisations and our societies at large.

The discussion in this book is mainly relevant to post industrial Western societies for a good reason. In these societies, sex equality discourses and closing the gap between women's and men's achievements are most advanced, as is the body of laws overseeing sex equality. As Archer and Lloyd put it: "(n)o longer is there an unquestioned consensus about what is the natural order regarding women and men."[3] Hence, the persistence

---

[3]   Ibid: 1.

of sex inequality in these societies is most illuminating in terms of the obstacles remaining to achieving equal outcomes in status between women and men.

I will rely mostly on data covering the OECD countries, and drill into the conditions prevalent in the Nordic countries, where sex equality discourses are most advanced; as is the policy framework guiding women's work and equality in the workplace . Looking at these countries makes it starkly obvious that assigning the role of care giving to women, which has been the hidden pitfall of policies in the Nordic countries', has seriously undermined their efforts to achieving sex equality. Consequently, even in countries like Sweden and Norway, that have a long history of supporting women's work, the male-female gap in pay and promotion remains stubbornly pronounced. The blind spot of assigning care primarily to women has fed into sex inequality the world over, and in this book I will explore the practical issues that can help transform this area of our lives, particularly in the workplace.

The book has six chapters. Each chapter is written as a standalone essay and can be read separately. However, the themes are highly interconnected and there is a logical main argument running from beginning to end. The main argument of the book cannot be fully understood without reading the whole book. Chapter I challenges traditional ways of looking at and comparing women's and men's achievements and brings in the new sciences of neuroplasticity and epigenetics to remove any remaining doubt about the inseparability of environment and behaviour, suggesting strongly that studies of sex differences that don't have this integrative framework are obsolete. Chapter II looks at the social construction of gender identities and the rigidities built into the constructs of femininity and masculinity that keep 'emotionally incompetent' men on the breadwinner track, and 'professionally incompetent' women on the mommy track. Chapter III looks at gender as a belief system. The chapter delves deeper into the social psychology of gender beliefs and into the human subconscious, revealing its amazing powers in keeping archaic gender beliefs intact in the 21st century. Chapter IV presents the state of play in educational and employment outcomes for women and men and looks closer at the reasons behind the persistence of an achievement gap between the two sexes. The chapter examines the social environment in which women and men make education and employment choices, and focuses on how Nordic countries' sex equality discourses have impacted professional outcomes for women and men. Chapter V examines in great detail the organisation of the workplace along gendered lines and the resistance to new ways of organising work and looking at leadership. The chapter re-examines our constructs of femininity and masculinity and questions the validity of the way in which we view men as masculine and women as feminine. In this chapter, I offer a new way of looking at, embracing and integrating the feminine and the masculine that promises to eradicate sexism not only from our self-concept, but from the work environment and from society at large. Chapter VI synthesises the why and how of the persistence of sexism in the 21st century; highlights the true cost of adhering to gender principles; offers a new way of viewing and embracing masculinity and femininity that not only frees the human mind from sexism, but also leads to fulfilment in our personal life.

I

WHY HAS EQUALITY
ELUDED WOMEN?

"When the mind took over and humans lost touch with the reality
of their divine essence, they started to think of God as a male figure.
Society became male-dominated, and the female was made subordinate
to the male." Eckhart Tolle (Spiritual teacher and author)[4]

Many of us wonder how come that in the 2nd decade of the 21st century, after decades of social transformation, relentless activism for sex equality and a sea of change in antidiscrimination laws, the workplace is still far more conducive to men's success than women's? And how come that men are still far more likely than women to engage in paid employment, to be fully employed, to have prestigious jobs, to secure high pay and to attain executive positions, even though young women exceed young men in secondary and tertiary educational attainment in OECD countries?

Inevitably, these questions can only be answered by looking, first, at how women and men make family and career choices during their life course, which in turn takes us down the difficult route of differences between men and women.

---

[4] Tolle, 2010: 165.

I.1   Equality *vs.* Sameness

"All through life there were distinctions - toilets for men, toilets for women; clothes for men, clothes for women - then, at the end, the graves are identical." Leila Aboulela (Author)

It should be obvious that equality doesn't mean sameness, and so the presence of difference between men and women does not mean they cannot or should not be equal. But the two issues have been muddled to a considerable degree over the last few decades, as one issue, namely sameness, is hijacked to prove or disprove the need for, or the plausibility of, the other, namely equality. On one side, the discussion of differences between men and women has been used to subliminally advertise men's superiority, and justify the exclusion of women from certain areas of public life. Such arguments tend to rest on the effects of hormones in shaping male and female brains in 'essentially' different ways. Boys' brains, it is argued, are best suited for 'systemising' due to the higher amounts of prenatal testosterone in a male, compared with a female, foetuses, giving them an advantage in maths and science skills. Lower testosterone in girls on the other hand predisposes their brains to 'empathising', giving females an advantage in childcare and other caring professions.[5]

On the other side, many feminist writers, lawyers, and activists vehemently deny the presence of any discernible differences beyond reproductive capacities between the two sexes, to make the case for equality more clear cut. For example, in a legal case brought by an employer challenging a California law that requires employers to provide pregnancy and maternity leave, lawyers representing the American Civil Liberties Union filed a brief in the Supreme Court opposing special treatment for women, arguing in part that pregnancy should be treated

---

[5]   See for example Baron-Cohen, 2004; see Fine, 2010, for an extended discussion with more references.

as one of a number of temporary disabilities warranting accommodation by employer. "This position reflected the belief that codifying 'difference' would work against women, since historically, women's capacity for bearing children has been the rationale for excluding them from public roles and high paying jobs."[6]

While the 'no difference' stance was behind the successful legislation of many anti discrimination laws and has had a profound impact on neutralising sex biased practices in the workplace, it does have its own set of problems. *First,* it contradicts ordinary men's and women's every day experience of thinking, talking, and behaving differently, of having different preferences and making different choices in life, and hence it alienates the very people it intends to help. *Second,* it has not been sufficient by itself in bringing about equality, because it doesn't pose a fundamental challenge to male-shaped institutions, since women are expected to follow a path forged by men to success. *Third,* by not tackling the issue of difference head on, many questions are left unanswered, the most important of which is why do mothers invariably assume the primary care position? The assumption of primary care responsibilities by women does not allow them to work as productively as men, in a man-made workplace, with profound consequences for their participation in public life.

The belief that there are *innate* differences between women and men is deeply ingrained in most of us that we don't question it as anything but the truth; to argue therefore that we are not different as women and men without explicating why and how we still *appear* to be distinctly different doesn't advance the equality conversation, let alone its practice. It is my intention in this book to elucidate why we appear different when we may not be in reality, and that the reason that makes us appear so different is the same as that which gives sexism a firm grip on our societies: namely our faulty, sexist system of thought.

---

6   Glenn, Chang and Rennie Forcey, 1994: 2.

Here is an example of a wholehearted acceptance of innate differences stated in deliberations that feed into the highest level of policy making, that of the Council of Europe which stated in 1998: "*it is important to understand that men and women have different living conditions which are only partly due to childbearing but also to their different make up emotionally, physiologically, and mentally. Ideally these differences should not have a negative impact on their position in society and in the work place*".[7] But that ideal has never been achieved, as women have not yet been able to assert themselves as different from men and yet equally deserving of the same status, with serious implications for every aspect of their lives.

I.2   Our Shameless Androcentricity

Historically, men were taken as the benchmark for human development and there has not been until recently a theoretical framework for understating women's development that wasn't based on a comparison to men. This is behind feminist scholarship scepticism of knowledge in general, because "while it claims to be universal and objective, it is in reality based on knowledge primarily from men's lives".[8] Even accounts of human evolution neglected the female side of human life until the mid- to late-1970s, when women anthropologists became active in the field.[9]

Our awareness of this history doesn't necessarily immunise us against applying andocentric norms when sex comparisons are made. Whenever we talk about sex differences, say in confidence, we automatically use men as the benchmark and assume that they are confident and women are under confident, rather than assume that women are confident and

---

[7]   Mosley, O'Reilly, and Schömannand, 2002: 114.

[8]   Tickner (2005), quoted in Halpern, 2011: chapter 1, section 5, subsection 2, para. 2.

[9]   Archer and Lloyd, 2002: 6.

men over confident, which may be closer to the mark – we could then deal with men's over confidence as *the* issue, as it may very well mask resistance to dealing with vulnerability, a subject that I will deal with in the next chapter.

No more is the andocentric bias relevant than in the highly masculinised workplace that is largely organised around an 'ideal' worker who is available to work long hours, has an uninterrupted career, and can respond promptly to organisational demands.[10] The underlying assumption is that this worker has no care responsibilities, or is 'care free'. Instead, it is assumed that someone else is taking care of the worker's family and his household responsibilities, including the worker himself, for no society has ever assumed that primary care is anything other than a woman's responsibility. This paradigm has meant that labour market outcomes do not necessarily reflect women's real, but highly constrained or *false*, choices.

Taking man as the template of human development has the implicit assumption that man is superior to women, which is still a strongly held belief in most societies, particularly when it comes to achievement. Achievement in a workplace that is designed with the characteristics of the ideal worker in mind would inaccurately measure women's success, because society is ascribing achievement according to a principle based on difference between women and men[11] - that of women being caring and men care free.

In their book that compares work-life balance in four European countries, Fine-Davis et al. (2004) argue that *"When one studies the life course of Europeans over the last 30-40 years, one is struck by an amazing asymmetry: beginning with educated women and eventually extending to most, we detect a clear masculinisation of women biographies. Women are*

---

[10]   Lyonette and Crompton, 2008.
[11]   See Bakan 1966: 113.

converging with men in educational attainment, in participation rates and, especially, in life-long employment. The amazing thing is that women have done all the changing while men stubbornly cling to a life course model that closely resembles that of their fathers and grandfathers."[12]

"It is not surprising therefore that, with few exceptions, those women who are intent on making it to the top tend to emulate male style behaviour and management, knowing full well that 'male-defined' strengths are the currency of promotion."[13] Studies have found that differences between men and women tend to diminish the higher up the organisation one went. Unlike their counterparts in middle management, women leaders who broke through the glass ceiling were seen both as strategic and as willing to take risk as men.[14] In many areas where differences are thought to be important in creating a wedge between women's and men's performance in the workplace, the gap between the sexes is closing, be it cognitive abilities, such as visuospatial and maths abilities,[15] or socio psychological behaviour, such as dominance and assertiveness.[16] Crucially, the single most important 'male-defined' strength is their ability to work full time, long hours and to have a continuous work history, which is made possible by the persistence of the ideal worker paradigm with its false underlying assumptions.

The stickiness of this socioeconomic paradigm has exacted a high price from women, businesses and the economy at large. Working full time while still largely responsible for managing family life creates considerable strain on women and diminishes the quality of their family life, dissuading many well educated, highly skilled women from persevering with their careers wholeheartedly. Many women, especially

[12] Fine-Davis et al., 2004: iv.
[13] Vanderbroeck, 2009.
[14] See Vanderbroeck, 2009, and references therein.
[15] Feingold, 1988; and Wai et al. 2010.
[16] Twenge, 1997a.

those with young families, either stop working altogether, take a career break, or scale back their careers by working part time or by taking on less demanding jobs. This makes illusive fulfilment in a genuine sense, i.e. pursuing careers they would have chosen had they not been constrained. For businesses and the economy, as women give up work or scale back their careers, considerable talent and skill is leaked out of economic production, at a time when economies the world over are scrambling for human assets to gain competitiveness in an increasingly globalised economy; what a "shocking waste of talent."[17]

The way forward is a *simultaneous* overhaul of: *1)* work norms and work organisation in a way that enables the full integration of home and work life; and *2)* society's archaic belief system about who women and men are and what their location in society should be, including dropping the assumption that women alone have the emotional capacity to assume primary care. Changing these two areas of our life would equalise the structural conditions within which women and men make life-career choices, bringing about level playing fields for their pay and promotion. Put *economically*, only by satisfying these two conditions will women's and men's productivity in the labour market be equalised. As women and men care equally, and as the workplace is reorganised to fully embrace the non-work aspects of life, care responsibilities will no longer compete with work responsibilities and will no longer entail career penalties on those who assume them. In other words, a successful overhaul of work norms and of society's gender beliefs would disappear two dichotomies: that of home life and work life and that of caring women and care free men. Only then will women and men be free to pursue as much or as little career advancement as they wish, and only then can we say that women have a *real* choice.

---

[17]   Sir Roger Carr, president of the Confederation of British Industry, quoted by http://www.startupdonut.co.uk/blog/tag/Hilary-Devey.

I.3   Are Men and Women Different?

> *"I think the important thing about my appointment is not*
> *that I will decide cases as a woman, but that I am a woman*
> *who will get to decide cases."* Sandra Day O'Connor (First
> *woman appointed to the U.S. Supreme Court)*

Given the huge advances women have achieved in the last century in terms of participation in higher education and public life, does the persistence of women's subordinated status in society mean that differences between men and women are hardwired in the brain or do they only reside in the mind?

The question of difference in our context doesn't concern itself with biological/physiological/morphological differences, on which the science is clear. Rather, the question is whether these biological differences entail sex-differentiated cognitive ability, competence, agency and overall fitness to participate in public life.

As many readers are aware, wars have been and are still being fought on scholarly pages and the popular media over the existence or absence of differences between the two sexes, in a clear indication of the strong ideological divide on the issue. This is hardly surprising, given the centrality of the issue to our social identity and who we are as women and men. Invariably, however, women are portrayed as right-brain dominant empathisers, with aptitude for the arts and verbal skills, and men as left-brain dominant systematisers, with aptitude for maths and science. The subliminal message is clear: the *status quo* of male dominance and success in public life is something the female cannot and should not aspire for, since her skills lie much closer to home. As men access powerful positions and high paying jobs, entailed by their intellectual supremacy, women are locked into subordinated socio-political and socio-economic positions that affirm male supremacy. This is precisely why arguments of 'no difference' are put forth, to undercut the male supremacy argument, underpinned by sex differences in intellectual and other capacities.

I.3.1   Sex differences in cognitive abilities

Sex differences usually refer to a statistically significant difference in the average values of performances between men and women on a particular measure.[18] Most sex differences exhibit overlapping distributions; take for example height, where the average height of men is larger than that of women, but there will always be some women who are taller than some men. The distribution of women's height (around the mean value) is said to overlap with the distribution of men's height. Similarly, when we talk about sex differences in general, be it in cognitive abilities, in psychological traits or in social attitudes, we are talking about overlapping distributions rather than separate distributions (unless you genuinely believe that men are from Mars and therefore their attributes do not overlap with those of Venus inhabitants!).

That said, the shape of the distribution curve is very important and it often (but not always) tends to differ between women and men, with significant implications. The distribution of males' cognitive abilities tends to be more widely spread around the mean than females, due to greater variability amongst men than amongst women in those abilities. This means there are more males at the very high and very low ends of cognitive abilities, and more females in the middle.[19] Small average differences combined with greater variability for males than females mean that for the same set of data, we can conclude that females and males are fairly similar when we consider the average performance, and dissimilar when we consider performance at the high and low extremes.[20]

---

[18]   Archer and Lloyd, 2002:8-9.
[19]   Halpern, 2011: chapter 3, section 2, subsection 1, para. 1.
[20]   Ibid.

With those points in mind, the complex truth about sex differences in cognitive abilities can be distilled in three broad statements:[21] *1)* There are no overall differences in intelligence between females and males; *2)* there *appears* to be sex differences on some cognitive abilities, *viz.* verbal fluency, maths and visuospatial abilities, with women better than men in verbal fluency, and men better than women in maths and visuospatial abilities; and *3)* while average differences in these areas appear to be small, at both the high and low ends of distribution, differences can be substantial.[22]

Data for the OECD countries suggest that around age 15, there are consistent gaps in cognitive skills between girls and boys: boys perform very slightly better than girls in maths in most countries (by 2%), and girls outperform boys moderately in reading in all countries (by 6.7%), while there are no significant differences in science literacy.[23] These small percentages should make it clear that there is considerable overlap between the female and male distributions in maths and verbal ability; that is, females and males are far more similar than different on these two aspects of cognitive ability. Tests for high ability boys and girls however give boys a significant advantage over girls, particularly in maths. Wai et al. (2010) looked at male–female ratio in the top 5% ability in maths across 30 years (1981–2010), and found that the ratio has declined from 13:1 in the 1980s to between 3:1 and 4:1 in the early 1990s, and has been stable since.

Average sex differences in visuospatial abilities seem to be more pronounced that both maths and linguistic, although the OECD-wide

---

[21]   See Halpern, 2011, for a thorough examination of sex differences in cognitive abilities, and considerable nuance in result interpretation.

[22]   See Halpern, 2011: chapter 3; Archer and Lloyd, 2002: chapter 9, sections 3 and 4.

[23]   OCED, 2011a:14; 22. Percentages are calculated from Chart 1.4: 23.

data is not available.[24] The main aspects of visuospatial skills are: *1)* spatial perception; *2)* mental rotation; and *3)* spatial visualisation.[25] Men tend to score higher than women on tests of mental rotation and spatial perception and orientation, whereas women tend to score higher than men on tests of memory for object locations in spatial arrays.[26] An international study by Lippa, Collaer, and Peters (2010) assessed mental rotation and line angle judgment performance in more than 90,000 women and 111,000 men from 53 nations. In all nations, men's mean performance exceeded women's on these two visuospatial tasks, with large variations among countries - interestingly, the scholars correlated these sex differences with sex equality,[27] and economic development,[28] and found counter intuitively that higher levels of gender equality and economic development were associated with larger sex differences.

Four critical points are often neglected in the literature on sex differences, particularly popular literature. The first is that just as there are more men than women at the top end of ability for maths and visuospatial abilities, there are more men than women at the low end of the distribution too. It is difficult to imagine then that male outperformance in occupational outcomes stems from cognitive ability differences.[29] The second and equally neglected point is whether we are measuring *ability* or *performance*. Ability implies an innate talent that is biologically driven, which is virtually impossible to measure because of interferences that range from psychological states (we all know how complex exam psychology is) to environmental conditions, both in terms of physical environment (comfortable chairs, dim lighting, etc)

---

[24] Visuospatial ability refers to the ability to imagine how an irregular figure would look like when rotated in space or the ability to discern the relationship among shapes and objects (Halpern, 2011: chapter 3, section 18).

[25] Halpern, 2011: chapter 3, section 7.

[26] Lippa, Collaer, and Peters, 2010.

[27] Assessed using United Nations indices (Lippa, Collaer, and Peters, 2010).

[28] Assessed using per capita income and life expectancy (Lippa, Collaer, and Peters, 2010).

[29] Archer and Lloyd, 2002: 186.

and in terms of cultural environment (beliefs about abilities relating to gender, class, race, etc.).

On the latter point, one of the main psychological differences between women and men is confidence; men tend to overvalue themselves, often beyond their true ability, while women either assess themselves realistically or undervalue themselves. This is to be expected in male dominated societies, where everything masculine is highly valued and everything feminine is devalued, and since confidence is something we are not necessarily born with but rather conditioned into. It follows that "given how we perceive ourselves and our own competence affects our perception of our chances of success, it is clear that lack of self-belief is a major factor holding women back."[30] In situations where they are being evaluated, women are more likely than men to worry, feel lower self-esteem, and become less willing to participate than men.[31] This becomes particularly acute in areas where women are believed to have inferior abilities than men, such as maths and visuospatial abilities. The confidence factor, combined with a whole array of other psychological aspects that I will discuss in greater detail in section III.3, has a profound impact on women's performance, cognitive and otherwise. Estes and Felker (2012) for example looked at the factors that might mediate sex differences in mental rotation of three dimensional figures (part of the visuospatial ability). They found that, among other factors, individual variability in confidence mediates performance in mental rotation and therefore sex differences in mental rotation appears to be a difference of performance rather than ability.

Confidence, linked in folk wisdom to testosterone, comes from self-belief. Moè and Pazzaglia (2006) experimentally manipulated women's and men's beliefs about their own spatial ability in a lab experiment. They divided a sample of 107 female, and 90 male, high-school students

---

[30]   Austin, 2000: 37.
[31]   Ibid: 35.

into three groups, and gave each group instructions to the effect that: *1)* men are better than women at mental rotation, *2)* women are better than men at mental rotation, *3)* general (no sex difference). Their results show that women who expect to be more able than men and men who expect to be more able than women outperformed their counterparts; mental rotation performance fell for those expecting to be less able. In other words, confident people, regardless of their sex, tend to outperform. In the study mentioned above by Estes and Felker, confidence mediated *within* as well as *between* sex differences in mental rotation.

A 2006 study published in the journal *Science* examined the maths scores of 220 female students who had read one of two different fake research reports. Half of the girls read one report claiming that scientists had discovered genes on the Y chromosome (the male chromosome) that gave males a 5% advantage over females in maths. The other half read a paper that asserted that men had a 5% advantage only because of the way teachers stereotyped girls and boys at an early age – implying that females are just as good at maths as males are. When the students were tested, the group who believed that the difference was due to stereotyping did much better than the group who thought they had a genetic disadvantage.[32]

The third critical point in interpreting data relating to sex differences is that of 'point of reference' and androcentricity; what if *all* tests are built on androcentric standards? In a series of studies, McClelland et al. (1976) found that women and men can be motivated in different ways to achieve better results when they are being tested, by manipulating pre-test conditions. When subjects were given an achievement test before and after an 'intelligence' test, there was a significant rise in the achievement scores for males but not for females. However, when the intervening experiment was a lengthy discussion about social acceptability and the subjects were informed that they were being secretly rated on that basis,

---

[32]   Hamilton, 2010: 21-22.

there were significant differences in achievement scores for females but not for males. The scholars conclude that women's achievement is tied up with social acceptability, while men's is tied up with leadership capacity and intelligence. It is not inconceivable therefore that *any* test has built in bias in that, unless told otherwise, 'being tested' implies to subjects that they are being tested for *intelligence*, which primes men for better results. A related point is that in male dominated societies where women and men are conditioned to be different, with males encouraged to be competitive and women encouraged to communal and to eschew competitiveness, test conditions would automatically put women at a disadvantage – unless the tests relate to an area where females have a positive stereotype such as literacy.

The last point to make on the subject of sex differences in cognitive abilities is that there are considerable cultural variations, even at the high ability end of the distribution: a cross-cultural examination of extreme giftedness in maths found that the proportion of women in this elite group varies depending on the extent to which girls' participation in maths is encouraged in their own country. Gallian, Kane, and Mertz (2010) found that some Eastern European and Asian countries frequently produce girls with profound ability in mathematical problem solving, in contrast to other countries, including the USA. The authors go on to state that there are many girls with profound aptitude for maths who are rarely identified because of socio-cultural and other environmental factors.[33] Wood (2009) too contrasts the US with other cultures, saying that in the US men tend to specialise in maths and science far more than women because men are encouraged to pursue careers in these fields, while in countries like China students of both sexes score better on maths' tests than American students; in Turkey too it is not unusual for women students to major in maths.

---

[33] Quoted in Halpern, 2011: chapter 8, section 2, subsection 3, para. 2.

I.4   Brain, Biology and the Environment: The Mind System

"Your beliefs become your thoughts. Your thoughts become your words. Your words become your actions. Your actions become your habits. Your habits become your values. Your values become your destiny." Mahatma Gandhi (Political leader)[34]

By biology we mean the effect of genes and hormones in generating differences not only in cognitive abilities but in psychological traits too, such as temperament, attitudes and behaviours, *via* their influence on the brain. Thanks to advances in neuroscience, we are starting to grasp how malleable the human brain is throughout the life course but particularly in young age. Neurobiological[35] systems are the foundation for how we think, feel, and behave, while simultaneously, how we think, feel, and behave shapes the workings of our brains.[36]

I.4.1   Brain and environment: neuroplasticity

"Simply put, your brain is what you do with it." Lise Eliot (American Associate Professor of neuroscience and Author)[37]

Modern science talks of 'neuroplasticity', a characteristic of the brain that means environmental events, such as infant care, child play, family relations and the physical and cultural environment shape brain development.[38] To give us an idea of the high degree of brain plasticity,

---

[34]   Quoted in Lipton, 2008: chapter 5, section 7, para. 9.

[35]   Neurobiology is a branch of biology concerned with the anatomy and physiology of the nervous system, especially the brain, under various conditions of health, stress, and pathology (Gilgun, 2012: part 1, section 1, para. 1).

[36]   Gilgun 2012: part 1, section 1, para. 1.

[37]   Eliot, 2009: 6.

[38]   Gilgun 2012: part 1, section 2, para. 3.

David Hamilton (2010) says: "Your brain is growing as you read these words.... Everything you see, hear, touch, taste and smell changes your brain and every thought causes microscopic changes in its structure. In a sense, thought leave physical traces in the brain in much the same way as we leave footsteps in the sand."[39] A study of London taxi drivers found that they developed a larger hippocampus (a key brain region for making visuospatial memories) since that part of the brain gets considerable workout as drivers navigate London's complex roads.[40]

Significantly, Bruce Wexler (2006) explains, the period of brain maturation and associated environmental influence is much longer in people than in other animals, and the parts of the brain that most distinguish the human brain from those of other primates are the last to mature and are subject to the longest shaping by the environment, including psychosocial and other sensory inputs.[41] The prolonged period of childhood in human beings combined with a high degree of brain plasticity at that age has significant implications for sex differentiated behaviour in adulthood, a subject that I will return to in sections III.1.2 and III.1.3.

Environmental influences on the development of the brain lead to a great increase in the functional variability among individuals.[42] This means, as Bruce Wexler (2006) puts it, "that rather than being locked into the rigid brain structure of our ancestors, our brain interacts with the environment by influencing and shaping it all the time, and this ability to shape the environment in turn shapes our brain. This makes room for human adaptability and capability to develop at a much faster rate than would have been possible through alternation to genetic code itself".[43] In this picture, biology is socially and culturally influenced as

---

39 Hamilton, 2010: 43.
40 Maguire et al. (2000), quoted in Hanson and Mendius, 2009: 5.
41 Wexler, 2006: 2.
42 Ibid: 3.
43 Ibid: 3-4.

it develops in a continuous interaction with, and response to, our minds and environment.[44]

The significant implications of brain neuroplasticity for sex differentiated learning cannot be over stated. David Hamilton (2010) give this example to illustrate the importance of repetitive action in shaping our brains: if we flexed the right hand repetitively over several days, without flexing the left hand, the right hand area of the brain would form several neural connections and would expand as a result. If we switched hands, the left hand area of the brain would grow and the right had area would shrink, because we are no longer using that hand.[45] It is easy to imagine what happens to brain structure and function from decades, centuries or even millennia of concentrating on one area of learning for one sex and another area of learning for the other sex. Given cultural beliefs about male superiority in maths, and relentless efforts in encouraging boys to develop those skills, it is quite surprising that sex differences are only around 6%. The fact that these differences are narrowing, as girls are more and more encouraged to concentrate on maths' skills, attests to the power of social culture in shaping our brain.

It is not only cognitive behaviour that influences the brain, but all behaviour. It has long been established that meditation changes the brain. A study of a group of meditators conducted at Massachusetts General Hospital in 2005 showed that meditation has increased the thickness of the prefrontal cortex of the brain – the area that controls concentration, free will and compassion.[46] Hamilton (2010) gives examples of how complaining behaviour and gratitude behaviour change the respective areas of the brain in as little as 21 days.[47] He also mentions that MRI studies of people undergoing talk therapies show that neurons in the prefrontal cortex light up (are activated) while activity in the

---

[44]   Fine, 2010: 178.
[45]   Hamilton, 2010: 43.
[46]   Ibid: 46; See also Hanson and Mendius, 2009: 85.
[47]   See Hamilton, 2010: 46, for references.

area that process painful emotions is reduced.[48] Recent studies have shown that we can even repair damage to the brain that resulted from childhood trauma; the process is called neurogenesis. Not surprisingly, neurogenesis takes place in enriching environments with considerable stimulation, as well as when we are exercising or experiencing new things, feeling excited, enthusiastic, fascinated, in awe, experiencing wonder or in a spiritual state, many of which are associated with strong, powerful emotions.[49] Hamilton asserts that neurogenesis continues throughout old age, to our very last moments. Scientists were able to observe newly formed neurons in terminally ill volunteers' hippocampi all the way to their final days, regardless of their age.[50]

Given the brain's amazing powers, it is quite clear that encouraging certain behaviour in girls and women and different and often contrasting behaviour in boys and men would have a profound impact on differentiating brain structure and function in each sex. Brain plasticity equally makes clear that reversing sexist behaviour in each of us is a distinct possibility, regardless of our age or how sexist the societies we grew up in were. Everything depends on our intention *vis-à-vis* eradicating sexism from our societies and our willingness to change our mind about who women and men are.

I.4.2   Environment and biology: control over genes

It is useful here to introduce the relatively new science of epigenetics, which is today one of the most active areas of scientific research that has completely changed our conventional understanding of genetic control. Epigenetics literally means 'control above the genes', and it studies how environmental signals select, modify, and regulate gene activity,

---

[48]   Ibid.

[49]   Ibid: 48-49.

[50]   Ibid.

so genes are no longer seen as our destiny.[51] This runs contrary to the conventional model of genetics which states that DNA controls all of life, and that all gene expression takes place inside the cell. Epigenetic studies on the other hand reveal that our genes are as changeable as our brains,[52] and that they are in a state of flux, constantly being remodelled in response to our experiences.

Joe Dispenza (2012) explains that there are experience-dependent genes that are activated when there is growth, healing, or learning; and there are behavioural-state-dependent genes that are influenced during stress, emotional arousal, or dreaming.[53] Environmental influences, including nutrition, stress, and emotions can modify genes without changing their basic blueprint; and yet, these modifications can still be passed on to future generations just as DNA blueprints are passed on *via* the double helix.[54]

Lipton (2008) elucidates that contrary to what has previously been believed, the cell membrane, rather than the nucleus, is the true brain of the cell that receives signals from the environment and translates those signals into cell behaviour. Lipton and Bhaerman (2009) explain that built into the cell membrane's structure are two types of proteins called receptor and effector that serve as switches that aid the translation of environmental signals into cell behaviour: when the receptor protein

---

[51] Lipton, 2008: prologue, para. 11; chapter 2, section 7, para. 1.

[52] Dispenza, 2012: 76-77.

[53] Ibid and references therein.

[54] Lipton, 2008: chapter 2, section 7, para. 1. The mechanics of this process are as follows: In the chromosome, the DNA forms the core, and the proteins cover the DNA like a sleeve. When the genes are covered, their information cannot be "read." But an environmental signal can spur the "sleeve" protein to detach from the DNA's double helix, allowing the gene to be read. Once the DNA is uncovered, the cell makes a copy of the exposed gene. As a result, the activity of the gene is "controlled" by the presence or absence of the ensleeving proteins, which are in turn controlled by environmental signals (Lipton, 2008: chapter 2, section 7).

receives a signal from the environment, it modifies its shape and connects with the effector protein. Effector proteins generate signals that go to the nucleus of the cell and change the way that the DNA makes proteins (the physical building blocks that assemble and interact to generate the cell's behaviours and functions) which gives rise to an alteration in gene expression.[55] Environmental signals can be both tangible and intangible: the air we breathe, the food we eat, the people we interact with and more generally the social culture we live in, all represent environmental signals that activate protein movement and generate corresponding behaviour. "Each protein responds to a specific environmental signal with the intimacy and accuracy of a key fitting into its matching lock."[56]

Dispenza (2012) states that epigenetics empower us to think about change more profoundly; the epigenetic paradigm shift gives us free will to activate our own gene activity and modify our genetic destiny. Just by changing our thoughts, feelings, emotional reactions, and behaviours (for example, making healthier lifestyle choices with regard to nutrition and stress levels), we send our cells new signals, and they express new proteins without changing the genetic blueprint.[57] In other words, our perceptions of life can shape our biology.[58] So while the DNA code stays the same, once a cell is activated in a new way by new information, the cell can create thousands of variations of the same gene. "We can signal our genes to rewrite our future."[59]

The view of the inseparability of gene expression from the surrounding environment is reverberated across the field: "Genes don't by themselves code for anything. Genes are expressed as part of an inseparable relationship to the environment in which they operate — both the external environment and the cellular environment in which they are

---

[55] Lipton and Bhaerman, 2009: 20-23.

[56] Ibid: 20.

[57] Dispenza, 2012: 78.

[58] Lipton, 2008: prologue, para. 11.

[59] Dispenza, 2012: 78.

suspended."[60] "Genes are under the control of epigenetics. Epigenetics are under the control of social behaviour. Social behaviour is under the control of culture."[61] But who controls culture?

I.4.3   The mind system

The missing link between brain and environment is the mind; because the mind is often confounded with the brain, we are constantly awe struck by the brain's ability to interact with the environment and to override genetics. If we think of the mind as a category or even a system that is not separable from the brain but nevertheless has its own sovereignty, many of the mysteries disappear. The brain interacts with other systems in our body, and the body in turn interacts with the external world,[62] which interaction then feeds back into our brain, our body and so on. All of these interactions combined make up the mind. So, in the largest sense, the mind has the brain, the body, the physical environment and the social culture as components integral to its functioning.

Hanson and Mendius (2009) acknowledge the power of the brain and its ability to influence the mind and vice versa. They give these examples: as the brain develops in childhood, so does the mind. If the brain is ever damaged so is the mind. Subtle shifts in brain chemistry will alter mood, concentration and memory. Using powerful magnets to suppress the emotion-processing limbic system changes how people make moral judgments. Even some spiritual experiences are correlated with neural activities.[63] The power of the brain is constantly being unmasked: new ways of thinking fire up new neurons in the brain; "when neurons fire

---

[60]   Daniel Povinelli, http://www.dnafiles.org/chimp-chat/day-four.
[61]   Terry Deacon, http://www.dnafiles.org/chimp-chat/day-four.
[62]   Thompson and Varela, 2001.
[63]   Hanson and Mendius, 2009: 10, and references therein.

together, they wire together;"[64] mental activities therefore create new structures in the brain and, as a result, "what flows through your mind sculpts your brain."[65]

The body too is critical to the mind system. The nervous system moves information throughout the body, mostly without our awareness. This information, such as signals that regulate stress responses, knowledge of how to ride a bike, personality tendencies and so on, is included in the broad definition of the mind.[66] A critical way in which we are made aware of the functioning of the nervous system (the state and strength of its arousal) is feelings, which are the subjective, conscious experience of emotions, or as Antonio Damasio et al. (2004) put it "a feeling is the perception of an emotional state, as enacted in the body."[67] Emotions are connected with, mainly but not exclusively, activities in the limbic system of our brain. Their purpose is to direct our attention, motivation and behaviour based on the significance of what is going on around us. Emotions are therefore our body's way of processing environmental events and a vehicle for shaping our relationship with the environment, making them a critical aspect of the mind system, linking brain with body and environment. Here is what Richard Lazarus (1991) has to say about emotions and human adaptation: "It is inconceivable to me that there could be an approach to the mind, or to human and animal adaptation, in which the emotions are not a key component."[68]

I.4.4   The epigenetics of belief

We are all familiar with the placebo effect, where some people get better when they believe (falsely) that they are taking medicine. The

---

[64]   See Hanson and Mendius, 2009: 4, for references.
[65]   Hanson and Mendius, 2009: 5.
[66]   Ibid, 2009: 6-7.
[67]   Damasio et al., 2004.
[68]   Lazarus, 1991: 4.

placebo effect is epigenetics at work: as the mind perceives the body to have received a drug, "the brain produces a natural drug that's tailor-made to combat the illness."[69] Placebo experiments started with pain relief placebo in 1978, and showed that the body has produced its own painkillers. More recently, a meta analysis in 2008, covering 35 clinical trials involving 5,133 patients, showed that the placebo effect of various antidepressants accounted for 81% of the drugs' effect.[70] Hamilton (2010) concludes in his book 'How your mind can heal your body': "with such a high placebo effect it is impossible to prove that the drugs actually work. ... the studies show that we have a much greater ability to heal ourselves than we'd ordinarily think."[71] Bruce Lipton (2008) calls the placebo effect the "perception effect", to stress that our perceptions, whether accurate or inaccurate, impact our behaviours and our bodies. He also calls it the "belief effect" to show the amazing ability of the mind to alter the body's reality.[72]

There are many experiments that show how environmental signals can override genetic programming. For example, studies show that mice with the breast cancer gene can develop breast cancer when brought up in normal stress level settings, but can remain healthy when put in low-stress, spa settings.[73] In real life, it is little known that many people who have the cancer gene do not necessarily develop cancer. The majority of cancer gene carriers, however, do develop cancer because they get into a stressed state on finding out about their condition, because of their perception that carrying that negative trait necessarily means

---

[69] Hamilton, 2010: 18.
[70] The only significant difference between the drug and placebo existed for severely depressed patients (Hamilton, 2010: 32).
[71] Hamilton, 2010: 32.
[72] Lipton, 2008: chapter 5, section 6, para. 1.
[73] Borysenko, 2013.

developing cancer,[74] when a different perception could have given them a healthy life.[75]

The Nocebo effect is diagonally opposed to the placebo effect, where some people develop a disease when they believe (falsely) that they have a medical condition or a negative physical trait that predisposes them to illness. Just as positive perceptions can promote healing through the placebo effect, so can negative perceptions powerfully influence health in the opposite direction, sometimes leading to death. Scientists have studied the fate of children adopted into families where there was a lineage of cancer running through the family. They found that the adopted children got the same family cancer as the natural siblings, despite the fact that they come from a totally different genetic pool.[76]

In their book 'Spontaneous evolution', Lipton and Bhaerman (2009) state that perception is key to altering genetic outcomes. As organisms interact with the environment, their perceptions engage epigenetic mechanisms that fine-tune genetic expression in order to enhance the opportunities for survival.[77] This environmental influence is dramatically revealed in studies of identical twins: at birth and shortly thereafter, twin siblings express almost the same gene activity from their identical genomes. However, as they age, their personal individualised experiences and perceptions lead to activation of significantly different sets of genes. Despite media reports to the contrary, twins rarely lead identical lives.[78] We actively control our genetic expression moment by moment, throughout our lives. We are learning organisms that can incorporate life experiences into our genomes and pass them on to our offspring, who will then incorporate their life experiences into the genome to further human evolution. Lipton and Bhaerman (2009)

---

[74] Ibid.
[75] For some powerful examples of the placebo effect see Lipton, 2008: chapter 5.
[76] Lipton, 2013.
[77] Lipton and Bhaerman, 2009: 29.
[78] Ibid.

conclude that perceptions and responses to life experiences dynamically shape our biology and behaviour.[79]

I.4.5   Mind, hormones and behaviour

Testosterone is king of sex differences. In folk wisdom, as well as in many scientific quarters, testosterone is seen as the hormone that creates an irredeemable wedge between women and men, with its effects starting *in utero*. Eisenegger et al. (2010) state that in some species like rats, higher testosterone *is* associated with aggression. However, folk wisdom transposes these finding to humans, suggesting that testosterone induces antisocial, egoistic, or even aggressive human behaviours.[80] Yet, "it is already clear that there is no simple one-to-one relationship between testosterone and machoism or aggressiveness or sexuality."[81]

Sophisticated tests suggest that testosterone domination does not create aggression *per se*, but only exaggerates what aggression already exists from socialisation. This is the conclusion that Robert Sapolsky (2011) reached in the 'Trouble with testosterone' in which he discusses the constant interaction between social conditioning and biology. Sapolsky describes how experiments that remove the source of testosterone only lead to a dramatic decline, but not total disappearance, of aggression and in some individuals it does not change at all;[82] "the more social experience an individual had being aggressive prior to castration, the more likely that behaviour persists sans cojones (without testes). Social conditioning can more than make up for the hormone."[83] He uses this to falsify the dichotomy between nature and nurture: "No biology. No environment. Just the interaction between the two"; "our behavioural

---

[79] Ibid: 30.
[80] Eisenegger et al., 2010.
[81] Mazur and Booth (1998), quoted in Eisenegger et al., 2010.
[82] Sapolsky, 2011: 44.
[83] Parenthesis and explanation added.

biology is usually meaningless outside the context of the social factors and environment in which it occurs".[84] The constant interaction between our genes and the environment to modify gene expression is after all the basis of our evolution.

Sapolsky discusses the "permissive effect" where varying levels of testosterone in the bloodstream within the normal range does not automatically alter levels of aggressive behaviour. So removing the testes leads to a plummeting of aggression, but reinstating testosterone to only 20% of pre-castration levels brings normal pre-castration levels of aggression back. If the normal level of testosterone is doubled, aggression also goes back to pre castration levels. So the brain doesn't seem to distinguish among a wide range of basic 'all normal' values. The conclusion is that knowing how much testosterone is in circulation in males will not help in predicting the degree of aggression they will exhibit.[85]

In another experiment, a group of five monkeys were put together and allowed time to establish social affiliations and the pecking order. The middle monkey was injected with considerable amounts of testosterone. Prior to the injection, the monkey was very aggressive to the two monkeys below him in ranking and diplomatic with the two above. After the injection, the result was intriguing: whilst he did engage in more aggressive interactions with the two monkeys below him, he was still judicious with those superior to him, suggesting that testosterone may not cause aggression, but exaggerates the aggressive behaviour that is already in existence.[86]

A meta-analysis by Archer (2006)[87] found that testosterone rose in men anticipating and playing sports and highly competitive games,

---

[84]   Wood, 2009: 44-45.
[85]   Sapolsky, 2011:43.
[86]   Wood, 2009: 43-44.
[87]   Quoted in Eagly and Wood, 2009.

especially among the winners, but did not rise in the absence of provocations calling for aggressiveness.[88] Although women have substantially less testosterone than men, female athletes still experience a rise in testosterone before a competition.[89] These experiments point to a different causation from that assumed in folk wisdom: rather than testosterone causing aggression, aggression raises the levels of testosterone. Furthermore, studies that experimentally injected men with testosterone or related synthetic androgens found no systematic rise in anger, aggression or hostility.[90] Booth et al. (2006) conclude: "Popular perceptions of the effect of testosterone on 'manly' behaviour are inaccurate. We need to move away from such simplistic notions by treating testosterone as one component along with other physiological, psychological and sociological variables in interactive and reciprocal models of behaviour."[91] In an interesting experiment, Eiseneggre et al. (2010) showed that the sublingual administration of a single dose of testosterone in women causes a substantial increase in fair bargaining behaviour, thereby reducing bargaining conflicts and increasing the efficiency of social interactions. However, subjects who believed that they received testosterone, regardless of whether they actually did, behaved much more unfairly than those who believed that they were treated with placebo. Folk hypothesis, therefore, seems to generate a strong negative association between subjects' beliefs and the fairness of their offers, even though testosterone administration actually causes a substantial increase in the frequency of fair bargaining offers in their experiment.

Hormones do affect cognitive abilities and behaviour, but their effects are complex and not fully understood, not least because of the difficulty of disentangling biological from environmental factors. For example, Booth et al. (2006) argue that high levels of testosterone are seldom

---

[88]   Eagly and Wood, 2009.
[89]   Ibid.
[90]   Ibid.
[91]   Booth et al., 2006.

associated with aggression because of the protective influence of the social environment and the resilience individuals develop by living in such an environment. Booth, Johnson and Granger (2005) attempted to find a link between testosterone and marital quality. In their study, neither husbands' nor wives' testosterone showed a direct connection with marital quality. In contrast, the association between husbands' testosterone and positive and negative marital quality (as evaluated by both spouses) was conditional on husbands' role overload. When perceptions of role overload were elevated, higher testosterone levels were associated with lower levels of marital quality. When perceptions of role overload were low, higher testosterone was linked to greater marital quality. The study shows that, depending on perceptions of the social context, testosterone enables positive behaviour in some instances and negative behaviour in others.

1.5   Conclusion: Sexism Seeded in Our Thoughts

"What we think, we become." Buddha (Ancient sage)

These studies reveal many interesting facts about human behaviour that are relevant to sex differences. *First*, genetic coding by itself is a poor predictor of behaviour. *Second*, the environment is critical in predicting behaviour, but what ultimately matters is the filtering of environmental signals through our minds, i.e. perception; the filtering process is the decoding of environmental signals through our system of belief. *Third*, given epigenetic control mechanisms, as well as brain plasticity, the dichotomy of nature *vs.* nurture is a fallacy. The only legitimate paradigm in studying behaviour, including differences between women and men, is one that allows the study of a three way interaction between brain, biology and environment.

We are genetically programmed to adapt to and evolve with the environment, including the social environment that we create and shape as we go through our evolutionary process. Advances in neurobiology and epigenetics increasingly show the high degree of articulation between environmental signals and body cells, leading to alterations in gene expression which are passed on to the next generation. The link between the two is the mind: how the mind responds to the environment, by way of beliefs, perceptions, emotions and attitudes, changes genetic expression.[92] This means that our minds, our bodies and our environment are inseparable; they are integral parts in what I called earlier the 'mind system'. We now know that epigenetic control mechanisms are those parts of the mind system that maintain coherence between the environment and behaviour. Epigenetic control mechanisms guarantee that our perceptions of environmental signals are translated into a corresponding behaviour that does not contradict those perceptions.

Sex differentiated behaviours, be it intelligence, psychological traits or even temperament are greatly shaped not only by our initial genetic endowment, but also by our socio-cultural environment. To the extent that the socio-cultural environment the world over, with varying degrees, has different expectations for women and men, these expectations must by necessity manifest as behaviourally different realities for women and men. Furthermore, to the extent that males more than females are encouraged and rewarded for developing those skills (maths, science, etc.) and engaging in those behaviours (competitiveness, achievement, economic provision) that are highly valued and more rewarded in society, while females more than males are encouraged and rewarded for developing those skills (literacy, the arts, etc.) and engaging in those behaviours (empathy, intuition, care and service of others) that are less valued in society, male supremacy remains the order of the day.

The epigenetic process that translates environmental signals into behaviour starts with a thought, which is the verbalisation of how the mind *perceives* an environmental signal. Thoughts are translated

---

[92]   Lipton, 2013.

by the nervous system into sensations/emotions, which are chemicals called neurotransmitters (epinephrine, serotonin, dopamine, etc.) that are transmitted between neurons. The purpose of neurotransmitters is to allow the body's chemistry to match the thought: negative and positive thoughts release the kind of chemistry that shapes the biology in a way that complements the thought, so that there is no contradiction between our thoughts and our feelings. Neurotransmitters in turn release different neurohormones, leading to a change in the tissue culture medium (the fluids that bathe the cells), which binds to the cell membrane,[93] leading to change in cell behaviour.

A man's perception of himself as intellectually competent, confident, competitive, aggressive, etc. mobilises not only his brain but every cell in his body to fulfil that perception, in order for him to be congruent with his social environment. A woman's perception of herself as warm, caring, communicative, etc. will similarly change her neural connections, her emotions, and her hormones to manifest those behaviours that are in harmony with society's beliefs about women. Cultural beliefs that men are inadequate carers and women are incompetent leaders create a corresponding behaviour at a cellular level, in order to maintain harmony between the mind's perceptions and life experiences. Lipton and Bhaerman (2009) say that cells, tissues, and organs do not question the information sent by the nervous system. Rather, they respond with equal fervour to accurate life-affirming perceptions as they do to self-destructive misperceptions. Consequently, "perceptions have a tremendous influence in shaping the character and experiences of our lives."[94]

To answer the question 'why has equality eluded women?', we must examine very carefully our thoughts and our belief system about the nature of women and men, their abilities, their roles in life, and their

---

[93] Borysenko, 2013.
[94] Lipton and Bhaerman, 2009: 26.

expected behaviours, demeanours, temperament, dispositions, etc. We may find when we excavate deeply enough into those beliefs that our outer reality of sex inequality accurately reflects a faulty system of thought that does not see women and men as equal, but sees men as superior to women, because the ways in which men are believed to be different are superior to the ways in which women are believed to be different.

The drive to achieve sex equality started more than a century ago, and to most of us the belief in male superiority is abominable. And yet, deep within our thoughts, rather than our stated opinions, there remains a seed of sexism.

II

GENDER AS A SOCIAL CONSTRUCT

In 'Conversations with God' (Walsch, 1995), God and Neale Walsch have the following conversation:

God: the purpose of life is to know and to recreate who you are. In so doing you do please god and glorify her as well.

Neale: why do keep saying her, are you a she?

God: I'm neither a he nor a she. Occasionally I use the feminine pronoun to jar you out of your parochial thinking. If you think god is one thing then you will think god is not another and that will be a large mistake.

Similarly, if we think someone is masculine then we automatically think they are not feminine and if we think they are feminine then we automatically think they are not masculine. And this is a large mistake, for what they are is both at the same time.

Gender is the collection of ideas that govern who women and men should be, as social entities, how they should behave, what attributes they should have and how they should organise the different aspects of their life that are directly or indirectly related to their reproductive capacities. Gender is also those aspects of life that support women and men while they are dealing with reproductive issues. Rules of engagement on sexual relations are part of the gender system. As is marriage, which as a system and an institution it not only deals with having babies, but also with organising family life along gendered lines: raising children in a manner that allows them to function well within the gender system; regulating adult intimacy in a way that fulfils them as gendered entities; giving men emotional and practical support while they 'provide' for their families; and channelling 'womanly' instincts for nurturing their families.

Gender therefore is an intellectual construction of a social system, of some sort, that is sophisticated, highly articulated and given to detailed descriptions and prescriptions of people's traits, attributes, dispositions and behaviours. Gender also prescribes the social structures and institutions that govern women's and men's behaviour and their reproductive activities. In a nutshell, gender is no more than a *conception* of that part of the social system that deals with women and men, and what kind of people they should be in order for society to function in a particular way.

As such, gender doesn't take into account people's humanity and who they really are as people, but only of whom they are as a product of society and actors or players in it. This is not where the real problem of the gender system lies, however, for all social systems are in part or in whole *conceptions* as such. The real pitfall of the gender system is that it assumes gender to be the totality of who we are, rather than a social superstructure laid upon who we are as human beings. As gender is acted and re-enacted, produced and re-produced over the millennia, it becomes invisible, seeming integral to the self rather than the thick layer of social conditioning that it is.

In fact, gender often detracts from our humanity, by prescribing highly restrictive personalities and roles for women and men. As societies advance in their quest for personal freedom, people become more and more disgruntled with gender's prescriptions, and they attempt to break out. This is manifested in fighting against heterosexuality as the norm for sexual relations; marriage for life as the template for family; men as sole providers for their families, and so on. And yet, gender prescriptions and proscriptions remain largely unchallenged, for the simple fact that it has not yet been unmasked as 'gender' in its totality, but is still largely believed to be part and parcel of who we are. Most of us still believe that the gender system is how nature has intended for women and men to live their lives, and that this is the way it will always be. Even in some societies with highly evolved gender discourses, like the Nordic countries, these discourses are focused on equity between women and men, leaving gender as such largely untouched and its built in gender hierarchies intact.

II.1   From a Woman to a Helpmate

> *"A woman who doesn't wear perfume has no future."*
> *Coco Chanel (French fashion designer)*

Men and women are who they say and believe they are, and this has changed over time. This may seem like a flippant remark, but it is truthful in as much as any identity is constructed in social discourse. Foucault's influential work in showing that all notions, including social notions, and all knowledge for that matter are not pre-existing, but are created in language through discourse. So what a woman, or what a man, *is* are not God given truths but are constructed through language and culture. We are born female and male (and this is the only God given truth) but only become girl and boy, woman and man, daughter and son, wife and husband through cultural experiences and alignment to social identities that normally come with a role that embodies a social meaning (daughter, son; mother, father; career women, house husband; etc.).

Gayle Rubin (1975) said powerfully: "a woman is a woman. She only becomes a domestic, a wife, a chattel, a playboy bunny or a prostitute in certain relations. Torn from these relationships she is no more the helpmate of man than gold in itself is money."[95] Raewyn Connell

---

[95]   Rubin, 1975: 179.

(2002) argues that we should not think of womanhood or manhood as fixed by nature, nor should we think of them as simply imposed from outside, by social norms or pressure from authorities. "People construct themselves as masculine or feminine. We claim a place in the gender order – or respond to the place we have been given – by the way we conduct ourselves in everyday life."[96]

One can think of gender as a 'social super structure', created on top of our 'humanness' as females and males. The core purpose of this super structure is to organise human endeavour in the areas relating to reproduction. Once created, however, this social identity cannot desist when dealing with aspects of life other than reproduction. Rather, gender extends far further than reproduction to include most aspects of our life that either intersect with reproduction (schools where our children are taught; home life where 'nurturance' takes place; the workplace where 'breadwinning' manifests, and so on), or are impinged upon by our femaleness and maleness (for example, male bonding often takes strong gender overtones when it becomes 'this is what men do'; pole dancing, beauty pageants, extreme sports, car racing, etc are all highly gendered interests and experiences). As the concept of gender expands to cover all these areas, the institutions in which it extends to are said to become 'gendered', as are the relationships that are created not only between people, but between people and institutions, and institutions and institutions.

Gayle Rubin (1975) saw gender as a socially imposed division of the sexes; a product of the social relations of sexuality.[97] This dichotomy however was cautioned against by Connell (2002): when gender is defined in terms of difference this "means that where we can't see difference we can't see gender. With such a definition we could not recognise the gendered characteristic of lesbian or homosexual desire (based on gender similarity), nor the powerful gender dynamic of an all male army. We

---

96   Connell, 2002: 4.
97   Rubin, 1975: 179.

would be thrown into confusion by research which finds only small psychological differences between women and men, which would seem to imply that gender has evaporated."[98] Furthermore, a dichotomous definition blinds us to patterns that are similar in women and men but are derived from gender. For example, differences between violent and non violent masculinity, or differences between males and females who are oriented to heterosexual relations and those who are not.[99, 100]

The key to understanding gender's enduring nature is to understand how it is constructed in the first place, what it consists of and how it is maintained. Gender is created through discourses; ideas, conversations and agreements that take place within certain historical and cultural contexts, about *who* and *how* women and men should *be* – traits attributes, behaviours and roles. These ideas turn over time into a cohesive system of thought, or a belief system. Once in existence, agreement over the rules of engagement creates a social system with multiple structures within which young females and males are socialised and become deeply conditioned over time. Gender is then acted and re-enacted through complex social and psychological processes, which I will discuss in the next chapter. Even when discourses about gender shift, the underlying socio-psychological processes are much slower to change. This is where the role of the subconscious becomes critical, since even when the conscious mind moves with the gender conversation, as often it does with varying degrees that depend on one's attachment to gender ideology, the subconscious mind does not necessarily follow suit, unless it is subjected to an external influence that disrupts its auto pilot

---

[98]   Connell, 2002:8.

[99]   Ibid.

[100]   Connell (2002) also speaks of gendered production relations, where the gender division of labour allows the dividend to accrue to men from the unequal shares of the products of social labour. She also points to the gendered character of capital: a capitalist economy working through a gendered division of labour is necessarily a gendered accumulation process. "So it is not a statistical accident but part of the construction of masculinity that men not women control the major corporations and great private fortunes (p74).

modus orperandi – more on this in the next chapter too. Fear of change is often lodged deep into our subconscious, preventing us from moving with the times. Even when we know change to be beneficial, we often resist change because we prefer certainty to uncertainty, no matter how pernicious the former and beneficial the latter. How many times have you heard the phrase 'one bird in hand..... ; the mind craves certainty.

The rigidity built into the main structures of gender, combined with our fear of changing them mean that in the areas where gender intersects with those aspects of life that have yielded to modernisation, there are contradictions and considerable confusion. For example, women's paid employment is an area that has experienced considerable change in the last fifty years, and yet the division of labour in the home remains stuck in last century mode, to working women's considerable consternation. Another area of great resistance is male dominated professions and men's dominance of top positions in society. The area where there is the highest amount of confusion is perhaps in men's intimate relationships, both with their children and their sexual partners, as marriage gives way to more modern forms and structures of family. The common denominator in all these examples is the rigid construction of femininity and masculinity.

II.2   Femininity and Masculinity

"It is important to understand clearly that the concepts of 'masculine' and 'feminine', whose meaning seems so unambiguous to ordinary people, are amongst the most confused that occur in science." Sigmund Freud (Austrian neurologist and founder of psychoanalysis)[101]

Our confusion around masculinity and femininity has not waned since Freud made that note in 1915. If gender is the social super structure for

---

[101]   Freud, Three Essays on Sexuality (1905), footnote, 1915, SE 7, quoted in Birksted-breen, 1993: 1.

human beings, femininity and masculinity are its two main pillars that arise from femaleness and maleness, to keep the super structure in place. Femininity and masculinity are the social constructions of what it is to be a woman and what it is to be a man, and how women and men deal, differently, with gender issues. So, femininity and masculinity are prescriptions of traits, attributes and behaviours of women and men. They relate not only to women and men as individuals, but to their location in society and the appropriate social identities associated with these locations. The gender system is created in order for marriage to take place, for children to be produced, for mothering to be done by women and for economic provision to be done by men. To achieve these gender goals, femininity and masculinity prescribe how women and men should be like, and what behaviours they should exhibit in order for gender goals to be achieved.

The insightful classic phrase of Simone de Beauvoir "one is not born, but rather becomes, a woman", holds true for a man: one is not born a man but acquires and enacts masculinity and so becomes a man.[102] Freud's psychoanalytic work was instrumental in showing how we are born female and male and only become woman and man through complex socio-psychological processes. It became clear from his valuable psychoanalytic accounts that femininity and masculinity are socially constructed over time, independent of biological sex.[103] Femininity and masculinity in this view are psychic formations that are shaped within, and critically dependent upon, family structure and family relationships, as well as the wider social culture, a subject that I will turn to frequently throughout this book.[104]

---

[102]   Connell, 2002: 4.

[103]   It's important to note here that this was not the stance that Freud himself took. Instead, his stance is fiercely debated in the literature and remains highly contested, but is more likely to have been one of biological determinism (See Birksted-breen (1993) for a discussion). The view that I express above is that of neo Freudian analysts, which however is based on Freud's own unique clinical accounts. See Chodorow, 1994; Rubin, 1975, and Birksted-breen, 1993.

[104]   Birksted-breen, 1993; Connell, 2002; and Rubin, 1975.

The terms femininity and masculinity, as commonly known, go beyond categorical sex differences, to include the ways in which women and men differ among themselves in matters relating to gender.[105] The concept is relational: femininity and masculinity arise only in relation to each other, and are only meaningful in a system of gender relations.[106] Connell (1995) emphasises the dynamic nature of constructing gender and within it femininity and masculinity, as they are neither fixed nor static.[107] Rather, "it is a *becoming* condition, actively under construction."[108] So when we speak of femininity and masculinity, we are relating them to a 'configuration' of gender practices. The process of 'configuring' is key here to understanding that the organisation of gender practices is an ongoing project, within which we write scripts for masculinity and femininity.[109] Taking a dynamic view of the organisation of practices, we arrive at an understanding of masculinity and femininity as gender projects.[110] Seen as such, one becomes more aware of one's involvement in these projects and in deciding what the feminine and the masculine constitute at any given point in time.

To show the fluidity of masculinity and its cultural specificity, Todd W. Reeser (2010) reminds us that heterosexual men's writings in Renaissance Europe included descriptions of their intimate love for other men. Instead of this being effeminate or homosexual, in their socio historical context it was more likely a reaffirmation of masculinity. Similarly, while French men might appear effeminate by the standards of other cultures, in context they are well within the masculine bounds. In India, it is common for men to walk arm in arm, which is not an acceptable masculine behaviour in Western cultures. Cross cultural and cross temporal differences make us aware of masculinity as both relative

---

[105]   Connell, 2005: 67.
[106]   Ibid: 71.
[107]   Ibid.
[108]   Connell, 2002: 4.
[109]   Ibid.
[110]   Ibid: 72.

and changing as a concept, since we come to see that what is taken for granted in one culture is not a given in another. This reveals the problem with considering masculinity or femininity, as we know them culturally, as 'natural' or 'innate'.[111]

Femininity is normally associated with softness, sensuality, emotionality, nurturerance, sensitivity, warmth, communality, attentiveness, intuition, empathy, care, devotion and self-sacrifice. Masculinity is normally associated with dominance, power, leadership, aggressiveness, competitiveness, physical strength, self-reliance, risk taking, toughness, resilience, rationality, objectivity, independence, and decisiveness.[112] These notions are also scientifically observed sex differences, as notions turn into social norms and societal expectations of how women and men should be. Through a whole array of psychological and sociological processes that I will explore in the next chapter, notions of masculinity and femininity turn into real life experiences by women and men.

A careful look at these descriptions reveals the main problem with seeing women in the gender system as only feminine, in order for them to fulfil their caring roles, and men as only masculine, in order for them to pursue economic provision. As a category, femininity and masculinity are not only different, but oppositional and therefore mutually exclusive. Prescribing femininity to women but not to men and masculinity to men but not women is "as if each sex is peculiarly deficient in the characteristic traits of the other sex."[113] This suggests that when it comes to societal notions of women and men, *difference* is pursued as a virtue in its own right.

Gender stereotypes portray women as self-sacrificial, nurturant, devoted and well suited for childcare and domestic services, but less competent

---

[111]   Reeser, 2010: 88.

[112]   Hanlon, 2012:1; Geis, 1993: 11.

[113]   Geis, 1993: 11

than men and unsuited for authority or leadership.[114] Men, on the other hand, are stereotyped as competitive, assertive, decisive and well suited for power and authority, but emotionally incompetent and unsuited for childcare and intimacy. The overarching gender difference is women's focus on 'other' rather than 'self', making them highly relational beings, while men's focus is on 'self' rather than 'other', making them highly independent, un-relational beings.

Gayle Rubin (1975) argues that far from being an expression of natural differences, an exclusive gender identity relies on the suppression of natural similarities.[115] It requires the suppression of whatever is likely to stain men as feminine or womanly, particularly tenderness, emotionality and care, and the suppression in women of any attributes that make them masculine or manly, particularly risk taking, toughness, rationality, independence, aggression, and even competitiveness and ambition. The gender system therefore is not only divisive but is also highly repressive of both women and men because of "its insistence upon a rigid division of personality".[116]

Neo Freudian psychoanalytic accounts shine considerable light on the oppositional and rigid nature of constructing women's and men's personalities, particularly men's masculinity. Chodorow (1999) for example explains that for children of both sexes, mothers represent regression and lack of autonomy, which they need to move away from. A boy associates these issues with his own gender identification at the same time, leading to the rejection of the feminine. The boy's dependence on his mother, which he must reject, and his attachment and identification with her, which he must deny, also represent that which is *not* masculine. A boy represses those qualities he believes to be feminine in himself and rejects and devalues women and all things feminine in the social world.

---

[114] See Geis, 1993: 11.
[115] Rubin, 1975: 180.
[116] Ibid.

This is why the socialisation of the masculine gender role is much more rigid than the feminine.[117]

With men's personality/masculinity rigidly defined as the antithesis of women's personality/femininity, it is inherently precarious and causes men great anxiety, for fear of appearing feminine, weak or homosexual. This puts men under relentless pressure to be seen as strong, virile, commanding and in control, which is why men feel particularly vulnerable in the context of illness and injury.[118] Kimmel (2000) says that boys learn that their status in the world depends on them distancing themselves from femininity and constantly proving that they are men, particularly among other boys and men. This results in a masculinity that is always willing to take risks, able to experience pain and not submit to it, and constantly driven to accumulate power money and sexual partners.[119]

There is a general agreement in the literature that gender is more restrictive of men than of women, and that gender socialisation is more rigid for boys than for girls, be that in traits and attributes, roles and actions or dispositions. For example, researchers have found more traits that are not permitted (proscriptions) for men than women, leading them to conclude that stereotypes are narrower, allowing fewer options and dispositional alternatives for boys and men than for girls and women.[120] To some extent this is true, for generally speaking it is far more deviant for a male to engage in traditional female activities (e.g., homemaker, nurse, or secretary) than it is for females to enter the traditional man's world (medicine, physics, trucking, or plumbing).[121] This trend starts at a young age when more *visible* restrictions are placed

---

[117] Chodorow, 1999: 181.
[118] See Hanlon, 2012: 62, and references therein.
[119] Quoted in Hanlon, 2012: 152.
[120] Prentice and Carranza (2002), quoted in Halpern, 2011: chapter 6, part I, section 6, para. 4.
[121] See Halpern, 2011: chapter 6, part I, section 6.

on boys' than on girls' behaviour. Messner (2001; 2007) for example found that males are much more insistent that boys do boy things than females are that girls do girl things,[122] projecting perhaps their own fear of violating the masculine code. Boys learn early on that fitting in with peers means they have to be strong, tough and aggressive. The ultimate insult for deviance from this norm is being accused of 'acting like a girl', with the embedded message that it is far more valuable to be masculine than it is to be feminine.[123]

That said, I believe that restrictions on girls and women are far more obscure than those on boys and men, and more overarching, and therefore far reaching, in their lives. Jeanne Block's (1984) observations of how parents deal with boys and girls led her to the conclusion that whereas the issues between parents and sons appear to be ones of authority and control, with daughters the emphasis is on relatedness, protection and support, with an overarching theme of "thou shalt not".[124] Girls' and women's natural impulses are therefore held in check to a far greater degree than boys' and men's, particularly those relating to focusing on the self, be it in pursuit of sexual pleasure or pursuit of self-actualisation. Because women are located in society *primarily* as wives, partners and mothers, their social identity is one of relation to and service of others, be it husbands, partners, children, or even bosses or society at large, entailing self-denial and self-sacrifice. Women who pursue careers wholeheartedly are thought of as 'selfish' and 'neglectful', because the starting point for a woman is serving others, rather than serving the self. These unspoken social judgements have a significant impact on restricting the dispositional alternatives available to women and on narrowing their choices in life, as reflected in putting their partners' careers ahead of theirs, in staying in unhappy marriages for the sake of the children, and more generally in not allowing themselves

---

[122] Quoted in Wood, 2009: 198.

[123] Wood, 2009: 198.

[124] Block, 1984: 8.

to find out what they truly want out of life in the first place, because society assumes childrearing *is* their calling.

II.3   Femininity, Masculinity and Power

"Women are the only exploited group in history to have been idealized into powerlessness." Erica Jong (Novelist, poet, and essayist)[125]

The most distinguished feature of gender relations is their hierarchical nature, for gender relations are not equal but stratified, with men in dominant positions and women in subordinate positions. The spread of gender equality discourses, with which most of us are in agreement, obscures the play of power and control between women and men.[126] Collective male power is often taken for granted, as white, middle class, heterosexual men are expected to hold dominant positions,[127] or as Hanlon (2012) puts it: "The gender order normalises male privilege which is taken for granted, expected and is invisible to its holders."[128]

Men's power and privilege, masculinity writers argue, is invisible to men because of their privileged social location.[129] However, women's under privilege too is invisible to them too, despite their disadvantaged social location (I will address women's unconsciousness to their under privilege in the next chapter). The invisibility of privilege works as an obstacle to uncovering domination, while the invisibility of under privilege is as an obstacle to opposing it. Both these aspects create conditions of 'unconsciousness', keeping women and men trapped in their gender roles, unable to free themselves in order to be truly fulfilled human beings.

---

[125]   http://www.religioustolerance.org/femquote.htm.
[126]   Seidler 2006: 62.
[127]   Kimmel (2000) quoted in Hanlon, 2012: 88.
[128]   Hanlon, 2012: 208.
[129]   Kimmel (1993) and Hanmer (1990) quoted in Hanlon, 2012: 89.

Traditionally, the power axis between women and men existed within patriarchal structures, where all men collectively gain a patriarchal privilege over women and children.[130] Although gender relations have moved away from this strictly patriarchal form, they are however constantly being reconstructed in a context of unequal power relations.[131] Power, or more accurately male dominance, therefore is a central dynamic in the construction of gender, femininity and masculinity.[132]

It is important to fully understand the power play within the gender system, for to say that all men are dominant and all women are subordinate is an oversimplification. Gender is not an isolated structure within the social order but integral to it, constantly interacting with race, ethnicity, religion, social class, education, and other aspects of the wider social culture. This interplay gives rise to various types of femininities and masculinities, leading to "massive hierarchies of power" amongst men.[133] Within this complex picture, Connell (1987; 1995; and 2002) identified 'hegemonic' masculinity as the masculinity that occupies the most dominant position in the gender hierarchy, defined in relation to not only femininity, but other subordinated or marginalised masculinities as well. Connell (1995) elucidates that hegemonic masculinity is socially constructed as an unachievable ideal that need not correspond closely with people in power, but could simply be exemplars. Hegemonic masculinity therefore can be seen as the 'culturally exalted' masculinity, a successful way of "being a man" in a particular place at a given point in time.[134]

What is the source of male power and privilege?

---

130   Connell, 1995:74.
131   Brandth and Kvande, 1998.
132   See Segal, 1990.
133   See Connell, 1995 for a fuller discussion.
134   See Pini and McDonal, 2008.

Male dominance is deeply embedded in the sexual division of labour,[135] where women are socially located in the domestic aspects of social organisation and men in the public aspects of social organisation.[136] Because legitimate masculinity for men derives from working outside the home, they are able to amass economic resources, and with it power and prestige; in modern times, resources are acquired through paid work. Legitimate femininity for women, on the hand, largely derives from focusing on and serving others. Therefore, despite the currently high level of participation in paid employment by women, many still feel that they can only fulfil their gendered identity through childcare and domestic duties, making those tasks more central to their lives than paid employment. Furthermore, when engaged in paid work, most women still occupy jobs that focus on helping and supporting others, such as secretarial work, nursing, teaching, community services, etc. In managerial positions too women tend to be concentrated in supportive services such as human resources. 'Supportive' jobs that are mostly occupied by women are invariably less prestigious and far less economically rewarding than jobs typically occupied by men. Generally speaking, men tend to be concentrated in jobs that are self- rather than other-focused, and that have the potential for self-promotion and self-expansion, giving men the chance to reach not only the pinnacle of their work organisation, but also the gender system.

The gendered character of women therefore is still underpinned by the ideology of 'mothering', which discourages women from focusing on

---

[135] Many scholars believe the separation of the home from the public sphere, and the ensuing sexual division of labour, dates back to the agricultural revolution in the Neolithic era (See for example, Eagly and Carli, 2007; Iversen and Rosenbluth, 2010; and Seabright, 2012.). In those days, women's work in the domestic sphere, even when it produced considerable economic value (baking, sewing, basket weaving, etc), deprived them of the opportunity to accumulate economic resources, which significantly impinged on their economic status and, as a consequence, their power and prestige. Women became dependent on men and needed their patronage, and were thus subordinated.

[136] Chodorow (2004), quoted in Polity, 2004: 2.

their own needs, wants and desires, and deprives them of the opportunity to expand their lives. Inequality, in other words, is structurally built into the gender system; attempting to achieve sex equality without the complete dismantling of the gender system is an exercise in futility.

In his interview of men with care responsibilities, Hanlon (2012) found that paid work gave men a sense of respect and recognition, allowing them to feel accepted, appreciated and admired.[137] Masculinity therefore is underpinned by men's economic provision for their families, even when they provide care, keeping breadwinning central to the configuration of masculinity. By a stark contrast, femininity is underpinned by primary care provision, even when women engage in paid work, keeping mothering central to the configuration of femininity.

Contending theories of the source of male supremacy include the role of culture and symbolism. Ortner (2004) for example believes the reason all cultures place a lower value on women than men is that women tend to be identified with nature, because of their specialised roles in reproduction and their involvement with child rearing. Men on the other hand are identified with culture, which is ranked above the realm of the physical world. Ortner stresses however that women's association with nature is not itself 'natural', but is a symbolic component of patriarchy.[138]

Ayers (2011) too highlights the role of ancient culture and symbolism in devaluing women. She shows how changes in ancient religious myths planted toxic gender conflicts which are at the heart of Western religions, philosophy, history and even psychology today. Specifically, the move from "mother" centred religions that see the earth as sacred, nurturing, and generative, to "father" dominated religions of a creator (God) who alone, without woman as a generative power, created matter, earth,

---

[137] Hanlon, 2012: 67-9.
[138] Polity, 2004: 9.

nature and "man" as separate from himself. A male sky God creating without woman and without the body of the earth (now defined as woman) has shame, which is projected onto women in the form of the succubus (the feminine demon that steals men's potency at night), Lilith (the sexually aggressive first wife of Adam in Hebrew myth), Medusa (the "mother" that devours instead of creates), and Eve (the origin of sin and sex, today's femme fatale and bimbo); all of whom are stereotypes of females preying sexually upon males.[139]

In neo Freudian psychoanalytic accounts, boys attempt to construct their sense of masculinity largely in negative terms, all that is not feminine, leaving their masculinity both fragile and elusive. It becomes important for the masculine identity, therefore, that certain social activities are defined as masculine and superior, and beyond the reach of women who are believed unable to do many of the socially important things. It is paramount to believe that women's economic and social contribution cannot equal men's. "The secure possession of certain realms and the insistence that these realms are superior to the maternal world become crucial both to the definition of masculinity and to a particular boy's own masculine gender identification."[140]

II.4   Femininity, Masculinity, Power and Emotions

> *"The modern, industrialized male tends to suffer a certain*
> *level of dissatisfaction in his relationship to women because*
> *he has unknowingly acquired a hardened and closed heart."*
> *Kevin and Donna Philippe-Johnson (Bloggers)[141]*

---

[139]   Rowland, 2012.

[140]   Chodorow 1999: 182.

[141]   http://earthstar.newlibertyvillage.com/awakening.htm.

II.4.1   Rationality *vs.* emotionality

Another area in which men distance themselves from women, to carve out and maintain a superior position in society, is rationality. One of the lynchpins of male dominance in Western societies, which is based on the power of white, middle class, Judeo-Christian men, is the belief that rationality is superior to emotionality and, at the same time, that men are rational and unemotional and women are emotional and irrational. Reason is defined in opposition to nature and so to emotions, feelings, needs and desires.[142] 'Ratio' is at the root of the word reason, which is the opposite of passion,[143] justifying La Bruyère's (2007) proclamation: "Nothing is easier for passion than to overcome reason."[144]

The 17th and 18th century Enlightenment, otherwise called the Age of Reason, created an unbridgeable schism between mind and body and rationality and emotionality. The body was associated with emotions, nature and animals and assigned a slave status to its master the mind, where reason resides. Seidler (2006) states that Kant fragmented the notion of 'human nature', where 'human' was identified with 'reason' and 'nature' was disdained as animal.[145] Consequently, "reason came to be marked as a sign of superiority that allowed a dominant masculinity to disdain emotions, feelings and desires located in a body itself regarded as 'animal'."[146] As women were deemed 'closer to nature', they were more likely to allow their behaviours to be influenced by emotions, which can be regarded as feminine and a sign of irrationality.[147] Women, Seidler (2003) argues, were therefore forced to subordinate themselves to men

---

[142]   Seidler, 2003: 15.
[143]   Elster, 2009: 1.
[144]   Quoted in Elster, 2009: 2.
[145]   Seidler, 2006: 4.
[146]   Ibid.
[147]   Ibid.

to anchor themselves in the new world of reason and science.[148, 149] The perception of difference from, and superiority to, women becomes a deeply held disposition for many men.[150]

II.4.2   Emotionality as a threat to masculinity

The association between rational thought and dominant masculinity means that men experience emotions as a 'moral weakness' and a 'threat to their identities'.[151] Men learn to fear their own emotions and feelings because they might betray their identity as heterosexual men.[152] Seidler (2006) states that since progress during the Enlightenment was identified with control and domination of nature, this control was something that men could exercise in relation to their inner nature, where they learnt to identify masculinity with self-control.[153] In their attempt to live up to the dominant masculinity, therefore, men hide feelings, beliefs, and intuitions that are incongruent with dominant images.[154]

Social norms therefore construct a highly gendered pattern of emotionality, where the stereotypical feminine is highly emotional, while emotional competence is written off from the masculine script,[155] leading men to experience discomfort in recognising and expressing emotions. Since it is not socially acceptable for 'real men' to display

---

[148]   Seidler, 2003: 14.

[149]   Seidler (2003) states that identification of masculinity with reason extends beyond relations of power between women and men into a more generalised conceptions of authority and legitimacy, such as the relationship between colonisers and colonised nations.

[150]   See Hanlon, 2012: 155, and references therein.

[151]   Ibid.

[152]   Seidler, 2006: 62.

[153]   Ibid: 5.

[154]   Seidler (1989) quoted in Hanlon, 2012: 71.

[155]   Hanlon 2012: 150.

emotions, public displays of care and intimacy are taboo among men.[156] Kierski and Blazina (2009) say that men do possess a rich tapestry of emotions and feelings, in particular extensive and strong fears relating to ill health, loneliness and lack of meaning in life. However, their masculine identity neither allows them to acknowledge these feelings nor reveal them.

Of the whole repertoire of emotions, those particularly incongruent with the masculine identity are fear, grief and shame.[157] When men do experience grief and vulnerability, they carefully manage emotional expression. Rationality, action and instrumental language become devices that men deploy to avoid the pain of self-revelation.[158] Bennett (2007) for example has shown how widowhood poses a serious challenge to emotional control in men. The widowers negotiate conflicting emotional experiences of widowhood with maintaining masculinity by resorting to rhetorical devices of emotional control like rationality, responsibility and successful action. Emotional expression may be permitted in private, but not in public.

Scheff (2003) states that in most male adults, fear, grief and shame are hidden, disguised or suppressed so that early in childhood being aware of them becomes problematic for boys. At the same time, men are socialised to pay less attention to relationships than women, particularly attachments to others, and are conditioned to be less interested in affectionate bonds.[159] The suppression of emotions *and* detachment from others are interrelated: the more emotions are suppressed, the more difficult others have in relating to us. But the more isolated we feel, the easier it is to suppress emotions. Suppressing emotions and distancing from relationship allow men to become 'mobile' and seek accomplishments outside the home. Such mobility however comes at

---

[156] See Hanlon, 2012: 146-147, and references therein.
[157] Scheff, 2003.
[158] Hanlon, 2012: 154.
[159] Lewis (1976), quoted in Scheff, 2003.

a high price: alienation from self and others, and a propensity for aggression and violence.

Continuing with the theme of trading off economic success, and therefore power and prestige, with emotional expression, Connell (2005) proposes that it is because of men's power and privilege that they experience 'toxicity' or an affective disadvantage. For her, it is the identities and relations of dominance which sustain the no affective relations of men.[160] Since losing power and privilege are at stake, there is considerable normative pressure on men to avoid emotional practices, particularly in public, leading men to actively police and control the boundaries of masculinity for emotional content.[161]

Clare (2000) argues that although femininity has been historically associated with weakness and illness, increasingly masculinity is associated with pathology. He suggests that men are like a bursting dam of unmet needs and consequently are often depressed and angry. A common way for men to deal with these unmet emotional needs is through denial and repression.[162]

II.4.3   Emotional repression and intimacy

Seidler states that because men treat 'control' as a form of domination, they develop very little ongoing relationship with their emotional selves, leading to what he calls 'inner vacuum'.[163] Men's 'affective disadvantage' creates a real crisis in intimacy, for to allow intimacy is to allow oneself to experience vulnerability, risking the failure of the masculine project that is predicated on rationality and self-control. Many men therefore balk at relationships that require them to be emotionally expressive, including

---

[160]   Quoted in Hanlon, 2012, 88.
[161]   See Hanlon, 2012: 147, for references.
[162]   Quoted in Hanlon 2012: 75.
[163]   Seidler, 2003: 48-52.

care practices and intimacy with adults. Hanlon (2012) states that since men need affection themselves, including care and nurturance, a conflict arises between these internal needs for nurturance and the rationale for power and dominance, which results in women becoming the 'emotional workers'.[164] Women as a result end up giving without receiving, while men receive without giving, emotional support. For a long time women tolerated men's avoidance of emotional reciprocity, but as Seidler (2006) says there is now a different vision of entitlement and a radical shift where it is no longer considered enough that a man is merely a good provider. Women have come to expect more emotionality for themselves within relationships and are increasingly dissatisfied with their partners' emotional absence. Marriage is no longer conceived of as an end in itself but as a framework within which identities can expect to seek their own fulfilment.[165]

Further pressure on changing the norms for masculinity comes according to Hanlon (2012) from the decline of the importance of group identity, such as social class, religion and race, and the rise in individual identity, and focus on self-interest and self-improvement. Within this dynamic context, intimate relationships transform as people look for a new sense of purpose and feelings of belonging, and love takes on particular salience. Children too are expected to fill the void felt as group identity dissolves, resulting in more emotionally intense child-parent relations that place great hope as well as great pressure on men. Compared to traditional fathers, children provide a focus for men's involvement in families.[166]

---

[164] Hanlon 2012: 71.

[165] Seidler, 2006: 63.

[166] See Hanlon, 2012: 59-62, and references therein.

II.4.4 The power of emotions

Emotionality is hugely misunderstood, and as a consequence denigrated, in Western cultural traditions, because it is seen as *base*, taking people away from culture, sophistication and, critically, rationality that remains the cornerstone of Western civilisation. Darwin for example, the godfather of human biology, thought of emotions as merely an aspect of the evolutionary history of human beings, tracing them back to animals and of no higher value in themselves to humans.[167] The Enlightenment was a critical period in advancing civilization through empiricism, scientific rigor and intellectual pursuits, and debasing anything that is to the contrary, including faith, spirituality and emotions.

As I have explained in sections I.4.3 and II.4.1, emotions are part of our nervous system and are therefore part and parcel of the human mind. They serve the important function of transmitting information (*via* neurotransmitters) to our bodies in response to the mind's cognitive processing of environmental signals. Feelings are the subjective experience of emotions, which direct our attention and motivate us to adopt certain behaviours in response to the events we encounter. Emotions are therefore integral to our understanding of and communication with the world around us, and it is inconceivable that we can deal with our environment through cognitive process alone. In their book 'Passion and reason: making sense of our emotions', Richard Lazarus and Bernice Lazarus (1994) state that one of the myths that still exist about emotions is that they are irrational and do not depend on thinking and reasoning, when in fact emotions and intelligence go hand in hand which is why humans, who are highly intelligent beings, are such emotional animals.[168]

---

[167]   See Oatley, Keltner and Jenkins, 2006: 5-6.
[168]   Lazarus and Lazarus, 1994: 3.

Antonio Damasio's (2008) remarkable book 'Descartes' error: emotion, reason and the human brain', challenges Descartes' main idea that the human mind is an incorporeal substance distinct from the body. Instead, he argues that pure thought untainted by emotions and other 'lower' mental functions is less useful than commonly supposed. Rather, personally beneficial decision making requires emotion as well as reason. He gives examples of how patients with damage to the brain's prefrontal cortex cannot make simple decisions because they lack the necessary emotional machinery. The brain often 'decides' among alternatives by 'marking' one alternative as more emotionally salient than another. Scientists tested this "marking" mechanism in controlled studies using gambling. Damasio writes: "certain aspects of the process of emotion and feeling are indispensable for rationality. At their best, feelings point us in the proper direction, take us to the appropriate place in a decision-making space, where we may put the instruments of logic to good use." "Emotion and feeling, along with the covert physiological machinery underlying them, assist us with the daunting task of predicting an uncertain future and planning our actions accordingly."[169]

Given the inseparability of reason from emotion, when we say men are rational and not emotional, this is not meant in a literal sense. With dominant masculinity underpinned by rationality, it is a certain kind of emotions and a certain manifestation of emotionality that are written out of the masculine script. Men allow themselves to feel and reveal pride for example, in themselves and in their loved ones. It is those emotions that are closely associated with women and femininity, such as fear, shame, vulnerability, and uncertainty than men distance themselves from. So too is the 'feminised' or 'gendered' ways of emotionality denigrated and denied by men, such as publically displaying emotions, or displaying emotions in an exaggerated way.

---

[169] Damasio, 1995, preface.

II.4.5   Vulnerability: the gateway to emotional freedom

Men are faced with a rising demand for 'care', as women fully engage in paid employment and as 'single fatherhood' rises too. Nowadays, men are expected to be involved fathers, emotionally competent and nurturing, and often times without the support of women who traditionally offered the emotional labour. As men increase their involvement in care, a golden opportunity presents itself in resolving the crisis in men's affective disadvantage. Chodorow's (1994; 1999) incisive vision into the structural and relational aspects of femininity and masculinity shows masculinity as an issue, in a way that femininity is not, as a direct result of a boy's experience of himself where he is parented by a woman, while the father is a more distant and less tenable source of affection. Given that gender ideology is premised on masculine superiority, masculinity is presented to a boy as less available and accessible than femininity, and at the same time more superior and hence more desirable.[170] The ego construction for boys then becomes one of distancing themselves from femininity and all things feminine, including the feminine aspects of their own psyche. Emotions are then associated with weakness, dependency and vulnerability, and are to be avoided at all cost.

Implicit in Chodorow's account is that rejection of the feminine and suppression of vulnerability in men is not inevitable; had the father been less distant and more involved in his children's nurturance, and had his social ranking been equal to that of the mother, ego formation would have taken an entirely different route. A common theme in gender equality literature is that fathers who care for their children and share more equally in household work tend to come from egalitarian families themselves.[171] Increased focus on child development since the 1980s has also contributed to calls for greater participation from men in their children's lives. Having two active parents is seen as providing

---

[170]   Chodorow, 1999:181.
[171]   See Coltrane, 2000; and Hanlon, 2012.

children with dual role models, allowing them to grow in a "richer, more complex emotional milieu", as children are provided with an extra source of stimulation and unique experiences.[172] Importantly, studies suggest that a high level of father involvement is associated with optimal toddler development, in terms of developing secure attachment, social confidence and problem solving.[173] Chodorow (1994) argues that beneath a fragile sense of masculinity is the conflicted need for men to identify with feminine values of caring, intimacy and emotional nurturance as a fundamental aspect of their human nature.[174]

But how can men access and fulfil these emotional needs within themselves?

In her famous talk 'The power of vulnerability', Brené Brown (2011) states that "vulnerability is having the courage to let go of who you think you *should* be and allowing yourself to be who you really are."[175] The *should* in a gender context comes from prescriptions dictating that men should be strong, in control and rational. Embracing who men really are entails by necessity desisting from repressing those 'tender' aspects of themselves which they denigrate as feminine and therefore "not good enough". This is why men who fail to achieve a socially viable masculinity have strong feelings of shame. Brown characterises shame in the following conversation with the self: "is there something about me that if other people know (..) or see (..) I won't be worthy of connection?"

Men inevitably 'feel' and 'experience' a whole range of tender feelings, especially as they engage in non-masculine endeavours such as caring, intimacy and nurturance, but more generally at times of uncertainty,

---

172 Haas, 1992: 9.
173 Ibid: 10.
174 Quoted in Hanlon, 2012: 57.
175 http://www.ted.com/talks/brene_brown_on_vulnerability.html, accessed on May 19th, 2013.

illness, grief, etc. Crossing over to this 'no man land' inevitably leaves men feeling vulnerable, which can be excruciating when they uphold the ideals of dominant masculinity. But vulnerability, revealing who we really are wholeheartedly according to Brown, is the gateway to connection and emotional freedom, and can therefore be a viable route for men to take in their journey of self-discovery. The more treaded this route is, the easier it becomes to rewrite a masculine script that embraces rather than suppresses emotions.

Vulnerability is universal and is experienced by everyone at different times and to varying degrees throughout life. However, to the extent that dominant masculinity, which is predicated on suppression and denial of the feminine aspects of the psyche, remains the ideal that most men aspire for, there is this tendency for men to experience vulnerable feelings as they enter care spaces. This deters the vast majority of men from engaging in care practices, knowing that what is at stake is loss of status. Staving off vulnerability in order to remain in control however exacts a heavy psychic price of disconnection and distance from 'others', creating feelings of shame that are never far beneath the surface for those espousing dominant masculinity. Embracing vulnerability, having the courage to let go of who we think we should be in favour of who we really are, is the only way to achieve an authentic self.

II.4.6   Fear and dread of the feminine

Within certain kinds of macho cultures in Central America, there is a visibly intense fear of the 'feminine'.[176] Gayle Rubin (1975) mentions many New Guinea societies[177] who are viciously oppressive to women. The power of the males in these groups is not founded on their roles as fathers or patriarchs, but on their collective adult maleness, embodied

---

[176]   Seidler, 2006: 62.
[177]   Rubin, 1975, lists Enga, Maring, Bena Bena, Huli, Melpa, Kuma, Gahuku-Gama, Fore Mrind Anim (see Rubin, 1975: 168 for references).

in secret cults, warfare, exchange networks, rituals and various initiation procedures. She also mentions many New Guinea groups where men and women are considered so inimical that men have to cleanse the effects of being in utero by consuming semen (usually through homosexual partnership).

These of course are extreme expressions of 'fear of the feminine', but many psychologists acknowledge the existence of such a psychological dynamic in the Western male psyche. Blazina (1997) states that fear of the feminine is a prevalent fixture in the western psychology, affecting men's definition of self as well as being a guiding force in the development of traditional male gender identity. Fear of what is labelled feminine characteristics has often been confused or miss associated with fear of actual women. Characteristics such as emotional awareness and feelings of vulnerability don't belong exclusively within the realm of women's experiences, but gender role socialisation tends to assume so.[178]

From his work with other men and from his own journey of self-discovery, Werner Kierski (2007) states that men are strongly affected by fear of the feminine, which is a mechanism that helps them avoid those feelings that are not endorsed by the masculine script. Effectively, fear of the feminine is a monitor mechanism that keeps men within the bounds of socially defined masculinity. Kierski further explains that the presence of entrenched notions of *difference* between men and women and the existence of detailed views of this difference heightens men's awareness of the non-masculine. This, combined with social demands placed on men to remain within masculine gender boundaries, creates a vigilant mechanism that polices conformity to gender identities, giving repeated opportunities for fear of the feminine to arise. Fear of the feminine in this instance performs as an internal check ensuring that men's emotions, cognitive processes and actions stay within the safe boundaries of gender identities.

---

[178] Blazina, 1997.

Kierski mentions Buss' (1994) global research that revealed the power of gender boundaries across most cultures in influencing behaviour such as mate preferences. Buss' research shows that men who do not seek to acquire wealth and status but instead reveal their vulnerability may have diminished chances to successfully attract a suitable mate. Kierski argues that these findings illustrate how fear of the feminine is not only a phenomenon related to men's inner worlds. The evidence instead confirms that the fear of the feminine is also a social regulating mechanism that ensures men stay in their prescribed tracks.

Freud describes the genesis of fear of the feminine in the masculine oedipal crisis: a boy's struggle to free himself from his mother and become masculine generates "the contempt felt by men for a sex which is the lesser";[179] "what we have come to consider the normal male contempt for women."[180] Horney (1932) says these phenomena are manifestations of a deeper 'dread of women' a masculine fear and terror of maternal omnipotence that arises as one major consequence of their early caretaking and socialisation by women: fear of total and incomprehensible control over a child's life at a time when the child has no reflective capacities for understanding.[181] To cope with their fears without giving up women altogether, boys and men develop psychological as well as cultural ideological mechanisms such as creating folk legends, beliefs, and poems that ward off the dread, by externalising and objectifying women: "it is not ... that I dread her, it is that she herself is malignant, capable of any crime, a beast of prey, a vampire, a witch, insatiable in her desires. ... the very personification of what is sinister."[182] We are again meeting Ayers' (2011) Succubus, the feminine demon that steals men's potency at night, as well as Eve, Lilith and Medusa, all of whom are depicted as evil women. Because the feminine

---

[179] Freud (1925), quoted in Chodorow, 1999: 182.
[180] Brunswick (1940), quoted by Freud (1925), who is quoted by in Chodorow, 1999: 182.
[181] Quoted in Chodorow, 1999: 183.
[182] Ibid.

is demonised, men are heavily invested in distancing themselves from the feminine aspects of their own psyche.

Jung (1953) suggested the archetype he labelled as anima represents the unconsciously repressed feminine side of the male, a part of men's personality that is often difficult to integrate into their conscious persona. For Jung, the feminine is the "other" of masculine consciousness.[183] Others suggest that men view the feminine aspects of themselves as *dangerous* and attempt to either deny or repress them. McCreary (1994) suggests that boys and men are dealt with more harshly than girls and women when they deviate from traditional societal gender prescriptions, so men risk societal punishment when employing cross gender role behaviours and are both directly and indirectly conditioned to fear and avoid behaviours that could be seen as feminine.[184] The thrust of these scholars' work is that the fear of the feminine is a deep seated structure in the male psyche that must be understood in order to understand men at all.

Kierski (2007) says fear of the feminine has internal and external triggers. Internally, fear of the feminine is an intra psychic defence mechanism enabling men to repress or split off vulnerable feelings, in order to remain in congruence with male identity. Feelings of vulnerability and emotional dependency, such as fear, uncertainty, loneliness, and depression are all deemed 'unmanly', 'weak' and therefore 'feminine'. These internal triggers, arising naturally in response to inner processes such as thoughts, sensations, memories, moods etc, leave men feeling exposed, threatened, uncertain or in need of support or closeness. Rigid masculine dictates however have no allowance for vulnerable feelings, hence these feelings are either denied or ignored by men. The fear of the feminine functions in this case like a barrier, preventing men from actually feeling even more helpless, out of control or dependent. "The

---

[183] Rowland, 2012.
[184] Blazina, 1997.

fear of the feminine can be experienced as feeling of discomfort yet it can also be a defence to stop emotional discomfort from becoming stronger."[185]

External triggers include masculine qualities that women posses which might threaten the inner normality and lead the man to an uncomfortable experience of himself, from which his fear of the feminine tries to protect himself. A successful woman might make a man feel less potent, out of control and vulnerable. Men shield themselves from fear of the feminine by keeping them secret from themselves, and projecting them onto women whom they then seek to control.[186] Seidler (2006) says that men feel they have to control 'their' women even if they can't control other areas of their lives. They can expect to give orders and be obeyed by their partners. Sometimes they will use violence to make sure of the obedience they believe they are entitled to.[187]

In a nutshell, fear of the feminine is fear of not *becoming* masculine, of *failing* to achieve a socially viable masculinity. Feelings of vulnerability, of emotional need and dependency and of not being in control remind men of how women are, and therefore of how they are not, or more accurately how they *should* not be. Any hint of those feelings therefore signals to men a threat to their masculine project, and triggers a defensive mechanism, be it denial, suppression or projection. Often times, men project those feelings of weakness on the women in their lives, and in extreme cases can result in violence toward others, including toward women who many men feel they need to control.

---

[185] Kierski, 2007.
[186] Ibid.
[187] Seidler, 2006: 61-62.

II.5 Femininity, Masculinity, Power, Emotions and Care

"I wondered if caring for children might not provide other
men with opportunities for fuller emotional lives. Could
men reclaim a more complete sense of manhood that was
not based on rejecting the softer often more "feminine" sides
of themselves?" Scot Coltrane (Scholar and author)[188]

II.5.1 The feminisation of care

Most of unpaid work but especially caring for children is feminised, given its association with affection, tenderness, empathy, intimacy, sensitivity, intuition and self-sacrifice,[189] and is subordinated to paid work, which is associated with instrumentality and agency and therefore power and prestige. For men to preserve their higher status in society, engagement in paid work and avoidance of unpaid work becomes central to the achievement of a valid, dominant masculinity. Hanlon (2012) argues that masculinity, culturally defined as rational, unemotional, inexpressive, and even emotionally incompetent, is antithetical to care; the oppositional definition of masculinity to femininity entails writing out femininity from men's lives,[190] and with it care practices. This is why being a good father is rarely associated with domestic chores. Seidler (2006) argues that men are still uneasy in domestic spaces, as if they don't really belong there.[191] Instead, fathers are more associated with agency and decision-making that comes with breadwinning, representing the family in the outside world, and consuming the services provided by women.[192] Men can feel more at ease with male friends and

---

[188] Coltrane, 1996: 96.
[189] Connell, 2002: 3; and Hanlon, 2012: 44.
[190] Hanlon, 2012:44.
[191] Seidler, 2006: 62.
[192] Hanlon, 2012: 44.

in work spaces, often ready to work long hours and overtime, but find this difficult within the space of the family.[193]

Hanlon (2012) states that since ideal caring qualities are highly "feminised", nurturing behaviour and practices are coded feminine and signify dependency, passivity, femininity and vulnerability; the antithesis of hegemonic masculinity. In the minds of men, caring is disassociated from recognition, respect, power, admiration and acceptance that men compete for and expect in the public sphere, and opting out of hegemonic masculinity to men means embracing an illegitimate masculinity.[194] In practice then, becoming a carer entails rejecting the stereotypical goals of masculinity, and embracing some aspects of femininity and status devaluation. Becoming a carer therefore can be experienced by men as emasculation, because it asks them to stop being 'a man'. Exiting one's comfort zone can then be experienced as exiting one's identity.'[195]

II.5.2   Studies of care

In his powerful study of Irish men engaged in various aspects of care, Hanlon (2012) shows that although the norms for masculinity and masculine care are changing, sex inequality persists mainly through men's resistance to care. The study gives valuable insights into the contradictions and conflicts in men's lives, as their masculinities transition to include feminine care, which impinges on the strict rules of dominant masculinities. Hanlon asks the pertinent question that since to be a valuable man is to be powerful, and to be human is to be vulnerable, how can men acknowledge their masculinity when feeling vulnerable and how can men acknowledge their vulnerability when feeling masculine? Hanlon contends that caring helps resolve

---

[193]   Seidler, 2006: 62.

[194]   Hanlon, 2012: 63.

[195]   Ibid: 194.

these tensions and contradictions, because equality in caring can create opportunities for men to deepen caring relations with others and create a healthier and caring society.[196] The emotional and relational gains men can experience as a result of caring can help compensate them for their perceived loss of power and status. When men acknowledge love and dependency, this reconnects them with vulnerability and challenges their masculine identities that are based on power, independence and being commanding. Experiencing vulnerability means that men are faced with the limitations of performing hegemonic masculinity and this can open spaces for change.[197]

Another study of the intersection between masculinities and care is Brandth and Kvande's (1998) who interviewed Norwegian couples during the fathers' time off work to look after their infants. The primary focus of the study was to see whether care becomes an extension of men's masculine identity, allowing them to preserve power and privilege, or whether care reconfigures men's masculinity when they embrace its fundamental qualities of tenderness, emotional connections, and self-sacrifice, and if so, does caring masculinities become subordinated to dominant masculinities?

II.5.2.1 Emotionally engaged fatherhood

The first interesting finding in Brandth and Kvande's study was that the fathers were striving to find out what it means to be a good father. Since in their family of origin their fathers were distant and uninvolved in family care, the fathers in the study felt they lacked role models. Implicitly, the question the men were pondering reveals the change in fathering norms and the cultural shift in masculinity discourses that now include emotionally involved fatherhood. Indeed, the fathers emphasised

---

[196] See Hanlon, 2012: 209, and references therein.
[197] Hanlon, 2012: 210.

the importance of intimacy in their fathering practices: closeness, showing interest and participating in their children's development were all important aspects of their fathering. Such an ideal, Brandth and Kvande conclude, has elements of 'ideal' mothering: closeness, care and contact, suggesting that caring masculinities encompass some aspects of feminine emotionality. Hanlon's study too found that masculinity is being slowly redefined to include emotionally engaged fatherhood; to act more like mothers; to shed their privileged outsider status and assume an active role in the routine care of their children.[198] In their study of fatherhood, Olmstead et al. (2009) show that contemporary cultural ideals of fatherhood include 'nurturant' fathers who are actively involved and responsive to all aspects of childcare. In "The normal chaos of love" Beck and Beck-Gernsheim (1995) observe how men are increasingly cognizant of the possibility that relationships with both their employers and their wives or partners maybe transient. For contemporary men, the notion of achieving either a job or a marriage that last a lifetime is somewhat optimistic. To these men, paternal bond is seen as superior to other liaisons.[199]

II.5.2.2 Devaluation of the feminine

Brandth and Kvande's interviews of the mothers in the study mentioned above revealed that although motherhood is usually taken to be the standard reference for childcare, the mothers believed the fathers' methods of caring was superior to theirs in many respects: the fathers were seen as practical, creating clear boundaries and not overly involved with the children. Several mothers went even further by saying that they attempted to 'emulate' the fathers' way of *being* with the children, thus attaching a higher status to paternal than maternal care practices. In some cases, the positive evaluation of male caring practices had a

---

[198]   Ibid: 44; and Coltrane, 1996: 5.
[199]   Quoted in Burnett et al., 2010.

corresponding devaluation of the feminine aspect of care. One mother described how she might spend her time with her daughter doing 'girl things'. This is not an isolated incident of women putting men on a pedestal, but another manifestation of the devaluation of the feminine in general, even by women themselves. What is poignant here is the context of the devaluation, namely childcare, the hinterland of femininity. This reveals strong ideological beliefs about men's superior competence that are brought to bear even on the idealised feminine practices of care.

Interestingly, both the mothers and the fathers in the study were critical of the mothers' ways of mothering. The fathers thought the mothers' over involvement with and over protection of the children deprived them of developing a sense of independence, and left the mothers too tired to engage in play with the children. The mothers agreed with these criticisms, particularly their emotional over involvement, but did not believe they could exercise any control in 'letting go'. Another point that reveals 'gendered' and highly conditioned differences in men's and women's attitude to paid work and care was the fathers' criticism of the working mothers' worry and guilt about not being able to spend enough time with their children. The fathers themselves did not believe their work took them away from the children. On the contrary, they felt that the children benefited from their work. This reveals women's anxiety in achieving the feminine ideal of mothering when they engage in paid work, which parallels men's anxiety in achieving dominant masculinity when they engage in care. In Doucet and Merla's (2007) study of stay at home fathers in Canada and Belgium, the fathers openly questioned whether a 'stay at home father' was also a 'good family man', highlighting the contradiction between evolving conceptions of caring fatherhood and the more traditional breadwinner masculine identity.

II.5.2.3 Resisting care: who cares and who doesn't?

Most of the men interviewed in Hanlon's (2012) study had an interest in having a 'care free' life and only a minority chose otherwise. The majority claimed more traditional and less hands on roles with their children. A minority were primary carers for their parents, or secondary carers for relatives. Being emotionally distant and practically uninvolved were more typical for older men, who provide care by providing education, a home and introducing their children to public masculine defined spaces.[200] The men drew on various discourses to support their gender ideology. Their care free stance was rationalised on the grounds that it was *unnatural* by conflicting with men's evolutionary and biological nature, *dysfunctional* by disrupting the natural social order, *impractical* by contradicting sensible economic considerations and *abnormal* by deviating from normative values and conventions.[201]

Equal sharing was seen as impractical, uneconomic or negatively sanctioned by their employer. It means claiming less advantage in the public sphere. While the men were prepared to engage in caring practices, they were opposed to sacrificing work-based masculinity while doing so. Fear of emasculation was evident when asked to give up paid work, believing they will feel insignificant and invisible to other men as they engage in care.[202]

The men also rationalised inequality in caring by using gender discourses that define caring in opposition to masculinity. Carers were thought to have chosen care work because it fits their psychological makeup, social interest and self-identity. Men's interests, roles, identities and basic capabilities on the other hand, were seen to be at odds with primary care and dissimilar to women's interests and identities. By imagining themselves to be inadequate, incompetent or uninterested nurturers, men easily distance themselves from feeling obliged to care.[203] Regardless of whether these differences were believed to be innate or to be socially

---

[200] Hanlon, 2012: 131-2.
[201] Ibid: 182.
[202] Ibid: 67.
[203] Ibid: 91.

constructed, they still made caring difficult for men.[204] Some admitted to limiting their caring practices within their comfort zone, by doing practical rather than intimate care tasks. However, as Hanlon argues powerfully, "(r)emaining in comfort zone is a privilege that allows many men to avoid the subordination of caring."[205]

At the same time, most of those interviewed by Hanlon were keen to declare their espousal of the socially valued ideals of gender equality. Often, the men used disclaimers like 'I'm not a sexist but' as a means of separating the principle of equality from its practice, enabling them to proclaim liberal ideas of gender equality while remaining complicit with dominant masculinity.[206] I will address this apparent contradiction between rhetoric and practice of sex equality principles in the next chapter. Suffice it to say here that what manifests in the world is a more accurate reflection of our deeply held beliefs than of our utterances. To this extent, men's resistance to care reflects society's belief, by both women and men, that it is still primarily a woman's job to care; and that care is subordinated to work.

II.5.2.4   Women's resistance to equal care

Women too work as gatekeepers to men's greater involvement in care, as they perceive care to be their own sphere of influence and seek to protect it from men's control. The feminine script is most restrictive when it comes to childbearing and childrearing, and for many women their gender identity is not fulfilled without bearing and caring for children and making them the focus of their life. For those women, engagement in the public sphere is secondary to their mothering activities, which they see as their real vocation. This mostly unconscious pattern is manifested in working women's guilt for not being at home with their children,

---

[204]   Ibid: 190.
[205]   Ibid: 193.
[206]   Ibid: 199.

and their inability to let go of being in charge of the household, their traditional fortitude. The idealisation of care and assigning it exclusively to women make it imperative for women to be the primary carers, even when they work; not fulfilling this gender identity can leave many women with a strong sense of inadequacy.

'Hormones' and 'nature' as well as economic and practical reasons are usually offered by women to justify their near monopoly of care. Since men have historically accumulated more human capital, their earning capacity tends to be invariably higher than that of women's, making the subordination of a woman's career to that of her male partner *appear* logical.

Some of the men in Hanlon's (2012) stated that women resist men's caring by labelling them 'emotionally unstable' and 'unable to plug in to their emotional side', in contrast to labelling women as 'naturally' caring. Others stated that it's an unspoken truth that men's care is a threat to womanhood.[207] In Brandth and Kvande's (1998) study, despite similar levels of engagement in paid work, the mothers were far more involved psychologically and emotionally with the children than the fathers, who had a more practical approach to parenting. The mothers' over involvement in childcare negated equality in caring between otherwise equal mothers and fathers (in employment, pay and occupational status).[208] This is a disheartening result given the advanced nature of gender discourses and practices in Norway, as reflected by the Norwegian men's willingness to take time off work to be sole carers of infants – more on this in chapter IV.

---

[207] Hanlon, 2912: 187-188.
[208] Ibid.

II.5.2.5 The abundant rewards of care... and its burdens

The men who undertook primary care roles in Hanlon's (2012) study had more empathy with the caring work done by women. It enabled them to identify with women's caring burdens and to appreciate how difficult, complex and underappreciated caring work can be. Caring enabled men to develop caring capabilities including practical, emotional and cognitive caring attributes and nurturant caring values. Caring also appeared to support men in developing a 'softer' masculinity, in reforming their lives and constructing other-centred sensibilities, and engaging with fears surrounding vulnerability.[209] The men were aware of the rewards they received from caring, including feeling loved and respected, experiencing emotional intimacy and feelings of self-esteem, respect and competence. Care for children particularly made the men feel 'responsible', 'competent', 'proud', 'challenged', 'joy', 'fantastic', 'happy', 'brilliant' and wanted.[210] Hanlon argues that sharing of care responsibilities provide evidence of 'gender convergence' by demonstrating increased levels of intimacy. 'Some of the men show how their involvement in the care of their children leads them to reflexively reconstruct their masculinity.'[211]

But there was no question that they also defined caring as burdensome in several respects. A significant theme relates to the amount of time that caring took, and some felt this was in competition with time dedicated to personal interests. Some believed it deprived them of the time to enjoy life, and believed that emotional rewards of caring were exaggerated. Nurturing masculinity is also challenged by the devaluation and invisibility men experience when doing nurturing work, by the worry of emotional work and by some of the demands of emotional intimacy. Nevertheless the sense that caring responsibility

---

[209] Ibid: 203.
[210] Ibid: 137.
[211] Ibid: 202.

is a burden is lessened when caring is undertaken by choice and when men take a professional and task oriented approach to love labour.[212]

II.5.2.6   Breadwinning as caring

Traditionally, men constructed their identities as fathers who care by undertaking paid work. As the gender equality discourse spread, a 'good father' has been re-defined as a successful breadwinner who is supportive of his partner's care activities and 'helps out' occasionally but is not expected to take any direct responsibility for childcare, spend equal time with the children as the mother, or develop the same type of close ties with children as mother's do.[213] So breadwinning remains central to realising a socially valued masculinity, and in keeping with this men understand that their principal role in caring is breadwinning.[214] The flip side is that childcare remains central to realising a socially valued femininity and in keeping with this, working women understand that their principle role in life is caring. The centrality of breadwinning to men, and of childcare to women, is at the heart of the sex inequality conundrum in contemporary times, as women's roles expand to include breadwinning but men's roles don't *equally* expand to include childcare. Therefore, despite popular discourses and media images depicting men as involved nurturers, providing for the family is still how men locate themselves in society and bearing and rearing children is still how women locate themselves in society.

When asked to describe their 'ideal father' role, the Norwegian men in Brandth and Kvende's (1998) study did not emphasise the role of a provider. However, some of them did stress the importance of providing material security as a basis for everything else in their family's life. Furthermore, the fact that all fathers in the survey had successful

---

[212]   Ibid: 138 -141.

[213]   Brandth and Kvande, 1998.

[214]   Hanlon, 2012: 109.

jobs and a relatively high income itself attests to the centrality of breadwinning to their lives.

The Irish fathers in Hanlon's (2012) study attached considerable importance to breadwinning, because it enabled them to define themselves as earners as well as carers. They understood that if men are able to meet the valued expectations as earners-breadwinners, they can achieve a sense of masculine caring respectability, as well as the status of fathering and the emotional satisfaction of a secure family life. This held true for men from different class and cultural backgrounds, although individual men assigned varying meanings to breadwinner masculinity. For all men, breadwinner masculinity did not exclude nurturing, nor the sharing of breadwinning and caring.[215]

In their study of fatherhood, Olmstead et al. (2009) found evidence to support the idea that fathering is increasingly complex and a multi faceted social role. The men they interviewed perceived their father status as multidimensional, consisting of a range of co-existing meanings and responsibilities beyond provider, including being available, sensitive, supportive, sharing in caretaking activities, disciplining and servicing as companions, confidants, and teachers. Like many other studies, they found that "providing" was integrated in the father role identity, instead of being perceived as a unique role identity. So, in the 21st century the idea of the father as merely a provider doesn't have the same validation it used to, or as O'Brien et al. (2007) put it: "'earning as caring' is not enough to validate being a good father".

---

[215] Ibid: 110.

II.6   Conclusions: Gender and the Illusion of Difference

> *"Losing an illusion makes you wiser than finding a truth."*
> Ludwig Börne (Political writer and satirist)

Gender as a social construct falters at more than one level. The mere fact of living life out of a socially constructed identity, a mental concept of the self, creates a disconnection from the reality of our humanness leading to alienation of the true self. The first pitfall of the gender system therefore is that it assumes gender to be the totality of who we are as human beings, rather than merely a social superstructure laid upon our humanness. As we enact our gendered identities and gender roles throughout life, without paying much attention to the real self, we become trapped in our own mental constructs, and we relate to each other and the world out of gender 'concepts'. It is as if we are in an invisible jail that we are unconscious of, although we are vaguely aware of not being completely free.

The gender system falters in three other significant ways. *First,* by assuming binary, opposing and mutually exclusive personalities for women and men, which leads to the denial and suppression of significant aspects of our human nature that we believe is incongruent with our sex. *Second,* by creating untenable ideals for femininity and masculinity, leaving both sexes feeling inadequate and unworthy. And *third,* by putting men above women in status, making inequality structurally built-in.

The gender system creates women's and men's personalities as oppositional and mutually exclusive, when in fact there is far more that unites women and men than divides them. The gender system therefore is made more toxic by what it leaves out than by what it includes. The exclusion of emotional competency from men's personalities and of agency from women's means that neither women nor men have access to the full range of attributes and capabilities that allow them to see themselves as whole and complete, and to connect at a deeper level with who they truly are. Women's economic dependency on men, out of their belief they don't have as much agency, and men's emotional dependency on women, out of their belief they are not emotionally literate, creates an unhealthy co-dependency between the two sexes. Embracing femininity without masculinity in women, and masculinity without femininity in men, entails the suppression of key aspects of our humanity giving us a sense of lack and feelings of inadequacy, neither of which is conducive to fulfilment or self-realisation.

Built around kinship and family,[216] the objective of the gender system is to organise sex and reproduction in a social context where kinship relations needed to be maintained and enhanced. And although these kinship systems have all but disappeared, the ideology of the gender system remains almost intact in the twenty first century. The *first* premise of the system is that men and women are *fundamentally* different, not just biologically but in every other respect. Therefore, we are either feminine or masculine but never both at the same time. The *second* premise of the gender system is that the masculine is the template for all creation, and hence it is superior, more important and has a higher intrinsic value than the feminine. The *third* premise of the gender system is that because of their biological sex and ability to bear children, women are believed to be more suited for child rearing and domestic chores, and men are believed to be more suited for work outside the home. Because of this division of labour, women are attributed with empathy, intuition and emotional connectedness, but are not thought competent enough to lead in the public sphere. Men, on the other hand, are attributed with agency and leadership but are believed to be constitutionally incapable of emotional connection and nurturance, and therefore cannot be trusted to look after babies.

---

[216]   See Rubin, 1975.

We have lived with this system for so long, some say approximately 8-10,000 years, that we accept all of its tenets as 'truths'. The relentless socialisation following these 'truths' means that women and men believe their gender-appropriate impulses and behaviours to be intrinsic expressions of their personalities rather than learned behaviour.[217] self-sacrifice and nurturance in women, and agency and competitiveness in men, are believed to be *innate* and remain largely unobserved as socially conditioned states and therefore unquestioned by the general public.

We can understand the gender system better by excavating deeper into what it represses, and the reasons for its repression. For men, the single most toxic aspect of gender repression is that of men's emotionality, in order to preserve their power and higher status above that of women. Rationality, objectivity, and intellectuality are seen as the lynchpin for men's superiority, distancing them from women's emotionality and their gendered activities, particularly childcare. Men's central location in public spaces also denies them relatedness and connectedness, in order to maximise their mobility as they pursue public sphere successes. The conflicted relationship between power on the one hand, and affect and relatedness on the other, has reached a point of crisis in men's lives as women increasingly reclaim their power and assert themselves in the public sphere and, as a consequence, are disaffected and less inclined to put up with unsatisfactory marriages and partnerships.

For women the repression is more obscure, but equally if not more far reaching. The overarching repression in girls and women is that of focusing on the self. Women's self-sacrifice is critical to the success of the gender project, because they are located in society *primarily* as wives, partners and mothers; i.e. in relation to others. Women who pursue careers wholeheartedly are judged as 'selfish' and 'neglectful', even by themselves, because the starting point for a woman is serving others. The imperative of caring for others entails that women measure their

---

[217]   Babcock and Laschever, 2008: 83.

success in terms of affective fulfilment, rather than fulfilment in non-relational endeavours, such as work. This gives considerable impetus to being overly focused on love relations, to the neglect of other areas of fulfilment. When women are faced with work-family choices, therefore, their choices are narrowed considerably as the internalisation of the feminine ideal, particularly the idealisation of motherhood, conspire to lower the value of achievement in public life.

It is those aspects of our personality that are suppressed by the gender system that are likely to unlock equality, for many reasons. As we move away from suppression, and allow our unbounded human nature to flourish, women and men will naturally move closer. The more similar people are the more affinity they have toward each other, a principle called homophily. When girls' and women's self-promotion and ambition is encouraged rather than suppressed, they are able to assert themselves in the workplace, in their intimate relationships and in work-family choices, without putting men's careers on a pedestal, or their children's' welfare ahead of theirs. Finally, as men are not restricted by masculine images and notions that preclude affect and intimate relations, childcare becomes an opportunity for personal growth and fulfilment, rather than something that is 'feminised', 'othered', and therefore devalued and avoided.

III

GENDER AS A
BELIEF SYSTEM

*"I know that you see it that way, and so that is the way it is
for you, for one thing that remains eternally true is that you
will always be given the experience that you believe you will
be given." Neale Walsch (Spiritual teacher and author)*[218]

Gender is the collection of ideas that people have about who females
and males should be, as social entities, including their roles, behaviours,
and attributes. The gender system even anticipates dispositions and
feelings, out of the schema it creates for women and men, girls and
boys. The gender system is born out of an ideology that is underpinned
by difference and division between women and men, including their
identities and their roles, and by male supremacy. Primarily, the gender
system assigns caring for women and earning for men, and prescribes
behaviours and attributes that facilitate the successful fulfilment of
these roles. Because of this stark division of roles, women and men are
prescribed personalities that are oppositional and mutually exclusive.
This is achieved by assigning femininity to women and masculinity to
men, with hardly any cross over.

As economic and cultural conditions change, sex roles change too
leading to a certain reconfiguration of women's and men's personalities,
and with them masculinity and femininity. For example, the advent of

---

[218] Walsch, 1998: 82.

women's liberation movements in the last century and the spread of sex equality discourses convinced most women to join paid employment, which necessitated some care contribution from men. Our ideas of what it is to be masculine for a man and what it is to be feminine for a woman are therefore constantly being challenged. As we attempt to reconfigure femininity and masculinity to adjust to new work-life conditions, conflicts and contradictions come to the surface. These contradictions mainly arise from our dogged belief that a woman's central location in society is one of service and care for others, and man's central location is one of economic provision, and that man is superior to woman. Our reluctance to let go of this ideology is reflected in a reality observed the world over that manifests women as primarily care givers, even when they engage in paid employment, and men as primarily breadwinners, even when they engage in care giving. This is true despite the fact that our stated opinions are invariably in line with sex equality principles.

If we believe, as we must, that nothing in life is haphazard, but the creation of 'Woman'/Man' herself/himself. And if we believe further that what we create is not created haphazardly but intentionally and purposefully, out of our system of beliefs, then we must also believe that our testable, observable reality reflects our unobservable thoughts and beliefs. This is why scholars often assert that there is always consistency between our environment and our inner world and that the events we align in our life resonate with our thoughts.[219] To this extent, failure to achieve equality between women and men is a result of failure in accepting sex equality in our thoughts. Put differently, sexism is the result of wrong thoughts about women and men and their entitlements in life. I am referring here to the *seed* thought, the thought behind the thought, or what Walsch (1994) calls the 'Sponsoring Thought', our basic guiding system that is responsible for what manifests in our lives; psychologists call it unconscious or implicit beliefs.

---

[219]   See for example Wexler, 2006; Lipton, 2008; and Dispenza, 2012.

III.1   Gender Ideology and Construction of the Gendered Self

"Concepts are learned. They are not natural. Apart from learning they do not exist.... Not one of them is true, and many come from feverish imaginations, hot with hatred and distortions born of fear. What is a concept but a thought to which its maker gives a meaning of his own?" Dr. Helen Schucman (Clinical psychologist and author)[220]

As women and men *act out* their gender roles, set within their gender identity, itself set within the overall gender system, they are guided in doing so by society's expectations of their rights and duties, and social norms of behaviour.[221] These expectations form a shared knowledge structure called stereotypes that specify what women and men should do, in order to fulfil their roles in society.[222] This leads to great predictability in women's and men's behaviour and the attributes they are likely to have, once they are located within society's gender system.[223]

Across the world, women spend considerably more time on unpaid work than men and men spend considerably more time on paid work than women.[224] Furthermore, across the world men occupy more dominant positions than women do, and even when women position themselves

---

[220] Schucman, 2007: 655.

[221] 'Role theory' is a perspective in sociology and social psychology that considers most of everyday activity to be the *acting out* of socially defined categories (e.g., mother, manager, friend, etc). Each social role is a set of rights, duties, expectations, norms and behaviours that a person has to face and fulfil. The model is based on the observation that people behave in a predictable way, and that an individual's behaviour is context specific, based on their social position and other factors (Hindin, 2007: 3959-3962).

[222] Eagly and Wood, 2009; Eagly and Carli, 2007: 84.

[223] The 'social role theory', which sprung out of role theory, bases its explanations of sex differences on social roles that women and men occupy (see Eagly, 1987, 1997; Eagly, Wood and Diekman, 2000).

[224] Eagly, 1987: 126.

in roles traditionally occupied by men, their status tends to remain below that of men. This is because the gender system is predicated on difference and division between women and men, by locating women in positions of care and service to others first and foremost, and men in positions of economic activity and economic provision first and foremost, which guarantees male supremacy in society. Once located in these positions and assigned their gendered roles, women and men act out society's expectations of the traits and behaviour that are in consonant with these roles.[225] Given that, we would expect women and men to exhibit distinctly different traits, attributes and behaviours, or what is called in the literature sex-typed behaviour.[226]

III.1.1   Living out others' expectations

"Your time is limited, so don't waste it living someone else's life. Don't be trapped by dogma – which is living with the results of other people's thinking." Steve Jobs (Co founder of Apple Inc)

One of the most powerful ways of translating society's beliefs and expectations into reality is our tendency to live our lives in alignment with what others expect of us, rather than from our own free choice. Similarly, gender beliefs and norms translate into actual behaviour when

---

[225]   This follows a psychological principle called *correspondent inference,* as identified by Gillbert 1998. See Eagly and Wood 2009.

[226]   See Eagly (1987) for great insights into the link between sex-typed behaviour and roles occupied by women and men. Eagly has a different slant than mine on the ordering and causation of gender beliefs, gender roles and sex typed behaviour. Her contention is that sex differences are directly related to the *contemporaneous* roles and occupations that women and men occupy in society. My contention on the other hand is that regardless of these roles and occupations, gender ideology dogmatically locates women in the care and service of others and men in providing, which better explains the persistence of archaic gender stereotypes that underlies sex inequality despite changes in sex roles.

boys and girls and men and women live out others' expectation of how they should be in order to fulfil their gender identity and gender roles.

There is strong evidence of how others' expectations determine how we behave toward them and how they in turn respond to us. In a landmark study experiment, the classic 'Pygmalion in the classroom', psychologists Rosenthal and Jacobson (1968) administered two tests, one real and one fake, to a group of elementary school children. The real test evaluated each child's general ability. In the fake test, the teachers were told that it was designed to predict which children were about to experience an "intellectual growth spurt". After the tests, the teachers were told which children (randomly chosen) are about to experience a leap forward in their learning abilities. A year and half later, the psychologists administered a general ability test to the same children. They found that the children who were randomly chosen but were marked out to experience a "spurt" had improved more than the rest of the students: while the non-spurters had gained an average of only 8.42 points on the general learning ability test, the pre-identified "spurters" had gained an average of 12.22 points, i.e. a 50% difference. In addition, the teachers gave the "spurters" higher grades in reading and reported that they were "happier and more intellectually curious" than their peers. The experiment reveals the significant impact teachers' expectations had on *a)* the teachers' own behaviour toward the students, and *b)* the performance of those children the teachers' believed' to be smarter.

The experiment clearly demonstrates how peoples' behaviour normally complies with others' expectations, without their awareness. It is important to note both sides of expectations in this experiment: those who viewed themselves positively and performed effectively when they were approached with high expectations, and those who performed less effectively when faced with low expectations. Given that each group was selected randomly, there may have been bright student in the underperforming group, just as there may have been underachieving students in the over performing group that was showered with high expectations. Put differently, others' expectations can have a profound impact on social outcomes, quite apart from innate ability.

This expectancy effect is mediated through a variety of behaviour, including nonverbal warmth, praise, frequency of interaction,[227] and by reacting positively when these expectations are confirmed.[228] In later work, Rosenthal (1989) proposed that an affect-effort dynamic mediates teachers' expectations and students' behaviour: teachers' expectations are communicated *via* affect, which includes verbal and nonverbal cues of warmth and liking, and effort, which includes spending more time and working harder with the students and teaching them more material.[229]

In a similar fashion, the expectation that females and males will exhibit distinctly different traits, attributes and behaviours, and that males will do better in maths and science and females in literacy and the arts translates into a corresponding reality of sex differentiated behaviour, as females and males comply with others' expectations through a variety of interpersonal experiences.

This process partly explains why many researchers like Schwartz and Rubel (2005) find scientific evidence of a correspondence between observed sex differences and traits that are thought desirable for each sex.[230] Similarly, Spence and Helmreich's (1972) study demonstrated that ratings of the ideal woman and man parallel those of the typical woman and man. Prentice and Carranza (2002) found that traits that were desirable for each sex were also believed to be typical of each sex. For example, it was desirable for men to be athletic and self-reliant, and they were also rated as being more athletic and self-reliant than women. A parallel example for women is that it was desirable for women to be

---

[227] See Harris et al., 1994, and references therein.
[228] Eagly, 1987: 14.
[229] Quoted in Harris et al., 1994.
[230] Eagly, 1987: 13.

warm and kind, and it was more typical for women to be warm and kind. These and many other experiments strongly indicate that beliefs and expectations about behaviours and dispositions that characterise females and males in society exert strong influences on their actual behaviour. This is because others' expectations become part and parcel of our social environment, which the mind perceives through the lens of gender and translates into a corresponding sex differentiated behaviour, through epigenetic control mechanisms (see section I.4.2), in order to keep coherence between our outer and inner worlds.

III.1.2   The social construction of the gendered self: The malleable 'I am'

What constitutes the self and how it is constructed is a subject that puzzled philosophers for millennia, particularly its apparent changing nature juxtaposed with an enduring and unchanging sense of who we are.[231] What seems to be plausible is that the self is both multi faceted and, at the same, has a central narrative that gives it an enduring nature.[232] I will only address the psycho social construction of the self here, insofar as it is impinged upon by gender beliefs, leaving the spiritual/ontological/philosophical questions of the self to their right place.

Cross and Madson (1997) state that the self *continually* and *dynamically* takes form through one's interaction with close others and with the social world, or as Mead (1934) explains "it is impossible to conceive of a self arising outside of social experience."[233] As individuals interact with others, in homes, schools, work and other social environments, they are bombarded with messages about who they are, who they should be

---

[231]   For an overview and a philosophical approach to the self see Baggini, 2011.

[232]   See Baggini, 2011, and Hood, 2012.

[233]   Quoted in Holstein and Gubruim, 1999: 5.

and how to construct their identity.[234] Individuals' views, emotions and motivations take shape and form within a framework provided by these cultural values, ideals, structures and practices.[235]

Our interactions with the social world become psychological experiences that build within us over time as a permanent narrative of who are. This *apparent* permanence allows us to know ourselves even as the self continually and dynamically takes form in response to life's situations. So our knowledge of who we are remains the same even as, paradoxically, the self is malleably taking shape. The continuous aspect of the self, the narrative that links our experiences over time,[236] is what scholars call the autobiographical self,[237] to which gender is central.

Florence Geis (1993) states that much of our self-identity is derived from social group memberships, such as one's nationality, ethnicity, religion and occupation, as well as from one's sex, as we adopt and internalise the norms, values, and attributes of our groups. Because sex and gender distinctions are central, important and pervasive in our culture, gender is the earliest, most central and most organising component of everyone's self-concept. As women and men internalise gender stereotypes,[238] society's expectation of them to be different and to exhibit sex-typed behaviours, becomes a reality – aided by epigenetic control mechanism (see section I.4.2). Cross and Madson (1997) for example state that women's self-construal tends to be interdependent, while men's self-construal tends to be independent, in line with society's expectations. We bring our gender coded expectations of ourselves and everyone else we interact with into every situation,[239] which influences how we behave toward others and how we expect others to behave toward

---

[234] Cross and Madson, 1997.
[235] Ibid.
[236] Baggini, 2011: 40.
[237] See Baggini, 2011: 32-33; Hanson and Mendius, 2009: 209.
[238] Eagly, 1987: 16; Wallis and Poulton, 2001.
[239] Geis, 1993: 15.

us. Built into this mirrored perception of the self, i.e. our perception of others' perception of us, is others' notions of who we should be as females and males, including temperament, dispositions, abilities, traits and attributes that go with our roles as daughter, son, mother, father, female student, male manager, etc.

Freud's insightful clinical accounts powerfully show how the social apparatus, through relentless conditioning, creates 'women' out of females, and how deeply embedded powerlessness is in women's self-concept. The powerlessness is a relational one, and comes from feeling the power of men and their lack of it.[240]

Lipton and Bhaerman (2009) state that up to around the age of six, we are like a blank tape recorder, merely downloading what is given to us about ourselves from our parents, schools and society at large. This is therefore a critical time for shaping our gender identity, based on our sex and society's gender beliefs and rules of engagement. This is also a critical period in the neo-Freudian psychoanalytic account of how the feminine and the masculine identity is formed. What gives the gendered self shape in this view is family relations within a cultural context where the mother, with whom the primary relationship is formed, is the same sex as the daughter but a different sex to the son. The father is a powerful but distant male love figure, and society values men more than women. In this cultural context, Chodorow (1978) explains how the family structure of a male breadwinner and a female homemaker, together with how society organises gender matters in general sends powerful messages to children about how they might successfully construct a socially viable identity, on top of their femaleness and maleness. Because the socially constructed feminine and masculine appear to be mutually exclusive, and because boys associate the feminine with lack of power and the masculine with power and authority, boys work harder to

---

[240] See Chodorow, 1994, 1999; Minsky, 1996; Rubin, 1975; and Birksted-breen, 1993.

renounce everything that is feminine, including emotions. Outside the home, the social conditioning machinery is relentless in confirming, consolidating, and further building on these nascent conceptions of the feminine and the masculine. Chodorow further argues that girls are able to continue their close ties to the mother well into puberty, and hence are able to base their feminine identity on this unbroken connection - the process creates a deeply internalised psychological impetus in women to reproduce the intimacy of their relationship with their mothers. Boys on the other hand, must break their identification with their mother in order to identify with the male in the relationship. As they pull away and lose their deep sense of attachment to this primary love their sense of maleness becomes connected to a sense of detaching from close relationship. As a result, women more than men will identify more closely with those relational issues that go into mothering – feelings of primary identification, lack of separateness or differentiation, boundary issues and primary love.[241]

Even in adulthood, the self remains ultra sensitive to the social culture and to others' responses, appraisals and expectations, giving it an aspect of flexibility that allows it to adjust to the rapidly developing challenges of modern life, making "the self ... socially responsive and undeniably malleable."[242] A malleable self makes sense of Rosenthal and Jacobson's Pygmalion in the classroom experiment mentioned above, as students perceive themselves as more or less competent depending on what is expected and reflected back to them by the teachers: "we come to know what we are through other's responses to us.......... The manner in which they act toward us defines our self we come to categorize ourselves as they categorize us, and we act in ways appropriate to their expectations."[243] Kupper and Zick study (2011) shows the extent of malleability of the gendered self and its hyper sensitivity to the socio-cultural context. They found that while in contemporary Germany the social construction of

---

[241] Chodorow, 1999: chapters 5 and 6.
[242] Holstein and Gubrium, 1999: 5; 8.
[243] Stryker (1998), quoted in Holstein and Gubrium, 2000: 10.

female and male identities follows traditional gendered lines, with men more socially dominant, the reverse was true of the older cohort that grew up in post war WWII Germany, when men were absent from the economy and the female ideal was an agentic one.

McCall and Dasgupta (2007) also argue for a malleable and context sensitive gendered self. They state that although men generally comply more closely with gender stereotypes than women do, there is evidence that men's gender related self-conceptions are highly responsive to gender salience in the environment. For example, men rely on stereotypically masculine traits in describing themselves when they are a minority in a mixed sex groups. More generally, men's self-description tends to be more gender stereotypical in the workplace and less stereotypical in sexual/intimate situations.

An important aspect of the self is agency which, combined with continuous social feedback,[244] allows the self to facilitate engagement in, and adaptations to, the social environment.[245] One facet of this agency is the self's powerful ability to regulate many aspects of human behaviour, such as directing perception, memory and inference concerning oneself and others. This allows the self to maintain a consistent autobiography. For example, when an ability or characteristic is especially important to an individual's self-definition, the person is likely to pay close attention to information relevant to the domain, to remember the information better than non self-relevant information and, equally importantly, to resist or ignore inconsistent feedback regarding the ability or characteristics.[246] More generally, people actively seek out information and experiences that confirm their existing self-concept and misinterpret or ignore information that contradicts their dominant beliefs about themselves.[247]

---

[244] Holstein and Gubrium, 1999: 5
[245] Cross and Madson, 1997.
[246] Ibid.
[247] See McCall and Dasgupta, 2007, for references.

This 'editorial' facet of our agency holds the key to unlocking gender dogma, since it is through this filtering process that we keep our bondage to social norms and gender stereotypes. I have already mentioned the powerful influence of childhood experiences, and their enduring impact in shaping the self. Growing up, we construct an autobiographical self, akin to writing a narrative of who we are (or more accurately who we think we should be) based on social conditioning and motivated by fulfilling others' expectations, including gendered expectations, narratives, discourses, images, myths, etc. Once constructed, we spend considerable effort filtering out inconsistent, and filtering in confirmatory, information of the core beliefs about ourselves, which when repetitively applied consolidates our beliefs into dogma.

Another dynamic of defending beliefs about the self is called 'compensatory cognition': expressing even *more* self-belief, when the self is under threat. Typically, the higher the status the more pronounced the compensation, since members of high status groups identify more strongly with their in group than members of low status groups. Men therefore are likely to be heavily invested in masculine self-conceptions, since deviation from agentic norms challenges the justification for their in group status. When agentic self-beliefs are threatened therefore, men are expected to compensate by expressing even more masculine self-beliefs to preserve their privilege.[248]

McCall and Dasgupta (2007) showed that when men experience low status conditions, through experimental manipulation, they automatically compensate for this experience of subordination by expressing a more stereotypically masculine pattern of self-beliefs, compared with high status conditions. Specifically, when men find themselves in a subordinate, i.e. a counter stereotypical, role that threatens their agentic and authoritative masculine self-concept, they respond either by automatically rejecting feminine attributes in

---

[248] McCall and Dasgupta, 2007.

themselves or by automatically rejecting masculine attributes in other people. Two points are important to make here, the first is that this compensatory cognition is an automatic, implicit or subconscious one leading to a conscious and reflective descriptions of the self – the over compensating statements. The second point is that the process takes place in order to protect the masculine self-conception relative to others, which is in line with creating a self-concept that is always in relation to others. McCall and Dasgupta think of the automatic compensatory response as a regulatory process that might pre-empt the need for changes in one's conscious self-conceptions. If compensation is effective, one would not expect any changes in descriptions of the self.

The experiment demonstrates clearly how and why men's gendered self-beliefs are particularly resistant to change, namely the rigid construction of the male identity that is allowed to be masculine but not feminine, in order to hold the higher status in society. In this set up, masculinity becomes confounded with high status, leading men to spend considerable energies defending their socially constructed agentic self, which creates genuine fear within men's psyche of failing to *become* masculine. Psychologists have identified fear of the feminine as those feelings of vulnerability that men repress, deny or split off to avoid dealing with the feminine aspects of their personality that might signal the failure of their socially constructed masculine project (see 'fear and dread of the feminine' in II.4.6). Compensatory cognition appears to be the cognitive aspect of fear of the feminine, triggered by a subordination of men's position that signals a threat to the superior masculine self-identity that confounds femininity with subordination.

III.1.3 Socialisation of the gendered self

Eagly, Alice (1987) argues that even if gender stereotypic behaviour is not internalised in the self-concept, people would still conform to gender stereotypes, because of the considerable social pressure on them to conform, including subtle nonverbal cues or more obvious methods such as monetary incentives, sexually harassing behaviour, etc.[249] In Niall Hanlon's (2012) study of men who took on care responsibilities, the men confirmed that they received negative reactions from other men, either by being censured, ignored, or simply treated with incredulity. The men themselves felt devalued and invisible in society simply for engaging in nurturing activities.[250]

These pressures are part and parcel of the social conditioning that targets conformity to society's rules, values and beliefs. There are two layers to social conditioning. The first is socialisation, which is the process of inheriting and disseminating social norms, customs and ideologies.[251] Socialisation's purpose is to encode society's values in individuals' systems of belief in order for them to become the social entities society has intended them to be: individuals capable of fulfilling their social roles while upholding society's morality and it's deeply held cultural beliefs. Socialisation therefore is the process by which society reproduces itself culturally. Pivotal to the socialisation process and quite inseparable from it is gender ideology that teaches young females and males how to become gendered adults.

Patterns and structures of socialisation include family, friends and relatives, schools, the workplace and the mass media. Parents' socialisation during the extended period of childhood in human beings is critical to the creation of the gendered self, given its presence in a child's life right from the beginning, when a child's mind is a clean slate. Sociologists have identified four ways in which parents socialise the gendered self in their children: *1)* shaping gender related attributes through toys and activities; *2)* differing their interaction with children based on the sex of the child; *3)* serving as primary gender models; and *4)* communicating gender ideals and expectations.[252]

---

[249] Eagly, 1987: 19.
[250] Hanlon, 2012: 137; 141.
[251] Clausen, 1968: 5.
[252] Epstein and Ward, 2011.

Conditioning goes deeper than socialisation, by modifying behaviour through manipulating its consequences. Wanted behaviour is rewarded (a positive consequence), and unwanted behaviour is either ignored or punished (a negative consequence). Behaviour that is reinforced, either by the application of a positive (appetitive) stimulus like praise, bribery, etc., or the removal of a negative (aversive) stimulus such as avoiding punishment, resuming pocket money, etc., will be repeated, while behaviour that is punished (time out, naughty step, etc.) will desist (becomes extinct). In essence, conditioning is *training* individuals in a society to act or respond in a manner that is approved by society. Behaviours followed by satisfying consequences tend to be repeated and those that produce unpleasant consequences are less likely to be repeated: a boy imitating his dad will repeat his behaviour if he receives appreciation (positive reinforcement), or will desist if there was no reinforcement. On the other hand, a boy wearing his mother's clothes or playing with dolls might be scolded, ridiculed or his toys taken away in which case his behaviour will desist too.[253]

Gender socialisation and gender social conditioning begin in childhood and are elaborated throughout childhood and adolescence:[254] girls are taught nurturance and domestic skills and boys are taught achievement related skills.[255] Through own observations as well as surmising from other studies that investigated gender socialisation, Block (1984) reported significant differences in socialisation emphasis between girls and boys, consistent with gender beliefs. With boys, socialisation stressed achievement and competition, and insistence on control of

---

[253] For a general discussion on social conditioning as it relates to gender see Rudman and Glick, 2008. For a technical discussion of operant conditioning, the most prevalent type of social conditioning, see Graham and Cullen, 1988. For a non technical discussion see http://www.zeepedia.com/read.php?theories_of_gender_development_2_the_behavioral_approach_gender_issues_in_psychology&b=88&c=10.

[254] Rudman and Glick, 2008 :20

[255] Eagly, Wood and Diekman, 2000: 126.

feelings and expressions of affect, and a concern for conformity to rules.[256] The emphasis with girls was on developing and maintaining close interpersonal relationships. They were encouraged to talk about their troubles and to reflect on life, and were shown affection physically and given comfort and reassurance.

Block observed that fathers direct and channel sex typed behaviour of both females and males to a far greater extent than had been assumed. In her own study, where mothers and fathers of preschool children were observed interacting with their children while doing a task, she noticed that parents of boys were more concerned with task-oriented achievements than were parents of girls. This suggested to her that from a very young age boys are more pressed for achievement by their parents than were girls, "from whom less is expected and from whom less is acceptable."[257]

Gender socialisation practices are so thorough and relentless that by the time females and males reach adulthood, they believe their gender-appropriate impulses and behaviour are intrinsic expressions of their personalities rather than learned behaviour.[258] Being nurturing, friendly, and selfless are thought to be innate qualities in women, and being competitive, confident, rational and unemotional are thought to be innate qualities in men, creating the imperative of care for women and the imperative of economic provision for men. This means that even when their choices are not constrained, women and men tend to have different interests, engage in different activities and chose different occupations. Put differently, while women and men believe themselves to be making free individual choices, the subtle but insidious powers of gender socialisation and conditioning steer them toward preordained paths of sex division and difference leading them to believe that they *are* different and have no choice in the matter. What make these

---

[256] Block, 1984: 9.

[257] Ibid.

[258] Babcock and Laschever, 2008: 83.

conditioned choices seem real are epigenetic control mechanisms that translate environmental signals into biological and behavioural realities in order to maintain harmony between mind and environment (see sections I.4.2 and I.4.4).

III.2   Gender Divisions and Differences

"Women, have as much to divide as to unit them, it would be inappropriate to write a book about them at all if it were not for a striking similarity in social attitudes toward women's roles throughout most of the world and over most of human history". Iverson and Rosenbluth (Scholars and authors)[259]

III.2.1   The different ways of 'being' for women and men

The single most important aspect in which women differ in their ways of being from men is the relation between 'self' and 'other' and the degree in the 'centring' of the self.[260] A woman's attitude toward life is seen as 'other' centred, in that she centres her feelings, her enjoyment, and her ambition in something outside herself. Lombroso's (1923) insightful remarks wrote all those years ago are still valid today: "she makes not herself but another person or even things surrounding her, the centre of her emotions."[261] Men on the other hand are seen as egocentric: "they make themselves and their pleasures and activities the centre of the world in which they lie."[262] Similarly, Kolb (1993) argues that men tend to focus on individual achievement and activities defined in terms of task and structure, while women see boundaries between themselves and others and between tasks and their surroundings as

---

[259] Iversen and Rosenbluth, 2010: chapter 7, para. 1.
[260] Bakan, 1966: 114.
[261] Quoted in Bakan, 1966: 114.
[262] Bakan, 1966: 114.

blurred or overlapping. A number of sex differences in interests seem to fall in line with this notion of degrees of self-other distinction and separation. Anastasi (1958), in her review of sex differences, concludes that interests, preferences, attitudes and values characteristically point to a greater *social orientation* of women.[263] Rosenberg (1989) found sex differences as early as adolescence, with girls evaluating harmony and sensitivity as more important than boys, and boys evaluating toughness and dominance as more important than girls.

All other differences between women and men seem to cascade, with varying degrees, from this fundamental difference in focus on 'self' *vs.* focus on 'other'. In their pursuit of enhancing the self, boys grow up to be more assertive and dominant men but less sociable and warm than women, and girls grow up to be more communal, having qualities like empathy, nurturing, and warmth, but also more prone to stress and anxiety than men.[264] Chodorow (1999) states that women's relatedness and men's denial of relation are in line with their differential participation in family reproduction and economic production. Women's location within the family defines them as wives and mothers, i.e. in a particular relation to someone. Whereas men's location in public life, away from the family even when they are husbands and fathers, removes this relational aspect from their self-definition. Consequently, beliefs about women define them as embedded in social interaction and personal relationships in a way that men are not. Women's family function stresses affective relationships and the affective aspects of family life. Being a mother and wife are centred on emotional and psychological functions, and therefore women's work is emotional work. By contrast men's occupational roles and the occupational work in general are increasingly without room for affect and particularistic commitments.[265]

---

[263] Ibid: 116.
[264] Becker and Grilo (2007), quoted in Halpern, 2011: chapter 5, section 5, subsection 3, sub subsection3, para. 1.
[265] Chodorow, 1999: 177-178.

Because *difference* and *hierarchy* are built into the gender system, even when women and men cross into each other's spheres, their roles remain different. Chodorow (1999) elucidates that within the family, being a husband and father is different from being a wife and mother. A father's first responsibility is to *provide* for his family, and his emotional contribution is rarely given equal importance to the mother's. Men's work in the home, with few exceptions, is defined in gender stereotyped ways: when they do 'women's' chores - the dishes, shopping, putting children to bed - this activity is often organised and delegated by the wife/mother, who retains residual responsibility - men babysit their children, women do not. The way fathers relate to their children is through creating 'independence'. This is facilitated by a father's own socialisation in repressing and denying relation, and his current participation in the non-relational public life. Fathers know their children more as separate people than mothers do.[266]

III.2.2   The feminine-masculine divide

Our beliefs and expectations about a group of people are contained in stereotypes, which are either expectations about what members of the group *are* like (descriptive stereotypes) or what they *should* be like (prescriptive stereotypes). Descriptive stereotypes are used to simplify people's understanding of other individuals and groups, making social interaction less demanding. Prescriptive stereotypes on the other hand are far more powerful in influencing human behaviour as they carry social condemnation in the absence of conformity. For example, a woman will not be ostracised if she was not into fashion (a descriptive stereotype), but she would be severely ostracised if she openly engaged in aggressive behaviour (prescriptive stereotype).[267]

---

[266]   Ibid: 179-180.
[267]   See Rudman and Glick, 2008.

The assignment of care and service to women and achievement and breadwinning to men lead to two broad clusters of stereotypic traits, which are either classified as communal *vs.* agentic, or expressive *vs.* instrumental. The fundamental modality of agency is concern with the self,[268] while that of communion is concern for others. Another way of looking at instrumental orientation is one of a *cognitive* focus on 'getting the job done' and expressive orientation as an *affective* concern for the welfare of others.[269]

The communal-expressive end of the spectrum entails the quality of warmth and care, within which we find traits like nurturerance, affection, devotion, compassion, kindness, empathy, emotionality, sensitivity and intuition. The agentic-instrumental end of the spectrum entails the quality of competence and task orientation, within which we find traits like confidence, risk taking, control, ambition, dominance, superiority, aggressiveness, toughness, resilience, rationality, decisiveness, forcefulness, independence, self-sufficiency, and individualism.[270]

Eagly and Carli (2007) state that despite some nuances specific to cultures, these gender stereotypes of communion and agency are quite similar across cultures.[271] Schwartz and Rubel (2005) study that covered 70 countries found that the majority of men tend to ascribe to power and achievement values while the majority of women tend to ascribe to benevolence and security values. In her comparison of gender stereotypes in six countries (Norway, Denmark, Finland, Sweden, England and the US) Block (1984) found remarkable stability in masculine and feminine identities as well as empirical verification of the different emphasis on

---

[268] Block, 1984: 5-6.
[269] Bem, 1974.
[270] Eagly, 1987: 15; Hanlon, 2012: 1; Gies, 1993: 11; and Halpern, 2011: chapter 6, section 7, para. 1. See also Bem, 1974; Spence and Helmreich, 1974, 1975; and Bakan, 1966.
[271] Eagly and Carli, 2007, 84.

agency and communion between the two sexes.[272] She also documents research that observed a sample of Norwegian mothers exert more pressure on girls to conform to social or communal norms, and other research that shows parents impose earlier and more rigorous demands on boys for conformity to societal notions of 'what is manly' and what is 'manly' is agentic.[273]

Prentice and Carranza (2002) examined the extent to which traits associated with one sex are permissible in the other, which they called 'relaxed' prescriptions or proscriptions, or not permissible in the other sex, which they called 'intensified' prescriptions or proscriptions. Intensified prescriptions (positive traits associated with one sex and rarely found in the other) include business sense in men and interest in children in women. Intensified proscriptions (negative traits associated with one sex and rarely found in the other) include 'arrogant' in men and 'melodramatic' in women. An examples of relaxed prescriptions (positive traits associated with one sex but also found in the other) are high self-esteem in men and friendliness in women, and of relaxed proscriptions (negative traits associated with one sex but also found in the other) include controlling in men and yielding in women.

Prentice and Carranza found that there are more 'intensified proscriptions' for men than for women. However, as I argued in the last chapter, restrictions on girls and women are more obscure but more far reaching than those placed on boys and men. Because women are seen as carers and nurturers, dispositions that are focused on the self are curbed and those that entail self-denial and self-sacrifice are encouraged. While women are encouraged to pursue education and paid employment, they are still seen as 'selfish' if they don't have children and 'neglectful' if they pursue their careers wholeheartedly once they do have children.

---

[272] Block, 1984: 11.
[273] Ibid: 7.

In a work environment, women are ostracised if they engage in risky or self-promoting behaviour, or if they negotiate as aggressively as men. Open sexual behaviour receives far more condemnation for women than for men, partly because of men's virility stereotype, but also because of women's "thou shalt not" conditioning.

III.2.3 Integrating the feminine and the masculine: is androgyny desirable?

"In a society where rigid sex-role differentiation has already outlived its utility, perhaps the androgynous person will come to define a more human standard of psychological health." Sandra Bem (American psychologist)[274]

As we saw in the last chapter, gender stereotypes are made toxic more by what they leave out than by what they include. Adherence to sex-roles as prescribed in the gender system can only be achieved by suppressing any behaviour that might be considered undesirable or inappropriate for the sex role adhered to: a narrowly masculine self-concept therefore necessitates the inhibition of behaviours that are stereotyped as feminine, and a narrowly feminine self-concept necessitates the inhibition of behaviours that are stereotyped as masculine.[275] It is precisely this suppression of the feminine in men and the masculine in women that leads to the social ills that I alluded to in the last chapter. Prominent among those is the exclusion of emotional competency from men's personalities and of agency from women's personalities, which means that neither women nor men have access to the full range of attributes and capabilities that allow them to see themselves as whole and complete. The suppression of those aspects of our personality that are thought to belong to the opposite sex gives us a sense of lack and

---

[274] Bem, 1974.
[275] Ibid, and references therein.

feelings of inadequacy, neither of which is conducive to fulfilment or self-realisation. So, does integrating the masculine and the feminine in each of us lead to superior results in terms of ego formation and a stronger sense of self?

Bem (1974) and Spence et al. (1974, 1975)[276] attempted to measure judgments made by people about themselves in terms of feminine and masculine qualities, by separately assessing the feminine and the masculine dimensions and developing an index for each.[277] Instrumental traits considered more socially desirable/typical for men included "assertive", "independent" and "analytical", and expressive traits considered more socially desirable/typical for women included "understanding of others", "loyal", "shy" and "gentle".[278] Any given person could be said to posses varying degrees of masculine and feminine traits. People who describe themselves as possessing masculine (instrumental) and feminine (expressive) traits to an equal extent were termed *androgynous*.

Bem (1975) argued that androgynous people might be better adjusted psychologically than sex typed people in that they are able to behave instrumentally or expressively as the situation demands. Sex typed individuals on the other hand, those who are either predominantly masculine or predominantly feminine, were limited in their behavioural repertoire by sex role expectations. In her experiments, androgynous subjects of both sexes displayed "masculine" independence when under pressure to conform, and "feminine" playfulness when given the opportunity to interact with a tiny kitten. In contrast, all of the non androgynous subjects displayed behavioural deficits of one sort of

---

[276] Quoted in Archer and Lloyd, 2002: chapter 2, section 6, para. 2.
[277] Those are the Bem Sex-Role Inventory - the BSRI by Bem (1974); and Personal Attributes Questionnaire - PAQ by Spence et al. (1974; 1975).
[278] Twenge, 1997a.

another, with the feminine females showing perhaps the greatest deficit of all.[279]

Lefkowitz and Zeldo's (2006) study revisited Bem's androgyny hypotheses to test how androgyny might contribute to wellbeing. The scholars used self-reports of wellbeing as well as clinical judgments of the mental health of their subjects, to add robustness to their findings. They found that masculinity is strongly related to measures of adjustment, but so is femininity which contributes to substantial self-esteem. Therefore, persons high in both masculine and feminine attributes have the highest levels of mental health, and those low in both masculine and feminine attributes have the lowest levels.

Generally, research that uses masculinity and femininity indices[280] portrays high masculinity people as high in social self-esteem, achievement motivated, extraverted, low in neuroticism and high in internal locus of controls.[281, 282] Similarly, Lefkowitz and Zeldo's (2006) study shows high masculine people as socially poised, assertive, and relatively free of both self-doubt and social anxiety. They have high aspirations and are productive, persevering, and not prone to existential concerns about the meaning of life or about committing to a course

---

[279] Bem's research on androgyny was challenged on two grounds. *First*, some argued that there was a clear association between masculine traits and mental health measures of adjustment, but no specific link with androgyny. This means that androgynous people tend to be well adjusted because they have masculine traits. *Second*, the measurement of many masculine traits is similar to that of self-esteem, making the statistical relationship between the two spurious. See Archer and Lloyd, 2002: 32-3, for a fuller discussion, controversies surrounding Bem's measure of androgyny and other references.

[280] Such as 'Personal Attributes Questionnaire' or PAQ, devised by Spence et al., 1975 (See Archer and Lloyd, 2002: 32).

[281] Lefkowitz and Zeldo, 2006.

[282] Locus of control is the degree to which people feel in control of their own destiny. A low locus of control is someone who believes others or fate to be in control of events in their life.

of action. The underside of these positive traits in the high masculine include being condescending, power oriented, and unafraid either to give unsolicited advice or to express hostility directly. Low masculine people on the other hand are described as moody, thin skinned, self-doubting, indecisive and full of dysphoric affects such as anxiety and guilt. They need and seek reassurance and advice, are prone to express their distress through somatic symptoms, and appear vulnerable to disorganisation under stress or trauma. On the other hand, scholars describe high feminine people as aesthetically reactive, cheerful, charming and likable. While attributes associated with the low feminine end of the continuum include being distrustful, hostile and aloof, prone to somatic components and fluctuating moods.

These findings and this genre of studies more generally, are interesting for many reasons. *First,* the researchers did not measure men's masculinity and women's femininity, as people are normally stereotyped, but rather the degree to which any person possesses masculine and feminine attributes. Cahill (2004) for example found that differences in the recall of emotional information existed between those individuals with masculine traits and those with feminine traits (as measured by Bem's 1974 index) rather than between females and males *per se.* *Second,* the researchers acknowledge than any person can possess *both* masculine and feminine traits at the same time, while we commonly mistakenly believe that a person is either masculine of feminine. *Third,* the researchers acknowledge that a high masculine doesn't negate a high feminine, whereas folk wisdom assumes that if a person is high in masculine they would be low in feminine and vice versa. Conversely, we believe that to *become* more masculine, is to become less feminine. In fact, although the number of studies looking at androgyny is extremely limited, these studies nevertheless portray people with a simultaneously high masculine *and* high feminine attributes as the epitome of mental health.

Both Bakan (1966) and Block (1984) advocated the integration of feminine and masculine attributes for the purpose of achieving a 'more mature ego formation'. A mature ego is able to move away from opportunism and hedonism toward universal principles of justice and concern for human worth (Block), and fulfil social viability (Bakan). Block argues that the achievement of higher levels of ego functioning is strongly associated with more androgynous, less sex typed, definitions of the self, that is able to integrate agentic concerns of self-enhancement and self-extension with the satisfaction derived from communion and mutuality. For women, integration of communion with agency required that concern for the harmonious functioning of the group, the submersion of self and the importance of consensus characteristics of communion be amended to include aspects of agentic self-assertion and self-expression that are essential for personal integration and self-actualisation. For men, integration of agency and communion required that self-assertion, self-interest and self-extension be tempered by considerations of mutuality, interdependence and joint welfare.

So for Block, the goal of identity development is not the ultimate achievement of either the masculine or the feminine, as popularly conceived, but acquiring a secure sense of self "that permits the individual to manifest human qualities that society until now has labelled 'unmanly' or 'unwomanly'."[283] For Bakan, the ultimate goal is "to mitigate agency with communion"; tempering masculinity with femininity, to achieve social viability.[284] For him, unmitigated agency, whether in exploitation or unrestrained economic expansion, represents evil.[285]

Maccoby (1966) offered reflections on the detrimental effects of unmitigated agency and communion on intellectual achievement.[286] In Maccoby's view, optimal cognitive functioning depends on a balance between the feminine/passive and masculine/active orientation. Children

---

[283] Block, 1984: 4-5.
[284] Bakan (1966), quoted in block 1984: 5.
[285] Quoted in Block, 1984: 6.
[286] Quoted in Block, 1984: 10.

manifesting extreme sex role typing are handicapped intellectually because hyperpassivity (supposedly a feminine mode) interferes with 'concept formation and manipulation', while hyperactivity (supposedly a masculine mode) 'militates against sustained and concentrated analysis,' suggesting that altering sex role typing may benefit cognitive functions in important ways.[287]

Hanson and Mendius (2009) say that compassion (stereotypically feminine) and assertion (stereotypically masculine) are a powerful combination that "get any relationship off the ground and keep it flying." "They support each other: compassion brings caring to assertion, while assertion helps you feel comfortable giving compassion, since you know your needs will be met." "Compassion widens the circle of "us" while assertion protects and supports everyone inside it. They both nourish the wolf of love."[288]

III.2.4   Trends in femininity and masculinity

Studies show that women in general are acquiring more masculine traits over time, without a diminishment in their femininity. Using the measures of the masculine-feminine spectrum mentioned above in a meta-analysis covering the period 1973 to 1994, Jean Twenge (1997a) found a highly significant rise in women's scores for masculine traits, as reported by the women themselves. To a lesser extent, men too reported endorsing more masculine personality traits.

Twenge (1997a) argues that this result may reflect changing cultural expectations of women, since the first cohort received the highly gendered messages of the 1950s, while the younger cohort grew up during the "unisex" 1970s. Eagly and Carli (2007) conclude from

---

[287]   Block, 1984: 10.
[288]   Hanson and Mendius, 2009: 137.

Twenge's study that a narrowing gap between women and men in instrumentality/assertiveness is due to women's move into new spheres of life and the change in their social roles. However, this cannot be the whole answer, Twenge (2009) argues, given the simultaneous rise in men's instrumental/assertive traits during the same period (1974-94). Instead, Twenge speculates that the rising endorsement of masculine traits by both women and men is due to a cultural trend in Western societies that emphasises the self over the group. Twenge (2009) found a significant rise in other masculine traits, including self-esteem, extraversion and even narcissism, among both women and men, which in her opinion reflects a culture that devalues expressive and communal traits, traditionally associated with women, and emphasises individualistic and even narcissistic values. She advocates encouraging communal traits among both sexes, since "(i)f no one cares, and people fail to nurture each other, collapse is soon to follow".

These cultural shifts, that increasingly see masculine attributes as the gold standard, are far more pronounced in cultural contexts that embrace capitalism wholeheartedly such as the US, the context for Twenge's research. Human welfare in purely capitalist societies is predicated on and measured by economic activity, which is underpinned by production in androcentric spaces. In this framework, masculinity is believed to be superior because of its association with economic production, and therefore competence, and femininity is believed to be inferior because of its association with care, and therefore incompetence. Bakan (1966) commented on the inevitable relationship of agency to capitalism, which requires the exaggeration of the agentic orientation.[289] Block (1984) observed that countries with a long and well established commitment to social welfare, such as Denmark and Sweden, are characterised with fewer sex differences and less emphasis on agency.[290] American women on the other hand describe their identity in more agentic terms,

---

[289] Quoted in Block, 1984: 13.
[290] Block, 1984: 13

including: ambitious, practical, assertive, self-centred, self-confident, shrewd and adventurous, indicting a link to capitalism.[291]

The other note worthy finding in Twenge's (1997a) study is the lack of change in men's feminine scale scores, despite the slight rise in their participation in housework and childcare. Twenge reports that her results parallel those of sociologists who found the increase in men's participation in the traditionally feminine housework and childcare to be incommensurate to women's substantial rise in participation in paid work (see section IV.5 'Equality in The Home'). Furthermore, as I will show in the next chapter, women don't only shoulder the lion's share in housework and childcare, but they do most of the routine, repetitive, less creative jobs over which they cannot exercise much control (cleaning, laundry, cooking, etc.), while men's contribution in domestic spaces tends to be more leisurely and less constrained. In other words, even when they participate in housework, men attempt to preserve their higher status by distancing themselves from lower status routine jobs.

Twenge (1997a; 2009) reports other areas of life that reflect the same trend in gender practices where women adopt more masculine roles while men seem to be prohibited from taking on more feminine ones: "women wear pants, play sports, repair cars, run for political office, and do many other things once the sole province of males. In contrast, it is not acceptable for boys and men to aspire to feminine pursuits, including too much expressiveness/communalism (e.g., being the one to stay home and care for children)." She concludes that males face harsher consequences for having feminine interests than females do for having masculine interests.[292] While at face value this seems true, as I have argued before, the constraints on women's gender practices are more obscure. It's true that women have been increasingly venturing in what used to be the male province, but they tend to do so within strict

---

[291]   Ibid: 12-3.
[292]   See Twenge 1997a, and references therein.

bounds: by remaining the primary carers and without abandoning their 'true calling' of serving others by concentrating themselves in caring and communal jobs, be it nursing, teaching, social and secretarial work, etc. - I will discuss this in more detail in the next chapter.

III.3 The Social Psychology of Gender Beliefs

> *"Projection makes perception. The world you see is*
> *what you gave it, nothing more than that." Dr. Helen*
> *Schucman (Clinical psychologist and author)*[293]

III.3.1 The stickiness of gender stereotypes

Women's lives have changed dramatically in the last half century or so, as reflected in the unprecedented accumulation of education and occupational skills. Furthermore, in the last few decades, women have been venturing in educational fields and occupations previously dominated by men, like science, maths, engineering, and accounting and many of them have secured executive positions in large corporations. Girls' and women's cognitive abilities in maths and visuospatial abilities have improved,[294] and women describe themselves as more assertive, dominant, self reliant and more ambitious than they did thirty years ago.[295]

Yet, two related aspects of women's lives remain largely unchanged. The first is that women's domestic role has not changed substantially over this time period, as they are still responsible for most of the housework and childcare (see section IV.5). The second aspect of women's life that remains constant is their concentration in lower status occupations that

---

[293] Schucman, 2007: 443.
[294] See Halpern, 2011: chapter 5, Section 8, sub section 2, para. 2.
[295] Eagly and Carli, 2007: 38.

require communal qualities, and their inability to reach top positions commensurately with their labour market participation. Both these aspects of women's lives reflect the persistence of gender dogma that still sees women's primary role in life as caring for and serving others, including during their engagement in public life, which is responsible for keeping women's status in society subordinated to that of man.

There has been a change in *stated* attitudes toward women's role in society, as they are now expected to undertake breadwinning as well as homemaking, as Twenge (1997a) has shown. Lottes and Kuriloff (1994),[296] measured Ivy League students' attitudes toward women during the period 1987-90 and found a favourable change in attitudes toward women.[297] This is to be expected, given the dramatic rise in women's participation in paid employment: our outer world is always in consonance with our mind. So it does seem that the second wave of women's liberation in the seventies has succeeded in shifting our *attitudes* toward women's social roles, but not our *beliefs* about the content of these roles, which in turn reflects the stagnation of our beliefs about the nature of women and what their social location should be. Williams and Best (1982, 1990) and Lueptow et al. (1995) studied gender stereotypes over these periods in the USA and found them to be fairly stable. A study by Catalyst in 2006 showed that both men and women believe that male leaders "take charge" while female leaders "take care". So what is behind the stickiness of stereotyping women as carers and men as leaders?

---

[296] Quoted in Jost, 1997.

[297] Using the Attitudes Toward Feminism Scale, the researchers reported that men scored between 1.21 and 1.42 standard deviations units *above* the scale's neutral point attitudes toward feminism, and between 1.52 and 2.01 standard deviation units *below* the neutral point on 'male dominance' (see Jost, 1997).

III.3.2 Stereotypes as a system of justification

Walter Lippmann posited that stereotypes, or the attribution of traits and characteristics to groups of people, are motivated by justifying one's status in relation to others.[298] For example, people with high socio economic status stereotype poor people as lazy and therefore deserving of their plight, to justify their privileged positions in society.[299] John Jost (1997) expands this notion to what he calls "system justification" which refers to the psychological process whereby prevailing social, political, economic, sexual or legal conditions are accepted, explained and justified simply because they exist. In other words, people are motivated to create beliefs that reinforce the *status quo*, to be able to see the social system in which they live as fair and legitimate; system-justifying ideologies emerge to maintain the *status quo*. The system justifying ideology for gender inequality is that women are *essentially* or *biologically predisposed* to care, freeing men to work and occupy the higher status in society.

But how and why does the *status quo* arise in the first place? Is it possible for any of life's conditions to manifest outside our consciousness? Doesn't the outside environment always resonate with our inner world, because they are both one and the same in the mind system? (see section I.4.3). Looking at things from this perspective, the *status quo* is simply mirroring our belief system in the first place, in which case justifications of inequality or injustice in general are merely statements of what we, consciously or unconsciously, believe to be appropriate. The justification aspect is needed when our deeply held beliefs are not in line with our stated values, with the latter generally tending to be more liberal than the former. Justifications are called for when our awareness is raised enough to know through reflection that inequality is objectionable, but

---

[298] Water Lippman is credited with importing the term 'stereotypes' in social sciences. He initially believed that stereotyping serve the cognitive function of simplification and categorisation (Jost, 1997).

[299] Jost, 1997.

not raised enough to change our unconscious or deeply held beliefs in line with our stated values. The gap created by incongruent conscious and unconscious beliefs creates a need for justifications.

When slavery was accepted as the norm, no justification of the *status quo* was needed. On the other hand, when liberal thought of equality to all human beings permeated our consciousness, justifications for slavery were called for. Yet, slavery didn't disappear overnight, because consciously or unconsciously many of us, especially those who benefited from it, believed they are better, and possibly altogether different, human beings than their slaves, in order to preserve their social status *and,* at the same, remain in line with the stated values of the time. Slaves too, according to system justification rationale, would have held inferior beliefs about themselves, in order to see life as just and fair. It follows that it is only when our inner beliefs, often held unconsciously, are aligned with our stated values that unjust conditions are corrected. Otherwise, if our consciousness has not risen at all, or if it has risen enough to alert us to the injustice but not enough to change our deeply held beliefs, the injustice will persist. It also follow that the first step to achieving justice is the uncovering of those deeply held beliefs that are incongruent with our social values.

Before the spread of gender equality discourses, the appalling treatment of women that barred them from most aspects of public life, including suffrage, education and paid work, was not justified, it was taken for granted as the correct and proper way. Our inner world, i.e. our deeply held beliefs, was in consonant with our outer world, outright discrimination against women, and we were deeply unconscious to the injustice. When gender equality discourses took root, the need for system justification arose and the argument of the *essential* differences between the sexes and the biological imperative of women's care was put forward.

As our collective consciousness rises enough to acknowledge, on reflection, that inequality is objectionable, but not enough to eradicate inequality, three things are important to note: *First,* the state of affairs at any given point in time accurately reflects our deeply held beliefs. *Second,* we may or may not be conscious of those beliefs, but most often we are not. *Third,* when we remain unconscious, a wedge is driven between our stated values and our deeply held beliefs. *Forth,* when this gap occurs, we rely on justifications to explain the discrepancy between our stated values and our practices that more accurately reflect our unconsciously held beliefs. This framework explains why although the vast majority of people state that they adhere to gender equality principles, invariably their practices reflects that they believe differently.

III.3.3   Gender beliefs, status and false consciousness

Jost (1994) emphasised the tendency for people to infer stereotyped attributes directly from information about status or position, mainly in order to justify differences in status or position. Ross et al. (1977) demonstrated this in a powerful experiment where they randomly assigned subjects to play either the roles of contestants or questioners in a variant on the game Jeopardy. The results were that people attributed greater knowledge to questioners than to contestants, simply because the former were in a more challenging position, despite the fact that they were randomly assigned to those roles. These false attributions persisted even when the subjects judged their own abilities: people judged themselves to be less knowledgeable when they were assigned to the contestants' roles than when they were questioners. In real life, seeing working class as 'unintelligent', 'incompetent', 'unreliable' serve the ideological function of rationalising their economic plight. Similarly, women as a group are seen as communal, ineffectual, and less instrumental compared to men to justify their lower status *vis-à-vis* men.

This distortion in social judgement is called false consciousness: falsely ascribing attributes to categories of people based on their position or status in society. False consciousness helps explain why although many

111

of the attributes assigned to women in society are positive, overall their attributes are seen as less positive than men. Looking at a number of studies that investigated gender stereotype attributes at various times, Archer and Lloyd (2002) note that those who are rating these attributes often ascribe greater value to male than to female attributes.[300] They give the example of a study by Williams and Bennett (1975) that put 15 adjectives in each list that had a positive or negative evaluation for women, 5 were positively valued and 10 negatively valued, while for men the opposite was true where 10 were positive and 5 negative. These findings suggest "that the greater societal power of men is reflected in the affective meaning of the words used to describe the traits most associated with them."[301]

Because "people are likely to underestimate the extent to which seemingly positive attributes of the powerful simply reflect the advantages of their social control",[302] false consciousness has profound implications for women's lives and the choices they make, particularly though not exclusively in relation to public arena pursuits. As I will show in chapter IV, women's belief that they are less able and less competent than men stops them from choosing fields of study that are known to be men's 'areas of strength', such as maths, science, engineering and medicine. Even when they do, if they are gifted and get the right encouragement, their belief in men's superior abilities stops many from performing as well as they might, had they attributed the correct abilities to themselves. Women generally avoid male dominated professions, or promoting themselves into higher positions where males are concentrated, fearing this will expose their 'incompetence'. Overall, women's false consciousness creates a crisis in confidence in areas outside the home sphere, leaving their performance well below their true abilities, and giving credence to the false belief of their incompetence.

---

[300] Archer and Lloyd, 2002: 21-2
[301] Ibid: 22.
[302] Jost and Banaji, 1994.

III.3.4 Gender beliefs and women's depressed entitlement

As women justify sex inequality and internalise gender ideology, they believe that they are entitled to less in life than men, who occupy the higher status in society. This effect is called 'depressed entitlement' and is thought to be one of the reasons for the prevalence and persistence of the 'gender wage gap' between women and men (see section IV.2.2.4). This phenomenon has been related to the paradoxical "contentment effect", whereby women are just as satisfied with their employment situations as men, despite large sex differences in earned wags.[303]

Major (1994) states that entitlement beliefs are key psychological mediators of how people react affectively, evaluatively, and behaviourally to their socially distributed outcomes.[304] There is considerable literature that shows that women feel entitled to less pay than men do. In experimental tasks in which women and men work together and they are asked to allocate a fixed reward between them, women tend to take less for themselves and to give more to their partners, even after outperforming their partners.[305] A survey exploring future pay projections found that comparably qualified and trained women consistently undervalue their prospects relative to men. Not only do women underpay themselves relative to men, but they also report that their underpayment is fair.[306]

Even when subjects' gender consciousness was expected to be relatively high, as in Jost's (1997) experiment involving female and male students in an elite North American University, this "depressed entitlement effect" was still present. In Jost's (1997) experiment, independent judges deemed the work produced by women and men to be of equal quality, and yet women still judged their own work to be worth 18% less

---

[303] See Jost, 1997 for references.
[304] Quoted in See Hogue and Yoder, 2003.
[305] Ibid.
[306] See Hogue and Yoder, 2003, for references.

than men did. Although Jost considers explanations advanced by other scholars to explain this depressed-entitlement effect,[307] he offers an overarching explanation based on his concept of "system justification " explained in the last section: driven by needs for rationality and in order to make sense of the *status quo*, women tend to explain and justify differences in their status, power, and prestige compared to men in a way that legitimises the overall system.

Babcock and Laschever (2008) state that women aged 35 and younger are just as likely as the older cohort to feel uncertain about what they deserve, and uncomfortable asking for more. Even more astonishingly, researchers were able to replicate the adult gender gap in entitlement among school children. Using first, fourth, seventh and tenth graders, researchers found that in every grade, girls paid themselves 30-78% less than boys paid themselves, despite the absence of any difference in the children's own evaluation of how well they performed the task.[308]

Hogue and Yoder (2003) demonstrated that it is not gender *per se* that is responsible for a depressed entitlement, but women's lower status *vis-à-vis* men. The scholars point that lower status has been linked to depressed entitlement effect independent of sex, for example for both women and men employed in low status jobs.[309] In this argument,

---

[307] Such explanations include: *1)* women may be using a standard of payment that is in line with their own past situations of disadvantage, which is lower than the standard that men hold based on their personal experiences; *2)* women may compare their wages to those of other women, resulting in a lower standard than that used by men; *3)* women and men may possess different value systems, whereby women value material rewards less than men; *4)* women may devalue their work inputs, assuming that their efforts are not as great as those of men; and *5)* women may perceive less of a direct connection between work and pay, so that their self-rewards may be more susceptible than those of men to contextual influences. Jost proposes that these mechanisms may be working in concert to produce depressed-entitlement effect (Jost, 1997).

[308] Callahan-Levy and Messe (1979), quoted in Babcock and Laschever, 2008: 78.

[309] See Hogue and Yoder, 2003, for references.

gender is merely a marker for status and anyone with lower status would allocate themselves less than higher status people, as they internalise their disadvantaged status.

Following this reasoning, Hogue and Yoder (2003) engineered a status enhancement in their experiment, to see if this would narrow or eliminate the gap in self-allocated pay by their student subjects. Information about status was manipulated in two ways. First, by telling participants that women have superior task abilities in comparison to men, which legitimates women's position as the more capable contributor. And second, by informing participants that college students have superior task abilities compared to less educated high school students. Hogue and Yoder report that enhancing women's status in these two ways led to the disappearance of the gap in self-pay: in both instances, the wage difference between women and men subjects disappeared as women subjects increased their self-pay relative to women in the control group, while men's allocation remained flat across all conditions. This was true despite the fact that in both cases neither the self-evaluations of the work produced nor perceptions of their own competence changed, and therefore neither can account for changes in women's self-pay. By reversing depressed entitlement effect for women, through manipulating their perceptions of their own social status, Hogue and Yoder (2003) have shown that it is not gender *per se* but status that accounts for depressed entitlement and that status is often confounded with gender.

An area that is intimately linked to pay entitlement is negotiations. Researchers conducting experiments in both natural (real life situations) and in lab settings have found that women tend to negotiate lower starting salaries than men,[310] aim less high and give in too easily in negotiations.[311] This impinges significantly on labour market outcomes because differences in starting salaries can have a significant and lasting

---

[310] See Barron, 2003, for references.
[311] See Babcock and Laschever, 2008, for references.

impact on employees' earnings, as well as advancement within an organisation. It has been shown that almost one third of the difference in men's and women's salaries in a large private firm could be traced back to differences in starting salaries. It has also been show that initial earnings had a significant positive effect on employees' advancement, after controlling for both individual attributers and initial job status.[312]

Barron (2003) carried out detailed post-negotiation interviews with the participants (business students) to glean their beliefs. Three aspects of her findings relate to women's depressed entitlement effect - or men's elevated entitlement effect, if we are to drop the androcentric yardstick! *First*, men indicated that they knew how much they were worth (85%) and women indicated they were unsure how much they are worth (83%). *Second*, men's belief, as gleaned from their remarks, that they were entitled to *more* than others (70%) and women's belief they are entitled to the *same* as others (71%). And, *third* that men believed they could prove themselves and their worth in the negotiations, to justify requesting a high salary, whereas women believed they have to successfully perform the job before they could justify asking for an above average salary. These beliefs were correlated with variations in men's and women's salary requirements.

One way for women to counter this unconscious depressed entitlement effect is by actively finding out what are the pay and promotion conditions and the rules that govern them. Scholars have found that differences in entitlement could be eradicated when women and men were both exposed to the same social comparison conditions or same performance feedback.[313] By educating themselves about comparison conditions, or insisting on them being made public when they are not, women can improve their financial position in labour markets.

---

[312] See Barron, 2003, for references.
[313] Ibid.

III.3.5   Stereotype threat and women's lower achievement

Another pernicious effect of false gender beliefs is what has come to be called in the literature as 'stereotype threat', first exposed by Steele and Aronson (1995) who showed in several experiments that black college students performed less well on standardised tests than white students when their race was emphasised. When race was not emphasised, on the other hand, black students performed better or equivalently to white students. The experiment demonstrated that performance in academic contexts can be harmed by the awareness that one's behaviour might be viewed through the lens of racial stereotypes. Similarly, when women and men are competing in areas that are stereotypically male-favoured, such as maths and visuospatial abilities, and gender is salient in the environment, women's performance is likely to be negatively affected by the psychological threat that a low score would confirm the negative stereotype about their group. Women's negative performance in maths becomes self-fulfilling. The problem becomes more acute the more underrepresented women are in the group within which they are performing, as the situation increases their self-consciousness,[314] or when the test is particularly difficult.[315]

Generally speaking, people have the motive to sustain a self-image of competence and of being able to secure important outcomes. Stereotype threat arises when these performance motives are jeopardized by the awareness of a negative stereotype relating to the ability of their group, in a situation where that stereotype can be confirmed by low performance.[316] Because most people are motivated to feel and to appear competent, nearly anyone can experience the pressure of stereotype threat in some situation or another and suffer the short-term consequence of impaired intellectual performance.[317] Nevertheless, research has given

---

[314]   Babcock and Laschever, 2008: 89.
[315]   Spencer, Steele, and Quinn, 1999.
[316]   Aronson et al., 1999.
[317]   Ibid.

us a better understanding of who is most vulnerable to stereotype threat and under which conditions. For example, stereotype threat has been shown to harm the academic performance of Hispanic students from low socioeconomic backgrounds, females in maths, white males when faced with the spectre of Asian superiority in maths, women in negotiations, homosexual men in providing childcare, and women in driving.[318]

Research also demonstrates that within a stereotyped group, some members may be more vulnerable to its negative consequences than others. Factors such as the strength of one's group or domain identification have been shown to increase vulnerability to stereotype threat. As does the salience of the stereotyped group identity:[319] when one views oneself in terms of a salient group membership (e.g., "I am a woman, women are not expected to be good at maths, and this is a difficult maths test"), performance can be undermined because of concerns about the possibility of confirming the stereotype of women's under performance in maths.

Spencer, Steele, and Quinn (1999) conducted three experiments that addressed women's performance in maths tests under varying conditions. In the first experiment, women were shown to perform equally well to men when the test was relatively easy, but men outperformed women when the test was difficult. This was true although both women and men were equally highly identified with maths (i.e., had a history of successful performance and valued performance in maths). In the second experiment, some participants, but not all, were told that the test would produce gender differences. In this case, women performed more poorly than men only when gender differences were highlighted. In the third experiment, the student population had a more varied background in maths but still produced similar results as the first two

---

[318] See http://www.reducingstereotypethreat.com for more references.
[319] Marx and Stapel, 2006; Marx, Stapel, and Muller, 2005.

experiments. The study demonstrates that gender stereotype threat can undermine performance of women in maths, particularly when a challenging task is confronted and when stereotypic assumptions are not neutralised.

Although the mechanisms behind stereotype threat and how do negative stereotypes lead to the demonstrated consequences is not entirely clear, scholars are beginning to better understand how stereotype threat is mediated. Generally speaking, psychologists believe that activating the stereotype either evokes a surge of positive self-esteem that enhances performance, if the stereotype is a flattering one, or rouses concern about confirming the stereotype, if the stereotype is an unflattering one. In the latter case, the fear of confirming a negative stereotype increases the person's performance anxiety and reduces their ability to concentrate on the issue in hand.[320] More specifically, research has shown that stereotype threat can reduce working memory resources, ultimately undermining one's ability to successfully complete complex intellectual tasks.[321]

All this suggests that negative expectations are an important force in pushing women's behaviour, into line with prevailing gender beliefs.[322] Geis (1993) argues for gender stereotype threat in a wider sense: stereotypes lower women's self-confidence in their ability to succeed at intellectual or "masculine" typed tasks, college courses and occupations, and lower self-confidence diminishes performance. This is the self-fulfilling prophecy at work: because of the biased attributions, employers are less likely to hire or promote women. And because people believe that decisions are fair, women's lesser success seemingly confirms the initial stereotype. The double whammy is that the same beliefs lower

---

[320] Babcock and Laschever, 2008: 87.
[321] Schmader and Johns, 2003.
[322] Babcock and Laschever, 2008: 89.

women's self-confidence causing actual poor performance and giving the stereotypes a gain of truth.[323]

III.4 How Conscious are we of Gender Stereotypes?

"We cannot change what we are not aware of, and once we are aware, we cannot help but change." Sheryl Sandberg (COO of Facebook and author)

III.4.1 Explicit *vs.* implicit gender stereotypes

One explanation for the stickiness of stereotypes is the fact that our conscious and unconscious gender beliefs don't necessarily match.[324] Bruce Lipton (2009) explains that the reason for the discrepancy between conscious and unconscious beliefs is that the actions of the subconscious mind are reflexive in nature and are not governed by reason or thinking. Physically, this mind is associated with the activities in the brain structures that are present in animals that have not evolved self-consciousness. On the other hand, Humans (and a number of other higher mammals) have evolved a specialised region of the brain associated with thinking, planning, and decision-making called the prefrontal cortex. This portion of the forebrain is apparently the seat of "self-conscious" mind processing. The self-conscious mind is self-reflective. It is a newly evolved "sense organ" that observes our own behaviours and emotions. Endowed with the ability to be self-reflective, the self-conscious mind is extremely powerful. It can observe any programmed behaviour we are engaged in, evaluate the behaviour, and consciously decide to change the program. We can actively choose how to respond to most environmental signals and whether we even want to respond at all.[325]

---

[323] Geis, 1993: 16.
[324] Ibid.
[325] Lipton, 2008: chapter 5, section 4, para. 6.

This elucidates the difference between what social scientists call implicit and explicit beliefs: implicit beliefs and actions are automatic and operate at the subconscious level, and explicit beliefs are reflective and operate at the conscious level. It has been shown that when we are *directly* asked about our gender views, i.e. made conscious of gender issues and can therefore exercise control over our thoughts, the majority of us will express a gender egalitarian view, since prejudice and stereotypes are considered socially undesirable.[326] On the other hand, our implicit representations of social groups are often remarkably reactionary, even when our consciously reported beliefs are modern and progressive.[327] When social scientists are able to tap into those implicit beliefs, they often find they are at variance with our stated liberal views, and in line with prejudiced stereotypes.

Phelps et al. (2000) were able to show the divergence in conscious and unconscious responses of White Americans subjects to pictures of Black Americans. Using brain imaging (fMRI) they showed that viewing pictures of Black Americans evoked the activation of the amygdala (a subcortical brain structure known to play a roles in emotional learning and evaluation) in White subjects, and that such activation was related to unconscious social evaluations (as measured by the Implicit Association Test or IAT and potentiated startle). This was in contrast to lack of any relationship between amygdala activation and the direct or conscious measure of racial attitudes (as measured by self-reported beliefs toward Black Americans).

In a gender context, divergence between conscious and unconscious beliefs was demonstrated by Concha and Garrido (2004). The scholars followed up on a study done at American universities in 1970's that demonstrated women's anxiety about their professional success compared to men. In their study, Concha and Garrido asked their subjects both

---

[326] See Geis, 1993:11, for references.
[327] Fine, 2010: 5.

directly and indirectly whether they are anxious: when asked directly, the women appeared as if they have indeed overcome anxiety. However, when a more subtle approach was used (using performance graphs), the women continued to attribute the best academic professional results to men instead of women, revealing the persistence of anxiety over professional success. The experiment demonstrates that women continue to prejudice themselves when they are compared to men, despite their utterances to the contrary.

These experiments show how in a state of unawareness we tend to rely on the general store of knowledge about the world, which includes old stereotypes as tacit or implicit beliefs, in guiding our perceptions and actions. Geis (1993) states that these implicit beliefs contain specific details that include personality traits, role behaviour, physical appearance, occupations and even interests.[328] But where does this store of knowledge come from?

Lipton (2009) states that while almost all organisms have to experience stimuli first-hand to gain experience, the ability of the human brain to learn is so advanced that we can actually acquire knowledge and perceptions indirectly from teachers. Once we accept others' perceptions as "truths", they become our "truths" and get wired in our own brains. "But what if our teachers' perceptions are inaccurate?" Lipton wonders.[329]

Indeed, what if we were told that men are dominant, rational, objective, independent, decisive, competitive, aggressive, capable of leadership, good at science and maths and interested in business, sports and politics? And what if we were equally told that women are submissive, emotional, gullible, dependent, sensitive, caring, nurturant, capable of devotion and good at domestic tasks and child rearing?[330] Even more

---

[328] Geis, 1993: 11.

[329] Lipton, 2008: chapter 5, section 4, para. 8.

[330] See Bem, 1974; Spence and Helmreich, 1979; Williams and Best, 1982; and Geis, 1993.

importantly, what if we were told, as we are, that what men do is more important than what women do, that men are more competent, more capable and more deserving of higher status? What happens when our brains are downloaded with such misperceptions?

Lipton (2009) explains that the subconscious mind is strictly a stimulus-response playback device; there is no pondering the long-term consequences of the programmes we engage in. Consequently, misperceptions programmed in our subconscious mind are not "monitored" and will habitually engage us in inappropriate and limiting behaviours.[331] In other words, unconscious stereotypical inferences happen automatically and without our awareness,[332] which is at the heart of the persistence of gender stereotype.

Given these cognitive processes, the literature has identified two types of gender stereotypes, explicit and implicit. Explicit stereotypes are collections of traits or attributes that people hold consciously and are explicitly associated with members of a social group.[333] Most conceptual treatments of stereotypes and all popular accounts have emphasised these explicit processes and their contents.[334] Implicit stereotypes, on the other hand, are traces of past experiences and learnt associations that mediate the attribution of qualities to members of a social category.[335] They are the remaining influence of past explicit beliefs that are consciously abandoned but remain unconsciously held and continue to influence our perceptions. Because implicit associations are beyond our conscious control, even when we explicitly disavow bias toward an out-

---

[331] Lipton 2008: chapter 5, section 4, para. 8.

[332] Geis, 1993: 11.

[333] White and white, 2006, based on Katz and Braly's (1935) definition of national stereotypes.

[334] White and White, 2006.

[335] Based on Greenwald and Banaji's (1995) definition, as quoted in White and White, 2006. Specifically, Greenwald and Banaji identified implicit stereotypes as "introspectively unidentified".

group, appropriate priming may trigger implicit stereotyped judgments allowing them to bias our perceptions of the group.[336]

Rudman and Greenwald (2001) argue that because implicit stereotypes operate without respondents' awareness, they bypass conscious processes that might otherwise serve as a defence against sexism. For example, women and men show similarly negative implicit attitudes toward female authorities, despite differences in their explicit attitudes. Moreover, implicit gender stereotypes may lead non-sexists to discriminate against female job applicants. In their study, Rudman and Greenwald investigated differences between implicit and explicit gender stereotypes that women and men hold. They found that men scored significantly higher than women on the explicit measure of sexism, suggesting that men far more than women hold more strongly to sexist stereotypes. Other research also shows that gender egalitarian beliefs and reduced sex stereotyping are observed more strongly among women than men,[337]which is not surprising given that women stand to benefit from reduced discrimination far more than men. When the scholars measured implicit stereotypes, however, there were hardly any differences between the two sexes, which is also in line with other research findings.

White and white (2006) compared explicit and implicit stereotypes for three occupations, engineering, accounting and primary school teacher, which represent the middle-to-end points of a masculine-feminine continuum of explicit occupational gender stereotypes. They found that while explicit measures of stereotypes put accountants between engineers and elementary school teachers in the degree of gender stereotyping, the implicit measure of stereotyping for accounting was not different from engineering, meaning that accounting is implicitly perceived to be a masculine profession.[338]

---

[336] White and White, 2006, and references therein.
[337] Rudman and Greenwald, 2001, and references therein.
[338] White and White, 2006.

This is a particularly interesting result since accounting is increasingly seen as a 'feminised' profession with the numbers of females in the profession exceeding that of males in the US: while only 25% of accountants were women in 1975, in 2006 the ratio rose to 59%.[339] And yet, as Lyonette and Crompton (2008) have shown in their study of the accountancy profession in the UK, female accountants suffer considerable under achievement compared with male accountants. Although women start out on a relatively equal footing to men, men forge ahead of women very quickly that by the age of 30, 51% of women are still working as non-managerial employees, compared with only 47% of men. The difference widens successively, leading to severe underrepresentation of women at the most senior level. Importantly, this is equally true for married and unmarried women, indicating that childcare responsibilities are not the whole answer to women's under achievement in this profession.

Marrying the results from White and White (2006)study with those of Lyonette and Crompton (2008) nicely brings the point of this book: we cannot rely on gender rhetoric or explicitly stated views to assess the extent to which we have freed ourselves from prejudice, for by this standard, we are fairly advanced in fighting sexism. Instead, taking stock of women's standing in society gives a more accurate reflection of our deeply held beliefs about the two sexes.

---

[339] Lyonette and Crompton (2008) point out that one of the reasons that accountancy is an attractive profession to women is that it requires occupationally specific qualifications which enables women to retain a closer attachment to the labour market during periods of family formation, which at the same time protects women from the drop in earnings typically associated with taking time out or working part time.

III.4.2   Stereotypes and conscious beliefs

Although the literature talks about implicit and explicit stereotypes, a more productive way perhaps is looking at these distinct knowledge structures as automatic/unconscious stereotypes and conscious beliefs. This distinction, made by Patricia Devine (1989), allows us in turn to distinguish between knowledge of a stereotype *and* acceptance or endorsement of it. Our personal beliefs may or may not be congruent with the stereotype, although there maybe overlapping features.

Devine says that to the extent that stereotypes and personal beliefs represent different and only potentially overlapping subsets of information about groups (ethnic, racial, gender, etc), they may have different implications for evaluation of, and behaviour toward, members of the those groups. In her study that examines how stereotypes and personal beliefs are involved in responses toward stereotyped groups, Devine elucidate how we all have knowledge of stereotypes, regardless of the degree to which we are prejudiced. This is because stereotypes seem to be well established in children's memories before children develop the cognitive ability and flexibility to question or critically evaluate the stereotypes' validity or acceptability.[340] Furthermore, automatic or implicit stereotype activation is equally strong and inescapable for high- and low-prejudice subjects. What *does* make a difference is engaging in controlled, stereotype-inhibiting thought processes. She found that low-prejudice subjects apparently censor negative, and what they consider inappropriate, thoughts since these thoughts detract from their goal of achieving a non prejudiced identity. Devine asserts that to stop automatic prejudiced thoughts from taking over requires *intention, attention,* and *time.*

Geis (1993) explains that despite the automatic and unconscious nature of stereotype inferences, their influence on our final conscious perceptions

---

[340]   See Devine, 1989, for references.

is not inevitable. Perception, she says, is a two- or three-stage process, proceeding from an earlier automatic and unconscious stage, to a later more controlled and conscious product. The early stage categorises and identifies the target person ('it's a women') and characterises her behaviour on the basis of relevant schemas and situational cues ('what she's saying is trivial'). The later, more conscious stage revises and corrects the initial result in light of conscious information[341] ('she may have something to add to this conversation'). At this later stage, perceivers may or may not revise their perceptions to correct the stereotypes influence.[342] "The conscious mind's capacity to override the subconscious mind's pre-programmed behaviours is the foundation of free will",[343] meaning we are not victims of our programming, but we must pay attention: as a pre-programmed behaviour is unfolding, the observing conscious mind can step in, stop the behaviour, and create a new response. "Subconscious programming takes over the moment your conscious mind is not paying attention."[344] This is why a significant part of feminists' agenda is "raising consciousness" on sexism, which I hope this book will contribute to. "Because humans have free will, we can choose to either rise to that new level of emergence or, in the manner of dinosaurs, fall by the wayside."[345]

III.5   Conclusion: Changing our Mind about Who Women and Men Are

"As a man thinketh, so does he perceive. Therefore, seek not to change the world, but choose to change your mind about the world."
Dr. Helen Schucman (Clinical psychologist and author)[346]

---

[341]   Geis 1993: 16-7.

[342]   Ibid.

[343]   Lipton, 2008: chapter 7, section 4, para. 5.

[344]   Ibid.

[345]   Lipton and Bhaerman, 2009, introduction, para. 10.

[346]   Schucman, 2007: 443.

"It's hard to fight an enemy who has outposts in your head." Sally Kempton (Teacher of meditation and tantric philosophy)[347]

The fact that we still hold implicit sexist stereotypes despite our egalitarian views points to the reason why sexism has persisted in the twenty first century. The disconnect between our implicit and explicit beliefs makes sexism, and any other form of prejudice, difficult to see since it is concealed by our liberal, progressive rhetoric. Crucially, women hold these beliefs equally to men, which explain why the march toward sex equality has been excruciatingly slow. In sex equality discourses, women are often presented as victims of society's androcentricity and its sexist beliefs and men's intransigence in giving up their privileged status. This is true in part, because institutions are far stronger than individuals and those in positions of power have more leverage in impacting societal change than those who are disempowered. Nevertheless, to the extent that our inner beliefs are far more powerful in shaping circumstances in our lives than our stated views, and to the extent further that women still prejudice themselves as much as men prejudice them, it is critical for women to recognise their responsibility in eradicating sexism by becoming more conscious of their own sexist thoughts and beliefs.

We should not be in doubt of the awesome power of the subconscious mind and its ability to run our life, if it remained uninterrupted. Pizzagalli et al. (2003) remind us that biologically and socially relevant information is processed in the human brain within the first 150 milliseconds after stimulus presentation, which strongly suggests that social cognition and evaluation operate in an automatic and pre-attentive way. Lipton and Bhaerman (2009) mention four more sobering facts about the power of the subconscious and its ability to keep playing out myths and misconceptions.

---

[347] http://www.religioustolerance.org/femquote.htm

First, as I have already mentioned, the subconscious is merely a record-and-playback mechanism that downloads life experiences onto behavioural tapes.[348] *Second,* compared to the conscious mind, the subconscious mind's ability to process information is breath taking: as an information processor, the subconscious mind is estimated to be one million times more powerful than the self-conscious mind.[349] *Third,* the most powerful and influential programmes in the subconscious mind are the ones that were recorded first: between gestation and six years of age. A child's perceptions of the world are directly downloaded into the subconscious during this time, without discrimination and without the filters of the analytical self-conscious mind, which doesn't fully exist at that time.[350] This is why Devine (1989) affirms that stereotypes seem to be well established in children's memories before children develop the cognitive ability and flexibility to question or critically evaluate stereotypes' validity or acceptability.[351] By observing the behavioural patterns of people in their immediate environment, children learn to distinguish what is acceptable and unacceptable for boys and girls women and men. "It's important to realize that perceptions acquired before the age of six become the fundamental subconscious programs that shape the character of an individual's life.[352] *Fifth,* these factors combined led cognitive neuroscientists to conclude that the self-conscious mind contributes only about 5 percent of our cognitive activity, leaving 95 percent of our decisions, actions, emotions, and behaviours to be driven by the unobserved processing of the subconscious mind.[353]

---

[348] Lipton, and Bhaerman, 2009: 40-41.
[349] Ibid: 32.
[350] See also Geis, 1993: 16-17.
[351] See Devine, 1989, for references.
[352] Lipton and Bhaerman, 2009: 37.
[353] Ibid: 33. We shouldn't forget that this alarmingly high percentage of the subconscious mind's responsibility for our behaviour includes directing our bodies' auto pilot functions, like heart beating, breathing, digesting, etc.

Lipton and Bhaerman (2009) state that perceptions acquired during the pivotal developmental period between 0-6 years can actually override genetically endowed instincts. They give the example of how newly born babies can instinctually swim like a dolphin the moment they emerge from the birth canal. And yet, we still have to teach children to swim for the very reason that parents' fear conditioning when their toddlers get anywhere near open water means that swimming is unlearnt by children as they start to perceive water as life-threatening. "Fear, acquired from the perception that water is dangerous, overrides the instinctual ability to swim and makes the formerly proficient child susceptible to drowning."[354]

Similarly, our perceptions of female nurturance and other-orientation, and male agency and self-focus, born out of society's fear conditioning when girls and boys veer away from gendered patterns, can override genetically endowed instincts in boys and girls. Our epigenetic mechanisms translate our gender perceptions (e.g. females' nurturance and lack of agency; males' competitiveness and lack of emotionality) into a corresponding gene activity, in order for us to adapt to our social environment and enhance our chances of social success. These genetic expressions can modify the readout of the genetic code,[355] that may very well include agency and competitiveness in girls and empathy and nurturance in boys, and are passed on generation to generation.

Our evolving brains dedicate vast numbers of cells to catalogue, memorise, and integrate complex perceptions, which are integrated into a powerful database.[356] The correspondence between perception and behaviour means that the complex and detailed nature of our perceptions in turn leads to intricately detailed behaviours. When it comes to gender, therefore, the multitudinous scenarios of gender actions, reactions, roles, sub roles, dispositions, mannerisms, etc., which

---

[354] Ibid: 39-40.
[355] Ibid: 29.
[356] Ibid: 31.

are stored in our perception database lead to highly differentiated gender behaviours in almost every aspect of life. This means that even when women and men cross over each other's gender territory, their behaviour can remain different.

Take for example childcare: women care for their children from an idealised mothering script, which is at the heart of gender organisation and as a result involves considerable fear conditioning, to dissuade women from detracting from it. Like the idealised notion of masculinity from which most men fall short, idealised mothering keeps most women feeling inadequate as mothers, prompting them to get even more involved in their children's lives. Ideal notions of mothering overemphasise the welfare aspects of childcare such as feeding, cleaning, educating, taking care of the home environment, etc., hardly leaving any time for mothers to have quality, one to one interaction with their children, which is crucial for child development. When men care on the other hand, and given the absence of a script for 'caring men' in the gender system, they experience considerable freedom in adopting a more practical approach to parenting, with the emphasis usually on encouraging their children's independence, and on enjoying their time with their children. The women in Brandth and Kvande's (1998) survey (section II.5.2) showed great awareness of the difference in the degree of freedom they experience in looking after the children, compared with their male partners who were able to integrate childcare with other practical aspects of their own life. Many of the women in the survey stated that they prefer the male way of parenting but at the same time, they didn't feel that they can 'let go.'

For men, idealised notions of masculinity that are underpinned by competitiveness and succeeding in public life can create the impetus to over work. And while engagement in paid work gives men the experience of self-respect, as they perceive themselves to be caring through providing, it can be a straight jacket too, as men find it hard to derive any self-worth from other sources of social engagement, least of which childcare. When mothers engage in paid work, and even if

131

it gives them self-fulfilment, they invariably feel guilty, out of their perception that they 'should' remain home with the children. Guilt seems to be the way in which women deal with their conditioning to be other oriented and to put everyone else's welfare before theirs: women more than men feel guilty when they leave a marriage, when they spend money on themselves, when they have leisure time, and so on. This is the obscure side of gender repression that affects women in ways that are not visible in society, regulating their impulses, dispositions and actions and significantly narrowing their choices in life. And it is in unlocking these obscure patterns of repressed/conditioned behaviour that sexism can be uncovered.

The only way to unconceal old, sexist patterns in our thinking is through "intention" and "attention". Only through our intention to fight sexism, and our constant, unrelenting attention to its insidious ways and means of shaping our thoughts, actions and choices in life can we eradicate it from our societies. This process involves the interruption of the familiar patterns of sex biased thoughts that emanate from our old reptilian brain (where our subconscious programming resides) and engaging the frontal lobe in our brain in controlled, stereotype-inhibiting thought processes. The frontal lobe is a relatively new part of the human brain and is the seat of thinking, planning, reflection and free will. Joe Dispenza (2012) explains that as we entertain new ideas, the frontal lobe surveys the rest of the brain and seamlessly combines all stored knowledge and experiences into a new model of thought. This helps create an internal representation that is different from our old representation of the world.[357] The process builds new neurological networks: remember that when neurons fire together, they wire together, and what flows through our mind sculpts our brain (section I.4.1). As we ponder new ways of looking at relationships between women and men that genuinely include an equal share of care and work, our neurons will begin to fire and wire in new sequences, patterns, and combinations

---

[357] Dispenza, 2012: 179.

because we are thinking *differently*. And whenever we make our brain work differently, we are changing our minds, literally.[358] As we do this repeatedly, we install new software and hardware programs into our nervous system, replacing the old, obsolete, prejudice filled programmes that have not served us so far. Epigenetic control mechanisms (see section I.4.2) will then insure that we exhibit a different behavioural reality that matches our new, equitable system of thought.

Epigenetic control mechanisms interact with the environment to regulate our biology and our genetic activity, in order to maintain harmony between our behaviour and our environment (both physical and cultural). The inseparability of behaviour, which involves our brain and our body, from the environment points to a mind system that is inclusive of all three: body, brain and environment, including our social culture. The integrative nature of the mind system (brain-body-environment) by necessity means that "by controlling our environment, we have the power to control our biology and become masters of our fate."[359] The next phase in fighting sexism therefore, after changing our mind, is to change our environment to one of sex equality, which will be reflected back onto our minds through epigenetic control mechanisms, eventually and through repetition leading to a change in our genetic expression to one of sex equality.

Deloitte's Women Initiative WIN is a good case to bring at this point. The company successfully squeezed sexism out of their work culture by, *first*, unconcealing hidden sexist patterns that were born out of stereotypes and biased assumptions about women and men, and, *second*, by creating a work environment that eliminated these biased assumptions and expectations, paving the way for a dramatic shift in the

---

[358] Ibid.
[359] Lipton and Bhaerman, 2009: 63.

proportion of women at the very top of the organisation (I will explore this in more detail in the chapter V).[360]

In summary, the cycle of sexist implicit perceptions creating sexist behaviour will continue *ad nauseam,* at it has done up till now, unless we: *First* unconceal and own up to our unconscious sexist patterns of thought. *Second,* create the intention of fighting sexism and sexist behaviour within ourselves, our communities, our societies and the world at large. *Third,* disengage from sexist, and engage in stereotype-inhibiting, thought processes. And *forth,* create a social environment that is in consonant with our stated, liberal beliefs that oppose prejudice of any kind.

---

[360] Interview with Michael Cook, previous CEO of Deloitte Touch (http://www.deloitte.com/view/en_US/us/About/Inclusion/Womens-Initiative/index.htm).

IV

THE STATE OF PLAY

"They used to give us a day--it was called International Women's Day. In 1975 they gave us a year, the Year of the Woman. Then from 1975 to 1985 they gave us a decade, the Decade of the Woman. I said at the time, who knows, if we behave they may let us into the whole thing. Well, we didn't behave and here we are." Bella Abzug (First Jewish female member of Congress; feminist, peace and civil liberty activist).

Compared to half a century ago, women's status in society has been considerably elevated, but it has not yet been levelled with that of men. The persistence of a 'status gap' between the sexes reflects our deeply seated beliefs about unbridgeable differences between women's and men's abilities and competences, themselves born out of beliefs about who women and men are, what their positions in society should be and what roles are entailed by these positions. It has been my contention throughout this book that nothing in reality can exist outside our consciousness, and therefore what manifests in reality is caused by and reflects our collective system of thought, albeit at an unconscious level. To glean into our deeply held beliefs about women and men, therefore, we need to examine our reality carefully which is my intention in this chapter. I will specifically examine women's status in the workplace and in the home, the two dichotomies that are a natural extension of the sexual division of labour, on which gender ideology is foundered.

IV.1   Education and Gendered Expectations

The starting point for pay, promotion and achievement in general is education, which is essential to advancing human capital, by developing knowledge and skills. High levels of education are often related to higher earnings and productivity, better career progression, as well as health and satisfaction with life.[361] Although secondary and tertiary attainment levels have increased for both men and women in most OECD countries, women's gains have exceeded those of men enough to shift the advantage in their favour. With few exceptions,[362] current secondary education attainment levels of young women aged 25-34 years in OECD countries are higher than their male counterparts, and 15% higher than education attainment levels of women born 20 years earlier. With even fewer exceptions,[363] the proportion of adults that complete tertiary education is consistently higher for women than for men in all OECD countries.[364]

Where the advantage is still distinctly in men's favour, is in the chosen field of study: despite the higher rate of women attending and graduating from college, young women are still shying away from those fields in higher education that offer better employment prospects, higher-pay and more prestige, namely science, technology, engineering and maths (STEM). The gap widens significantly as we move toward tertiary study. Examples specific to the US show this trend very clearly, as females progressively drop out of maths and science as they progress in their education: women earn 22.6% of undergraduate degrees in physics but only 15.5% of doctorates; they earn 46.7% of undergraduate degrees in maths but less than 29% of doctorates; and only 10% of faculty

---

[361]   OECD (2010), quoted in OECD, 2011a: 12.

[362]   These include Austria, the Czech Republic, Germany, Mexico, Switzerland and Turkey (OCED, 2011a: 18).

[363]   These include Chile, Switzerland, Mexico and Turkey (OCED, 2011a: 18).

[364]   OCED, 2011a: 18.

in maths and science are women.[365] For the OECD as a whole, while the majority of degrees awarded in maths, engineering and computer science in all are given to men (average of 75%), women account for the vast majority of graduates in the arts and humanities (average of 71%).[366] The massive accumulation of human capital by young women, therefore, is not being converted into economic and social capital, as young women steer away from the fields that have traditionally given men an advantage in labour markets.

Furthermore, even when women complete STEM studies, they are less likely than men to work in these sectors:[367] the majority (about 55%) of male graduates in sciences work as professionals in physics, maths and engineering, as opposed to only 33% of the female graduates. Overall, only 7.5% of women work in these fields while physics, maths and engineering are the second favourite fields for men.[368] This trend has serious implications in hindering women's careers and lowering their future earnings, not to mention depriving businesses of a source of talent and innovation and rendering investment in education for the economy at large an inefficient one.[369]

Evidence suggests that ability differences are not the primary reason why women quit sciences and engineering: while the advantage men have over women in maths' performance at age 15 is merely 2%, the male to female gap in the proportion of tertiary degrees awarded in maths and computer sciences are on average 64% in OECD.[370] This points to other factors than ability in influencing young women's choices in selecting fields of study, such as gender stereotyping within and outside the

---

[365]   Wood, 2009: 192-193.
[366]   OCED, 2011a: 15; 25.
[367]   Ibid: 25-26.
[368]   Ibid: 26
[369]   Ibid.
[370]   Ibid: 15; 25.

school,[371] which may erode their self-belief and their ability to achieve competently in male dominated fields. A report entitled "Women's experiences in college engineering" states: "Many young women leave (…) for reasons other than academic ability. These reasons can include their negatively interpreting grades that may actually be quite good, diminished self-confidence or reluctance to spend all of their waking hours 'doing engineering."[372] The report states that many women who left mentioned negative aspects of their school's climate such as competition, lack of support and discouraging faculty and peers.[373]

Diekman et al. (2010) used the agency versus communion gender stereotyping to explain why women opt out of STEM field careers. They provided undergraduates with a list of careers that are primarily occupied by either women (e.g., social worker, nurse, education administrator) or men (e.g., lawyer, architect, and physician). The students were asked to consider how well each career would fulfil agentic goals (power, achievement, excitement) or communal goals (intimacy, affiliation, altruism). They also had students indicate their interest in various careers and rate the extent to which they endorsed communal and agency goals. They found that when individuals endorse communal goals, who invariably were women, they are less interested in STEM careers.[374]

The negative stereotypical belief about women's low ability in maths and science held by academic staff was uncovered to the world when Larry Summers, president of Harvard University in 2005, suggested at an academic conference that *innate* differences might explain why so few women major in the sciences.[375] Sex stereotypes affect not only

[371] Sikora and Pokropek (2011), quoted in OCED, 2011a: 26.
[372] Goodman et al. (2002), quoted in Niederle and Vesterlund, 2005: 41.
[373] Quoted in Niederle and Vesterlund, 2005: 41. The authors mention that similar effects have been found by Felder et al., (1994).
[374] Quoted in Halpern, 2011, Kindle locations 5701-07.
[375] Wood, 2009:189.

how others evaluate women's maths and science skill but also women's self-confidence and how they perform on maths and science tasks: "when females are aware of a detrimental stereotype according to which females do less well at maths, they score lower than males on maths tests."[376]

The reference here is to stereotype threat that I discussed in section III.3.5. Evidence on how stereotype threat undermines standardised test performance and school outcomes is well documented.[377] The threat arises because members of the stereotyped group experience extra psychological pressure in situations where their behaviour can confirm the negative reputation that their group lacks a valued ability. "The fear of confirming others' stereotypes is presumed to create anxiety and distraction, robbing the stereotyped person of cognitive resources."[378] This psychological pressure, or "stereotype threat", can undermine the intellectual performance of virtually anyone whose group is targeted by a negative stereotype about their ability in a particular domain.[379]

Since Steele and Aronson's (1995) paper, research has shown that the consequences of stereotype threat extend beyond under achievement on academic tasks to include self-handicapping strategies, such as reduced practice time for a task,[380] and to a reduced sense of belonging to the stereotyped domain.[381] Chronic exposure to stereotype threat, such as that faced by women in academic environments regarding their maths performance, can prompt a long-term defence strategy against the exposure, by devaluing, disengaging, or disidentifying with the threatening domain. This would explain why women disidentify with

---

[376] Monastersky (2005), quoted in Wood, 2009:193.

[377] See 'Bibliography' page in http://www.reducingstereotypethreat.org.

[378] Eagly, Alice, personal communication in March 2013.

[379] Niederle and Vesterlund, 2005.

[380] Stone, 2002.

[381] Good, Dweck, and Rattan (2008), quoted in http://www.reducingstereotype threat.org.

maths as a domain that can bolster their self-esteem, given the maths' ability-doubting stereotype about women.[382] In education, therefore, stereotype threat can lead students to steer away from domains of study associated with negative stereotypes, and consequently limit the range of professions that they can pursue. In the long-term stereotype threat might be a major contributor to educational and social inequality.[383]

In addition to stereotype threat, Aronson et al. (1999) suggest the possibility of long-term exposure to devaluing stereotypes engendering feelings of inferiority that have been 'hammered into one's head' by persistent stigmatising conditions, which in turn can result in a stigmatised personality. In other words, prejudicial treatment can lead to internalised inferiority.[384] Even without internalising feelings of inferiority *vis-à-vis* maths' skills, the long standing belief that females innately have less aptitude and ability in maths and science can help erect barriers to women's participation in education as well as in careers in those fields.[385] Because cultural stereotypes of femininity do not include being skilled at science and maths, social disapproval or distance may greet women who excel in those skills. Nor do cultural stereotypes of femininity include the assertiveness and drive required to succeed in fields historically associated with maleness. Consequently, women in the sciences often face a double bind: if they are *not* extremely successful, they are judged as incompetent and if they *are* successful they are often perceived as cold, selfish and manipulative and are disliked for those reasons.[386] The same phenomenon, of social ostracism for violating

---

[382] Aronson et al.,1999. See also Aronson, et al., 2002; and Steele, 1997.

[383] Good et al., 2008; and Schmader, Johns, and Barquissau, 2004.

[384] See Aronson et al., 1999, for references and extended arguments. According to social role theory (Eagly, 1987) women and men internalise desirable personal attributes that are associated with their social roles. It follows that, to the extent that maths' skills are not considered essential for the fulfilment of women's social roles, women would internalise the negative belief that their maths' skills are inferior to men's.

[385] See Wood, 2009:192, for a review of the literature.

[386] Dean (2006), quoted in Wood, 2009: 193.

gender stereotypes, is observed when women attempt to get to the top of organisations as we shall see later in the chapter.

Together with stereotyping, and perhaps part and parcel of it, is the lack of professional role models for girls and young women in these fields, which sends a powerful message that it is gender inappropriate for girls and women to go into them. In addition, girls and young women may perceive the occupations that these fields lead into to be difficult to combine with family life.[387]

IV.2   The Gendered Workplace

> *"Women are a substantial part of the paid workforce, lower down the hierarchy." R. W. Connell (Australian sociologist and author)*[388]

IV.2.1   A spectacular rise in women's employment

One of the most profound labour market developments in OECD countries over the last five decades has been the significant rise in women's paid employment, leading to a substantial narrowing in the gap between male and female participation and employment rates.[389] In addition to joining the labour market, women's attachment to the labour market was significantly prolonged over the same period.[390]

In 2011, the average female employment rate in OECD countries was 60%. Much higher rates were seen in the four Nordic countries (Sweden, Finland, Norway, and Denmark) where the average stood

---

[387]   OECD, 2011a: 26.
[388]   Connell, 2009: 2.
[389]   See for example OECD, 2002: chapter 2.
[390]   OECD, 2002: 8.

at 70.8%,[391] which compared with an average rate of 40.5% in 1960, implies a spectacular 75% rise in Nordic countries' female employment rate.[392] The same trend was observed in most OECD countries, albeit at more subdued rates: in the US for example, the female employment rate rose from 39.5% in 1960, to 62.0% in 2011 (a 60% rise) and in the UK from 43.1% to 65.3%, in the two respective years (a 50% rise).[393]

The rise in mothers' employment was far more dramatic, contributing to most of the narrowing in the gap of female employment compared to men. There is no OECD comprehensive data, but taking the US as an example is indicative: while in 1960 only 25% of all married women with children under 18 years were participating in employment, the number rose steadily without interruption until the early 1990s, when it peaked at nearly 70%; it has come off its peak slightly since, standing currently at around 68%.[394]

On average for OECD countries, the gap between maternal employment and that of women without children is around 4% in the case of mothers with one child, and 13% for women with two or more children.[395] Differences across countries are large. In seven countries (including Denmark, Portugal and France), employment rates of mothers with one child are higher than those of childless women, while differences in employment rates between the two groups of women are also marginal in Sweden and Canada.[396]

---

[391] OECD, 2011a, Annex to chapter 2: Background data on employment, Table A2.2: 58.

[392] Pissarides, et al. 2005, Table 2.1: 71.

[393] Numbers and percentages are calculated from OECD, 2011a, Annex to chapter 2: Background data on employment, Table A2.2: 58; and Pissarides, et al. 2005, Table 2.1: 71.

[394] Cohany and Soki, 2007, Chart 1: 10. These calculations use different age brackets from those mentioned above relating to US so they are not strictly comparable. The intention here is to show order of magnitude.

[395] OECD, 2007b, Figure SS3.1 and SS3.2: 57.

[396] Ibid.

By far, the most important factor in driving up women's employment rates is the dramatic rise in women's educational attainment, which has been experienced by all OECD countries. Bassanini and Duval (2006) who sampled twenty OECD countries, found that 50% of cross-country variation in the growth of female employment rates between 1982-2003 can be attributed to rising educational attainment, while only 28% was due to policies and institutions. This stands to reason, since higher education is likely to give women access to well-paid occupations, making paid employment more attractive and formal child-care arrangements more affordable.[397] In all OECD countries, female employment rates are highly correlated with educational attainment: for example, while average female employment for women aged 25-64 in 2008 was 48% for those with less than secondary education, the rate was 80% for those with university/tertiary education. In Norway, which boats the highest average female employment rate in all OECD countries of 79%, those with tertiary education had a rate of 89% of female employment.[398]

IV.2.2 The persistence of difference

Across the OECD, compared to men, women are less likely to work for pay, more likely to be employed in lower-paid occupations and sectors, and more likely to have temporary employment contracts. Women are also likely to work fewer hours, are less likely to progress in their careers and are underrepresented in decision-making positions.[399]

IV.2.2.1 The employment gap

On average across OECD, the gap in employment between men and women (the employment to population ratio) stood at 18% in 2009,

---

[397] Altonji and Blank (1999), quoted in OECD, 2008:188.
[398] OECD, 2011b, table LMF 1.6.A.
[399] OECD, 2011a: 9.

with the gap less than 10% in the Nordic Countries (as well as Canada and Estonia).[400] As stated above, the higher educational qualifications are, the higher too is the employment rate amongst women and, as a consequence, the lower the employment gap between women and men. The employment gap therefore narrows to 10% for women with tertiary education, while it rises to 22.8% for those who have not completed upper secondary education (and 17.2% for those who have completed upper secondary or post secondary non-tertiary education).[401] Finland appears to be one of the countries in which educational attainment is the highest and where women have the greatest educational lead compared to men, and at the same time the employment gap between women and men at 3% is the smallest in all OECD countries.[402]

Sex differences in working hours are even starker than those in employment rates: if we take the full-time equivalent employment rate across all OECD countries,[403] the gap widens to 32%.[404] This is mainly explained by the higher likelihood of women working on a part-time basis compared to men.[405] For all OECD countries, just over one-quarter (26%) of women worked part time in 2011,[406] compared with only 8% of men. There are great variations among OECD countries in women's part time work: while it stood at the exceptionally high levels in Netherlands of 60% in 2011, it was 38.8% in the United

---

[400] OECD, 2011a, Annex to Chapter 2, Background data on employment, Table A2.1: 58.

[401] OECD, 2011b.

[402] OECD, 2008: 144; OECD, 2011a: table A2.1: 56.

[403] Full-time equivalent employment rates are calculated by multiplying the employment to population ratio by the average weekly hours worked by all employees and dividing by 40 (OECD, 2011a, Annex to chapter two, Background data on employment, Table A2.2: 58)

[404] It is lowest (below 15%) in Estonia and Finland and highest (above 50%) in Chile, Mexico and Turkey (OECD, 2011a, Annex to Chapter 2).

[405] OECD defines part time as working 30 hours or less a week (OECD, 2011a).

[406] The average for the EU is lower at 20.3% (OECD, 2011b).

Kingdom,[407] and only 18% in the US.[408] Part time work is also highly variable within the Nordic countries, with the highest incidence of women's part time work in Norway at 30.4% (with only 12% for men), and the lowest in Finland at 18% (10% for men). Denmark is interesting in that while women's part time work is close to OECD's average of one quarter, men's part time work at 10.9% is significantly above the 8% men's average for OECD countries,[409, 410] which has significant ramifications for the wage gap, as we shall soon see. The reason for the high variation in part time work in OECD countries is that it depends on many variables relating to economic and social policies, particularly income tax, social security contributions, family allowances and child care provisions and subsidies.[411]

In most OECD countries, prime-age women (25-34 years) are also more likely than men to have a temporary rather than a permanent employment contract; nearly 20% less men than women on average have temporary employment.[412] Temporary jobs tend to pay less than permanent jobs and often offer less access to training and to fringe benefits.[413] Women's relatively weak position in the market for paid

---

[407] OCED 2007: 3. On the other hand, part-time employment is rare in the Czech Republic, Hungary, and the Slovak Republic and is less than 15% of employed women in Finland, Greece, Korea, and Portugal (OECD, 2011b).

[408] OECD, 2011b: Chart LMF 1.6A: 1.

[409] And well above that for EU at 6.5% (OECD, 2011b).

[410] OECD, 2011b, interpreted from LMF1.6: Gender differences in employment outcomes.

[411] See David and Starzec's, 1992, for an insightful comparison between the UK and France of the effect of their welfare, tax and childcare policies on part time work.

[412] OECD, 2011a, table A2.1.

[413] In European countries, statutory benefits are provided to all workers. In principle therefore, temporary workers are entitled to the same benefits as permanent workers. Invariably, however, these workers do not accrue the necessary minimum contribution period and are therefore denied access to the benefits. In North America, on the other hand, most fringe benefits are voluntarily provided by employers who seldom extend them to temporary workers (OECD, 2011a: 33).

work is largely due to their intensive involvement in unpaid work: on average across OECD, women spend about 2.4 more hours (50% more time) on unpaid work per day than men.[414]

IV.2.2.2 Occupational segregation

In OECD countries, women tend to be concentrated in fewer occupations compared with men. On average, 24 occupations accommodate half of all employed men, whereas only 12 occupations accommodate half of all employed women.[415] Concentration in only a few occupations curtails women's opportunities of advancement throughout their career cycle and leads to skills' mismatches.[416] Interestingly, the widest sex gap in occupational concentration is observed in Sweden (as well as the Slovak Republic and the United Kingdom),[417] indicating that Nordic countries' success in achieving sex equality is more apparent than real, a subject that I will address later in this chapter.

Women are overrepresented in the helping professions, such as teaching, nursing, and social work, as well as in clerical occupations and sales, while men are overrepresented in maths, science, engineering and chemistry. Men and women do however approach equality in other job categories such as medicine, law and journalism.[418,419] These skewed choices mirror those made in education: in 2009, on average for OECD, only 26% of graduates in engineering, manufacturing and construction were women, compared to more than 75% of graduates in health and

---

[414] OECD, 2011a, table A2.1.

[415] OECD, 2011a: 46.

[416] Ibid.

[417] The lowest gaps are observed in Greece and Ireland (Ibid).

[418] Halpern and Murphy 2005: 5; OECD, 2011a: 46.

[419] Women are also under-represented in manual and production jobs as they tend to steer away from manufacturing (OECD, 2012a).

welfare degrees.[420] In other words, most occupations are "sex typed" in that they have a high concentration of either females or males and they become identified as masculine or feminine jobs. Technically speaking, stereotypically male characterised occupations are those in which at least 60–75% of the workers are males, and the same is true for female characterised occupations. Generally speaking, male characterised jobs are more highly paid than female characterised occupations.

Occupational segregation appears to be more pronounced for low-skilled workers, as well as for mothers, who are more likely than other women to work as service and sales workers.[421] This might be the result of self-selection by mothers into occupations that are more compatible with their family responsibilities, or might be related to employers' biased selection and promotion practices, where they are less likely to offer mothers career and employment opportunities.[422] In a diagonally opposed fashion, fathers tend to be more concentrated in occupations where men are over-represented, which are in general more likely to be management positions with higher earnings.[423] This too might be the result of self-selection into occupations and positions that are more compatible with family financial demands, or might be related to employers' biased perception of fathers as more 'authorities', more on this issue later.

Ideas about the suitability of certain jobs for women and men, which tend to run along gendered, stereotypical lines, start from a young age. A survey of 508 children and young adults (aged 13 to 18) was conducted in England by Miller and Hayward (2006).[424] Participants

---

[420]   Ibid.
[421]   OECD, 2011a: 46.
[422]   Ibid.
[423]   Ibid.
[424]   Quoted in Halpern, 2011: chapter 6, section 2, sub section 1.

were presented with a list of jobs and asked, "Who should do this job: men, women, both?" and "Who mainly does this job: men, women, both?"[425] With only one exception, the girls and boys agreed on which jobs are appropriate for each sex: while most jobs were seen as appropriate for men (airplane pilot, architect, civil engineer, biotechnologist, forensic scientist, financial advisor, computer programmer, webmaster, etc.), only very few, communal occupations were thought to be appropriate for women (hairdresser, nurse, occupational therapist, physiotherapist, secretary, and a slight preference for maths teacher). The lone exception is "dentist," which was seen as equally appropriate for both sexes – although the differences for this occupation were too small to be meaningful.[426]

The experiment unveils society's agency-communion conversation about women and men, where women are seen as relational beings, whose calling in life is to serve and care for others, and men as rational, non-relational, agentic beings whose job in life is to provide. Chodorow (1998) argues that women's work in the labour force tends to extend their housewife, wife, or mother roles and their concern with personal and affective ties (as secretaries, service sector workers, nurses, teachers, etc.), whereas men's work is less likely to have affective overtones (craft workers, operatives, professional and technical workers).

IV.2.2.3 Vertical segregation

Despite the large increase in the proportion of managerial jobs going to women in the last few decades, the "vertical" component of occupational segregation persists as women are still under-represented in managerial

---

[425] Halpern commented on the study's consistent listing of the term "men" before "women" in the questions, as well as listing male responses before female responses, suggesting an androcentric bias in the study that might have influenced results.

[426] Quoted in Halpern, 2011: chapter 6, section 2, sub section 1.

jobs, especially at the most senior level.[427] On average across the OECD, only one-third of the managers were females in 2011;[428] while the average percentage of female board directors across the EU was only 13.7% in 2011.[429]

So it seems that not only do women gravitate toward lower paying professions, but they also tend to be concentrated into the lower-ranked and lower-paid positions within a given profession. Even when women occupy management positions, they are more likely to be concentrated in personnel than in marketing professions, with the median salary in the US for a marketing manager £66,000, while for a personnel manager it's £60,000.[430] Another example occurs within the medical field. Female doctors are much more likely to be heavily concentrated in the family practice (with and average salary in the US of $211,083), obstetrics/gynaecology (with and average salary of $312,257) or paediatric specialties (with and average salary of $210,678). However, men are more likely to become surgeons and highly specialized medical practitioners, with salaries upward of $400,000.[431]

IV.2.2.4 The wage gap

The wage gap between men and women (as measured at 50% of median earnings) declined over time, but remained significant at 16% on average

---

[427] Ibid.

[428] This is subject to considerable variation across countries: while the proportion of women managers is high in France, Poland and the United States, where more than 35% of managerial positions are held by women, women find it particularly difficult to progress up the career ladder in Luxembourg where only around one in five mangers are women.; in the UK the proportion is 34% (OECD, 2011b).

[429] http://www.europeanpwn.net/index.php?article_id=29.

[430] http://www.indeed.com/salary?q1=personnel+Manager&l1=United+States.

[431] http://www.healthcareers.about.com/od/compensationinformation/tp/Doctor-Salaries.htm.

across the OECD in 2008.[432, 433] These are unadjusted hourly wage gaps,[434] and do not account for sex differences in hours worked,[435] sector of employment, experience, and so on. Research shows that when these differences are controlled for, the 'gender gap' is smaller but still positive; the unexplained part of the gap is attributed to sex discrimination.[436]

The Institute for Women's Policy Research (IWPR) in the US found that in 2010, the ratio of annual average wage for women full time workers compared to men was 77.8%.[437] If part time workers were included, the gap would be much larger since women far more than men work part time.[438] This overall number for the wage gap masks substantial differences between occupations: for example, according to the US Census Bureau (2005), women's earnings as a percentage of men's were 65% or less in legal occupations, sales, health care and technical occupations.[439] The gap starts to widen considerably when men and women are in their early to mid-thirties and peaks when they are in their fifties.[440]

An analysis of the earning gap by the US Council of Economic Advisers in 1998 found that even after controlling for variables like career breaks, return to part-time or fewer hours in full time position, or sliding down

---

[432] OECD, 2011a: 35 and chart A2.1: 56.

[433] This overall number masks considerable variation between countries, with the largest gaps of over 30% in Japan and Korea and the lowest in Italy and Hungary, where the gaps are negligible (OECD, 2011a:35 and chart A2.1: 56).

[434] Country coverage of the adjusted gaps is much less comprehensive (OECD, 2011a:35 and chart A2.1: 56).

[435] The difference between women and men in the number of hours they spend in paid work tends to increase when children are young, as mothers of young children tend to cut back while fathers sometimes increase the hours worked on the arrival of children (OECD, 2011a:35 and chart A2.1: 56).

[436] OECD, 2011a:35 and chart A2.1: 56.

[437] Quoted in Halpern 2011: chapter 1, section 9, sub section 2, para. 1.

[438] Ibid.

[439] Ibid.

[440] Halpern and Cheung, 2008: 9.

the career ladder to accommodate family (going into teaching rather than engineering or social work rather than financial institution) the evidence is that labour market discrimination against women persists.[441] A more recent study by the US government Accounting Office in 2003 estimated that approximately 20% of the earning gap between women and men cannot be accounted for by occupation, hours worked, and other relevant variable. The researchers found that jobs that offer more flexibility also offer lower pay and fewer opportunities for advancement, which they took into account when estimating the unexplained portion of the pay gap, reaching the conclusion that "there is a lingering bias against paying women at same rate as men."[442]

In Europe too a significant part of the gap remains unexplained. Arulampalam, Booth, and Bryan analysed pay gaps across the wage distribution in eleven European countries. They controlled for the effects of individual characteristics at different points of the distribution and calculated the part of the gap attributable to differing returns between men and women (i.e., pay discrimination). The economists found that pay gaps typically widened toward the top of the wage distribution, and in exceptional cases it also widened at the bottom. In 2008 the OECD concluded that "30% of the variation in gender wage gaps across OECD countries can be explained by discriminatory practices in the labour market."[443]

Lower earnings and later on lower pensions, are largely responsible for the higher incident of poverty amongst elderly women than men; as is lack of participation in paid employment. A study by Dex and Bukodi (2010) of 1958 and 1970 cohorts found that women more than men in both cohorts are more likely to be living in social housing in adulthood. Similarly, in both cohorts more women than men were likely to receive non-universal benefits (means-tested).

---

[441] Quoted in Halpern and Cheung, 2008:16.
[442] Ibid.
[443] OECD, 2008.

IV.2.2.5 The care gap

I will address the issue of sex differences in care in more detail in following sections. Suffice it to say here that in the vast majority of OECD countries, women engage in much more unpaid work than men, mostly in care activities.[444] Even non-working fathers devote less time to caring than working mothers. There are also clear divisions in the type of care provided by men and women: mothers typically provide physical personal childcare and housework, while fathers spend proportionally more time on educational and recreational childcare activities. "In countries with high rates of female employment, more men spend time on unpaid work. This suggests that to mobilise more female labour supply, men would have to participate more in unpaid work in the home."[445]

IV.3 Social Discourse, Public Policy and Sex Equality: Lessons from the Nordics

"Beliefs can easily cause us to become blind to the obvious."Dean Radin (Researcher in parapsychology)[446]

The Nordic countries are often seen as a paradigm of sex equality, meriting a closer examination of their achievements to glean insights into advancing women's careers. The distinguishing factor of the Nordic example is that both social discourses, particularly the gender equality discourse, and public policy are fully supportive of women's work. In the rest of the OECD countries, government policy is not necessarily in step with the 'gender equality' discourse. This is partly, but not entirely,

---

[444] More time is spent on caring for and educating children rather than caring for elderly and disabled relatives OECD, 2011a: 40).

[445] OECD, 2011a: 40.

[446] http://blog.gaiam.com/quotes/topics/blind-spot.

influenced by the whole hearted adoption of welfare state policies by the Nordic countries, while policies in the rest of the OECD countries, is more laissez faire, with varying degrees. The single most important outcome of this difference between socially oriented and free market oriented policies is the degree to which childcare is supported by the state. Countries that are unapologetic about their laissez faire approach to social policy, such as the US, see childcare as a purely private issue. Consequently, parents don't only have to organise and pay for their own childcare privately, but they also have to take parental leaves out of their own personal holidays.

In the Nordic countries, on the other hand, public policy in the late 1960s and throughout the 1970s and 1980s focused on securing the wellbeing of children while promoting employment of both parents. This includes paid child-related leaves (maternity, parental, and paternal leaves, and sick children leave); shorter working hours when children are young; subsidised early care and education services, and out-of-school hours' care until children enter secondary school. There are in addition widely available community based institutions to share the care of children and the elderly, either as public or subsidised services. Further, in Sweden, the development of the social welfare state greatly expanded employment opportunities for women in the caring professions and situated these activities in the public sector.[447]

So how successful have these welfare policies been in closing the gap between men and women's careers in the Nordic countries?

In all four countries (Sweden, Norway, Denmark, and Finland), women's participation rate (employment to population ratio) in 2009 was 8-14% higher than the average for the OECD countries. When we take the full time equivalent measure of women's participation rate, the Nordic countries advantage over the rest of OECD countries

---

[447] OECD, 2011a: 44; and Apelbaum et al., 2002: 145.

narrows to 6-9%, because there are more women working part time in the Nordic countries than the rest of the OECD.[448] A higher rate of women's participation means a lower gap between men's and women's participation in the labour force in the Nordic countries than the rest of the OECD: in Finland, men have a mere 1% advantage over women, in Norway and Sweden 5%, and in Denmark 7%, compared with an 18% average for the OECD.[449]

The picture is less clear cut when we consider the earnings' gap (as measured at 50% of median full time earnings). In Finland at 20.5%, and Sweden at 18% in 2011, the average earnings' gap remains higher than that of the OECD's at 17.5%, but in Denmark and Norway at just over 15%, it is below the OECD average.[450] Crucially, however, taking the top quintile in Norway's earnings gap reveals a different picture, as the gap widens to 16%, which is closer to the OECD average of the top quintile of 17.5%, revealing that most of the progress in closing the wage gap in Norway has come from lower level earnings; indeed, the gap between men's and women's pay in the bottom quintile in Norway is as narrow as 5%.[451]

Time spent on unpaid work is the area where the Nordic countries have unequivocal advantage in bringing about sex equality reflecting more clearly their sex equitable social norms: while the gap between time that women and men spend on unpaid work in the OECD countries is on average 50%, it is roughly half of that in the Nordic countries, with Denmark having the narrowest gap at 23%.[452] The reason is that men spend considerably more time, and women considerably less time, doing unpaid work than their counterparts in other OECD countries, which

---

[448] Calculated from OECD, 2011a, Annex to chapter two, Table A2.2: 58.
[449] Ibid: 56.
[450] OECD, 2011b, Chart LMF1.5.C: 3.
[451] Ibid, Chart LMF1.5.B: 2.
[452] OECD, 2011a, Annex to chapter two: 56.

perhaps is not surprising, given women's higher than OECD average participation in paid employment in the Nordic countries.[453]

The massive efforts in shifting care work from the private to the public domain in the Nordic countries, through extensive welfare policies, has had a significant impact on raising women's participation in paid employment. It has also contributed to relieving stress and ameliorating work-life conflict in those countries. In a cross country comparison of the effect of having children and household responsibilities on working women's levels of stress, Compton and Lyonette (2007) found that women in Portugal are most likely to have a stressful home life, followed by Britain, and France, while Norway is two times less likely, and Finland three times less likely than Portuguese women to find life stressful at home.[454] "These findings lend support to the argument that positive dual earner policies in the Nordic countries contribute to 'societal effect' resulting in lower levels of work-life conflict."[455]

In conclusion, sex equality discourses in the Nordic countries have successfully influenced their public policies and work norms in supporting women's continuous work. This has lead primarily to a significant reduction in the gap between women's and men's labour market participation. These policies have also contributed toward a less conflicted work-life organisation, allowing women to reduce, and men to increase, time spent on unpaid work, leading to a reduction in women's share in unpaid work.

Where the Nordic countries' success has been less spectacular is in narrowing the gap in pay and promotion. Apart from Finland, women in the Nordic countries remain concentrated in few, relatively low

---

[453] Ibid, interpreted from tables in Annex to chapter two: 55-58.

[454] 46% of all Portuguese working women find life at home stressful, as compared to 39% in Britain, 30% in France, and only a very small minority of Norwegian and Finnish women do (Compton and Lyonette, 2007).

[455] Compton and Lyonette, 2007: 131.

paying occupations, such as care, health and education. For example in Sweden, just over 10 occupations accounted for half of all women's employment in 2007, compared with over 30 occupations for men.[456, 457] By contrast, in the US 50% of women's employment is spread amongst 24 occupations, compared to 28 occupations for men.[458] Furthermore, women remain under-represented in senior position in the Nordic countries. The proportion of women with managerial responsibilities stood at 30% in 2007 in the four Nordic countries, which is below the OECD average of 32.1%, and significantly below that in the US at 36.7% and the UK at 34.4%,[459] both of which have public policies that have shied away from the public provision of childcare, particularly the US where childcare remains entirely a private concern.

These lacklustre outcomes in Nordic countries are due to the distinct nature of their equality discourses and the ensuing strategies that focused entirely on 'continuous work' for women, rather than sex equality *per se*. Where the 'gender' conversation has gone amiss in the Nordic countries, therefore, is in their failure to challenge the founding assumption of the gender project that it is women who care. Given this blind spot, it was thought appropriate to integrate women in the labour market through part time work, mainly in the public sector and in care and education professions. Women in the Nordic countries in other words were not afforded equality of opportunity to men, inevitably making equality of outcome in labour markets unachievable.

---

[456] The comparable numbers for the rest of the Nordics are: in Norway, 9 occupations for women, and 23 occupations for men; in Denmark, 7 occupations for women, and 15 occupations for men; and in Finland, 15 occupations for women, and 33 for men, account for 50% of all employment (OECD, 2011b, Chart LMF1.6.E).

[457] The spread of employment among occupations in any given country is related to the economic structure of that country, hence of itself is not an indicator of women's advancement *per se*; what is relevant, therefore, is women's position relative to men.

[458] OECD, 2011b, Chart LMF1.6.E.

[459] Ibid, Chart LMF1.6.F.

Clearly then, sex equality discourses in the Nordic countries have not yet fully incorporated the structural aspect of equality that involves equality of status. It is telling perhaps that in the Nordic counties, and the world over, that sex equality discourses are still described as 'gender equality', not realising perhaps that to accept gender in the first place is to accept it's *built in* inequality. The gender system, which aims to organise women's and men's productive and reproductive social practices, is predicated on assigning caring to women and earning to men, creating a permanent structural inequality in status, power and prestige between the two sexes. To accept 'gender' as our social identity is to accept that women and men are 'different' by nature. And given that the 'nature' we assigned for women is a caring one while that we assigned for men is an agentic one, we must therefore remain unequal and to speak of 'gender equality' is an oxymoron. The real blind spot perhaps comes for believing that we need a social identity in the first place, it is as if without a conceptual identity of who we are we will not recognise ourselves as women and men, when nothing could be further from the truth. It is precisely because we live our lives out of mental constructs of who we 'think' we are that we forget who we truly are as simply human beings. Until we get this point about the nature of human beings, of boys and girls and women and men, we would not have unmasked gender as a thick layer of social conditioning that aims to alter our nature to one that helps society organise sex and babies.

IV.4   Barriers to Women's Advancement

In recent years the term glass ceiling has been discredited, as it gives the illusion that women advance to a certain level in work organisations and then hit resistance at management level. Research has shown that women face disadvantage in obtaining promotions at *all* levels, including entry level, leading to a dwindling effect as they move higher up the organisation.[460] To help give a more accurate representation of obstacles facing women as they pursue their careers, Eagly and Carli (2010) summoned the image of negotiating a labyrinth to describe women's difficult route to the top since "with continuing change, the obstacles that women face have become more surmountable, at least by some women some of the time. Paths to the top exist, and some women find them;"[461] however, these routes can be circuitous and difficult to discover.[462]

IV.4.1   Unexamined assumptions and biased expectations

That said, the glass ceiling concept has stirred up emotions and instigated valuable research into the obstacles facing women as they attempt to advance their careers. The Glass Ceiling Commission set up by the US Congress in 1995 identified two major societal barriers that cause and reinforce a glass ceiling that restricts women's access to higher-level employment opportunities: the supply barrier, related to educational opportunity and attainment, and the difference barrier which manifests itself as conscious and unconscious stereotypes, prejudice, and bias related to gender – as well as ethnicity.[463] The commission also listed internal structural barriers within the direct control of businesses, some of which I will discuss in section VI.4.

Catalyst (1989) expanded on the difference barriers to include 'misperceptions' and 'unexamined assumptions' about women's career interests, abilities and long-term commitment, and to 'unquestioned policies and practices' that pervade the corporate culture. "In combination, these artefacts of a traditionally white male occupational culture work against the career progression and retention of talented

---

[460]   See Baxter and Wright, 2000; and Elliot and Smith, 2004.

[461]   Eagly and Carli, 2007: 6.

[462]   Ibid.

[463]   Federal Glass Ceiling Commission, 1995: 8.

female managers."[464] Gorman and Kmec (2009) looked specifically at law firms and found that key factors like high status, work uncertainty, and the historical predominance of male incumbents, characterise highly ranked positions and heighten the 'gender bias' of decision makers.[465] A necessary first step therefore in creating a work environment that is as conducive to women's success as it is to men's, is uncovering unconscious beliefs and unexamined assumptions that lead to different expectations, and as a consequence differential treatment, of women from men in work spaces.

In 1991, Deloitte and Touche decided to tackle the problem of low representation of women at executive level (only 5% of the firm's partners were women at the time). The company performed an audit of workplace practices and found a great number of unexamined and unfounded assumptions being made about men and women that clearly disadvantaged women.[466] The biggest assumption the company made was that women who left them did so in order to take care of their families, when in fact the women simply moved on to other companies. This family care assumption underlies all other misguided expectations of women's preferences and abilities. One firm-wide practice for example was the tendency to give men and women different work assignments, with serious repercussions for their advancement. This was based on assumptions such as women would not be comfortable in manufacturing environments, or that they would not want to travel too much. The latter assumption is particularly career–damaging in a company that relies heavily on travel to serve its clients. More damaging is the finding that while men were being typically evaluated based on their 'potential', women were evaluated based on their 'actual performance', with the result that men were being promoted considerably faster than women. The accumulation of these assumptions, all of which are based on archaic gender stereotypes, amounted to firmly held beliefs that disfavoured

---

[464] Quoted in Halpern and Cheung, 2008: 4.
[465] See also Purcell, et al., 2006.
[466] Quoted in Babcock and Laschever, 2008: 16.

women and limited their advancement, as well as made the working environment inhospitable,[467] prompting those women to leave to other companies. Interestingly, in line with other research findings, Deloitte and Touch found that both men and women wanted the freedom to balance work and family better. No one wanted what was then the standard 80 hour week.

So it appears that when organisations are running on auto pilot and not paying *attention*, they rely on old beliefs that include gender stereotypes. These are practically past generations' way of thinking that remained unexamined in our contemporary times, and therefore still run our lives. Old, obsolete, and dysfunctional ways of relating to women and men will continue to dictate behaviours in the workplace, until they are *unconcealed, interrupted* and *replaced* with a fresh, new way of thinking. When organisations *do* pay attention, as did Deloitte and Touch did, they become more conscious of practices that are based on erroneous assumptions that slam the breaks on women's careers.

IV.4.2　Bias against women?

A Catalyst study (1998) attempted to uncover the reasons behind women managers leaving corporate America to set up their own business. They found the following as the main reasons for women's departure: failure to have their contributions recognized (47%); not being taken seriously (34%); feeling isolated (29%); seeing others promoted ahead of them (27%); excluded from informal networks (21%) and excluded from training opportunities (21%).[468] Moore and Buttner's (1997) study also found that 27% of their sample of women cited a "desire for increased responsibility and recognition" as a reason for leaving the corporate environment.

---

[467]　Babcock and Laschever, 2008:17.
[468]　Catalyst, 1998: 17, figure 9.

Even in academic environments, the bastions of intellectual integrity, scholars found differential pay and promotion tracks for men and women. A study by McDowell, Singell and Ziliak (2001) investigated faculty promotion in the economics profession. After controlling for quality of Ph.D., training, publishing productivity, major field of specialisation, current placement in a distinguished department, age and post-Ph.D. experience, they found that female economists were still significantly less likely to be promoted from assistant to associate and from associate to full professor than male economists.

In a class action sex discrimination lawsuit against Wal-Mart in 2004, which included 1.6million current and former female employees of Wal-Mart, expert statistical evidence presented in the case showed that women earned less and received promotions less often than men, despite having superior qualifications and records of services. At every level of management, women were promoted less often than would be expected based on their representations in the 'feeder pools' of employees having credentials suitable for promotion. The statistical consultant in the case summarised this quantitative evidence on behalf of the plaintiffs as such: "Women employees were concentrated in the lower paying jobs, are paid less than men in the same job, and are less likely to advance to management positions than men. These gender patterns persist even though women have more seniority, lower turnover rates and higher performance ratings in most jobs."[469]

Part and parcel of gender stereotypes is attributing men's success to their 'ability', an internal, stable factor that is likely to continue into the future, and women's success to 'luck', an external, unstable factor implying little likelihood of repeat performance. Failures follow the opposite pattern: men's failures are attributed to external factors and women's to lack of ability. Consequently, men's successes are seen as indicative of future performance and their failures discounted as

---

[469] Eagly and Carli, 2007: 74.

temporary, but women's successes are discounted and their failures interpreted as diagnostic. Inevitably, this creates the bias of seeing a man with an identical record of successes and failures to a woman as more likely to succeed in the future.[470] This biased belief against women leading to a greatly disadvantaged position in the workplace is no clearer than when men achieve quicker promotions in female dominated professions, such as nursing, librarianship, elementary school teaching and social work, which sociologist Christine Williams dubbed as the *glass escalator.*[471]

Attributing women's success to luck entails that women have to work considerably harder to achieve similar results to men. In a study conducted with 448 upper-level employees, Lyness and Heilman (2006) found that women were less likely to be promoted than men, and if they were promoted they had stronger performance ratings than men. This suggests that women have to be far more competent than men to be considered eligible for the same leadership role. In a number of longitudinal studies that track comparably qualified men and women, such as graduates of the same MBA program or law school, it has been shown that over time there is degradation of women's compensation that cannot fully be explained by differences in qualifications, work history, experience, or career interruptions.[472] Wood, Corcoran, and Courant (1993) for example studied male and female lawyers 15 years after graduation from the elite University of Michigan Law School. They found an 18% salary gap between men and childless women, i.e., those women who were unlikely to show weak labour force attachment, which is a common explanation for a wage differential.

It does seem that prejudice against women in the workplace is caused by, as well as reflects, societal bias. For example, Hekman et al. (2010)

---

[470]   Geis, 1993: 15-6.

[471]   Eagly and Carli, 2007: 74

[472]   For example Olson, Frieze, and Good, 1987; Strober, 1982; and Wood, Corcoran, and Courant, 1993.

found that white men receive significantly higher customer satisfaction scores than equally well-performing women and minority employees. Customers viewed videos featuring a black male, a white female, or a white male actor playing the role of an employee helping a customer. The customers were 19% more satisfied with the white male employee's performance and were even more satisfied with the store's cleanliness and appearance when served by a white male. This despite the fact that all three actors performed identically, read the same script, and were in exactly the same location with identical camera angles and lighting. In a second study, they found that white male doctors were rated as more approachable and competent than equally-well performing women or minority doctors. They conclude that customer ratings tend to be inconsistent with objective indicators of performance and should not be uncritically used to determine pay and promotion opportunities.

What are the specific assumptions made about women and men in a work environment that lead to those biased expectations of competency?

IV.4.3   Femininity incongruent with leadership

The workplace still favours those traits and skills that are associated with being male and devalues those that are associated with being female. The underlying reason is that people hold different beliefs about the *nature* of women and men and therefore assign the caregiver-family role to women and the assertive-career role to men, with attendant stereotypes and perceptions about their abilities and statuses in society. A logical conclusion to the assignment of agency to men and communion to women is that leadership roles, and success more generally, are collapsed with agentic traits leading people to believe that men possess the necessary leadership traits. Women's communal qualities of warmth and niceness, on the other hand, tend to be inconsistent with the attributes believed to be required for success.

Eagly and Karau (2002) state that this disparity between communal female stereotype and agentic leader stereotype leads to two forms of prejudice. *First,* women's potential for being endorsed as leaders is less than men's, since the male stereotype is closer to the leader stereotype. *Second,* women's actual leadership is evaluated less favourably than men's actual leadership, because women's assertive behaviour is perceived as undesirable or threatening particularly to men.[473] Crucially, because individuals are normally assimilated in group stereotypes, this evaluative penalty is exacted even from women who do not possess the qualities that are stereotypical of their group but do possess those regarded as necessary for success in the job role. "Discrimination is a behavioural expression of this evaluative penalty."[474]

Eagly and Karau (2002) further argue that when gender is salient in the environment, the only way for women to be influential with men is to conform to prescriptive stereotypes and be tentative (communal trait) rather than assertive (agentic trait). Role congruity proponents believe that there is an asymmetry between women and man in the way they perceive women leaders. They state that compared with men, women generally have a more androgynous construal of leadership and they are more influenced by assertive rather than tentative female speaker, because of the perceived agency of the speakers.[475]

Heilman and Eagly (2008) mention natural setting audits that confirmed the lack-of-fit theory: there was a high incidence of sex discrimination against women in the more senior jobs that yield higher status and wages, as well as against both sexes when they applied for jobs dominated by the other sex. Goldin and Rouse (2000) conducted a powerful quasi experimental study by auditing the hiring process of musicians in a major symphony orchestra, where most positions are traditionally held by men. They used a screen to hide the identity of

---

[473]   Reid, et al. 2009.
[474]   Heilman and Eagly, 2008.
[475]   See Reid et al., 2009, for references.

the musicians who were auditing, and compared the success of women and men under these conditions with those when the Orchestra did not use a screen. They found that the screen increased women's success by approximately 50% in the initial round of auditions and made them 1.6 times more likely to win an orchestral position.[476]

In academia too, the assumption that women's communality is incongruent with success prevails. Madera, Hebl, and Martin, (2009) examined letters of recommendation for faculty positions in higher education and found that women were more likely to be described with adjectives that connote communal terms (e.g., affectionate, warm, kind) and less likely to be described with agentic terms (e.g., assertive, confident, ambitious). Critically, the scholars found a negative relationship between communal characteristics and hiring decisions in academia.[477] White, Bagilhole, and Riordan (2012) looked at career trajectories into university management in Australia, South Africa and the United Kingdom (UK). They found that the typical career path was modelled on male academic careers. In South Africa and the UK the perception of top university leaders was of a man but in Australia, where more women have been Vice Chancellors, there was no such assumption. Characteristics valued in university leaders in Australia and South Africa were 'soft' leadership traits, but in the UK 'hard', 'aggressive' and 'competitive' leadership prevailed.

IV.4.4   Lower status and biased expectations

A broader perspective on how gender stereotypes might bias hiring and promotion decisions against women links expectation of competence to status, rather than to attributes, which takes us back to false consciousness (see section III.3.3). In their interaction with each other,

---

[476] Quoted in Heilman and Eagly, 2008
[477] Quoted in Halpern, 2011: chapter 6, section 2, sub section 1, para. 4.

people look for status markers to form expectations about the person's competence.[478] Gender, like ethnicity, religion, race and education are general status characteristics, which are used in conjunction with individual characteristics to form a judgement on the status of the person. Even physical attractiveness is said to be used as a status marker, as is one's occupation. Generally speaking, people have higher status in society if they are: male rather than female, physically attractive rather than physically unattractive and more educated rather than less educated.[479] Therefore, depending on the salience of these factors, women will be perceived as either more or less competent than men. If gender *is* salient, they will be assumed to be less competent than men and expected to behave in a communal, or less assertive, manner, otherwise they will lose their ability to influence others. If on the other hand education or professional affiliations are salient, women will be expected to behave in an assertive manner, and as they do they will become more influential.[480]

Reid et al. (2009) state that because status characteristics are based on consensual beliefs, people's behaviour is shaped through a collective process that defines who can legitimately enact influence. The result is that high status people are permitted to enact assertive but not tentative behaviour, whereas low status people are permitted to enact tentative but not assertive behaviour. Behaviour that is inconsistent with this legitimated order is viewed as a status violation and sanctioned by the groups. For example, women who attempt to enact an assertive role will be *perceived* as lacking in the prescribed level of communality, and they will be resisted, disliked, and lack influence, particularly with men.[481] For women to be influential when gender is salient they have to

---

[478] This is called 'expectation states theory', a branch of which is called 'status characteristics theory', formulated by Berger et al. (see Reid et al., 2009; and Miles and Clenney, 2010).
[479] Ridgeway and Diekeman, 1992.
[480] Miles and Clenney, 2010.
[481] Reid et al., 2009; and Miles and Clenney, 2010.

soften their suggestions with tentative language to convey recognition of and deference to status hierarchy and this deference enables a female speaker to be somewhat influential.[482] Surprisingly, research suggests that tentative women are not just modestly influential, but highly influential with men despite being evaluated low on competence and agency.[483] Men maybe particularly influenced by tentative women when gender is salient because the latter confirm men's social advantage, giving their collective self-esteem a boost.[484]

Status characteristics have been used to shed more light on why women achieve inferior results in negotiations compared to men. Babcock and Laschever (2008) highlighted how in negotiations, women start from a lower position, aim less high and give in too easily. The authors believe that one of the reasons is women's focus on maintaining good relationship with their interlocutor and being too self-conscious of how they might appear if they were to negotiate more aggressively, which violates gender norms.[485] I have shown in section III.3.4 that women's lack of self-belief, given their order in the gender hierarchy, lowers their confidence in their ability to assert superior outcomes and creates a false consciousness of low entitlement.

Miles and Clenney (2010) examined the possibility that women's lower gender status constrains their ability to reach outcomes that are equal or superior to men, which further perpetuates men's higher status in society. Specifically, they argue that gender operates as a status characteristic in negotiations, which means that women are viewed as less competent than men and are therefore more constrained in their behaviour. Communal, cooperative behaviour is perceived as acceptable for women, while assertive behaviour is not. Men on the other hand,

---

[482]   Miles and Clenney, 2010.
[483]   See Reid et al. 2009 for references.
[484]   Ibid.
[485]   Babcock and Laschever, 2008: 113-114.

who have a higher status than women, are perceived as more competent and therefore more influential in negotiations.

Negotiations involve using the twin strategies of *competing* and *cooperating*, both of which need to be deployed at different times, in order for negotiations to succeed. During negotiations, if women behave in a masculine manner (competing) their motives will be questioned, whereas as Eagly et al. (1992) suggested, males' motives are not questioned when they behave in a communal manner (cooperating). Therefore, proposals that involve both benefit to the self (competing) and benefit to the counterpart (cooperating) are more readily accepted from men than from women. Men's higher status legitimates their right to engage in actions and make proposals that simultaneously cooperate and compete, while women's lower status creates a perception that such actions are illegitimate.[486] If women chose to violate the norms by acting more aggressively, this will have a 'backlash' effect as they are viewed negatively (less likeable), for having violated gender stereotypes, met with great resistance and lose their ability to influence others. Because of these tendencies, and in an effort to establish likeability in salary negotiations, women have a tendency to accept lesser economic outcomes, offer more concessions and accept the first salary offer presented by employers.[487]

IV.4.5   Homophily and exclusion

Homophily is the tendency for individuals to associate with others who are socially and culturally similar, and this is believed to influence women's occupational mobility.[488] Rosabeth Moss Kanter's (1993) classic work, 'Men and women of the corporation' reveals the importance of conformity in corporation settings, particularly at management level,

---

[486]   Miles and Clenney, 2010.
[487]   See Miles and Clenney, 2010 for references.
[488]   Purcell et al., 2010.

where uncertainty pressures drive men in management to reproduce others in the organisation in their own image, in order to be able to trust them. Lack of conformity in large corporations is not tolerated even in appearance, and "if differences in appearance were not easily tolerated in the ranks of those called managers, neither were a wide range of other sorts of differences".[489]

The higher up the organisation one is located, the greater the uncertainty and the need for predictability and routine, making interdependence and rapid communication between mangers and their subordinates critical. Under these circumstances, managers value traits such as trust, discretion and predictability in their hiring decision and they seek to find these traits by hiring employees who are similar to them socially and culturally.[490] They carefully guard power and privilege for those who fit in and are seen as 'their kind'. Kantor quotes Wilbert Moor who uses the metaphor of 'bureaucratic kinship system' to describe the corporation where the kinship system is based on what he calls "homosexual reproductions" as men reproduce others in their own image.[491] "Management becomes a closed circle in the absence of better, less exclusionary responses to uncertainly and to communication pressures."[492] This system usually leaves women out, along with a range of other people with 'discrepant' social characteristics. The same "tendencies that lead to insisting that trust means total dedication and non-diffuse loyalty, also serve to exclude those, like women, who are seen as incapable of such a single minded attachment."[493]

Kanter says there is a self-fulfilling prophecy buried in all this: the more closed the circle, the more difficult it is for outsiders to break in. Their difficulty in entering may be taken as a sign of incompetence, a sign that

---

[489]   Kanter, 1993:48.
[490]   Purcell et al., 2010.
[491]   See Kantor, 1993: 48, for references therein.
[492]   Kanter, 1993:68.
[493]   Ibid: 68.

the insiders are right to close their ranks. The more closed the circle the more difficult it is to share power when the time comes, as inevitably it must when the control by one type of people is challenged, and the greater the tendency for a group of people to try to reproduce themselves, the more constraining becomes the emphasis on conformity.[494] Judy Rosener (1995) states that one of the benefits women bring to the workplace which adds significant value is creating work environments in which people can be themselves and don't have to 'fit in' to a 'one best model' of managerial behaviour.[495]

The description Kanter gives of the corporation environment is the microcosm of sexism in the outer world, where men with dominant masculinities jealously guard power and prestige for those who fit in their 'masculine' image, the only image they see as deserving of status and power. Women and those with subordinated masculinities are kept out of that privileged system, and 'others'' inability to break into this ring fenced masculine world of power is seen as proof that they are undeserving of inclusion.

IV.4.6   Work entitlements and equality

Scandinavian countries such as Norway and Sweden are leading the way with generous parental leave for both mothers and fathers. Introducing parental rights that are shared equally between fathers and mothers would help alleviate the prejudice that 'men have careers and women have children'. It would encourage fathers to take on a bigger share in unpaid work and adjust their work patterns to accommodate family responsibilities. Employers would start getting used to male employees, not just female employees, needing to take a substantial amount of time for parental responsibilities at some point in their working lives.[496]

---

[494]   Ibid.

[495]   Rosener, 1995: chapter two.

[496]   Maitland and Thomson, 2011: 24.

And yet, despite the fact that work entitlements, which include maternity/parental leaves as well as flexible working arrangements, are progressively targeting men, they are still taken up predominantly by women, reflecting our conviction that it is women who should care. Work entitlements are therefore a double edged sword: on the hand they afford women work continuity, which is critically important for career progression, earning potential and access to benefits such as superannuation and long service leave. As Dex's (1986) work has shown, women's ability to remain with the same employer is critical to their upward mobility, and the reverse is true. On the other hand, work entitlements institutionalise and exacerbate the differential trajectories of men's and women's careers, precisely because they either target women or, when they target men as well as women, they are taken up far more by women than by men.

IV.5   Equality in the Home: To Divide or not to Divide.... Housework and Care

"(Women) got a very raw deal to the whole equality thing (because) they expect there to be sharing the breadwinning role 50% with their husbands and to have a career but they are also supposed to ... come home, make the dinner, look after the kids, put them to bed, even look after their own elderly mother down the road, whereas men don't take on that role automatically." John (47 years old interviewee)[497]

"...men's support for feminism (can) no longer be a matter of supporting women in their own struggles for equality, but involve(s) men learning to name their experience as 'masculine'." Victor Seidler (Scholar and author)[498]

---

[497]   Interviewee in Hanlon's survey, 2012: 179.
[498]   Seidler, 2006: Preface and acknowledgments.

Nowhere is gender status and hierarchy more visible than in the home, as reflected by the rigid division of domestic labour, with housework and childcare integral to a woman's, but incidental to a man's, role. Although women's widespread entry into the labour market has increased men's involvement in housework and care, the increase has not been commensurate with that in women's overall workload.[499] This reflects that while "beliefs about the appropriate roles of women and men in the workplace have undergone substantial shifts in the past several decades, assumptions about who should perform unpaid family work have changed more slowly. And changes in domestic behaviour have been slower still."[500]

Even women who deny that they are constrained by stereotypes report that they do most of housework.[501] As we have seen above, the resilience of these traditional ideas about women's and men's roles is also reverberated in the labour market, where males are still dominant in leading roles while women in the majority are still in supportive roles. Put differently, women's fundamental location in society as one of service and care is reverberated both in the home and in the workplace. Research shows that the decision to hire domestic help doesn't depend on how much money a dual earner couple have available, but solely on how much money the woman earned, with wives who earned high income more likely to hire household help that lower income wives. "It is as though the wives fulfil their gendered roles by buying themselves out of housework".[502]

It is important to appreciate the full implications of these traditional conceptions of sex roles on women's careers and their standing in public life. Women's domestic labour doesn't only support their dependents but to a large extent their male partners' too. Furthermore, in any

---

[499]   Hanlon, 2012: 45.

[500]   Coltrane, 2000.

[501]   Ibid.

[502]   Halpern and Cheung, 2008: 52-53.

heterosexual partnership, and as we have seen in chapter III, women are also the emotional workers. This practical and emotional support of men by women frees men to engage in public life pursuits unencumbered, often working hours that are beyond the reach of many 'caring' women. This in turn allows employees to adopt more rigid work practices than would otherwise be the case, since men are both able and willing to put in the hours. By taking on the primary responsibility for domestic work therefore, women are hindering their own chances of advancement in the workplace both because of the burden of their dual role and because of the extra, artificial boost they give to men's careers. Within the constraints of rigid gender constructs, therefore, women's career choices are twice false: *once*, from the imperatives of care and domestic responsibilities, and *twice*, from rigid work norms made possible only through their provision of care for children and men.

IV.5.1   Trends in sharing housework

Empirical evidence from time diary studies (that record activities during each hour of a twenty-four hour day) in the US suggests that men did increase their share of domestic work following the second wave feminism in the 1970s and up until the mid 1980s, when the rise in their contribution started slowing down, reaching about eleven hours a week in 2005. Women's contribution dropped rapidly in the 1970s and 1980s but the drop slowed down from the mid 1990s, bringing their contribution to around nineteen hours a week in 2005.[503] The convergence in men's and women's contribution to domestic work since the mid 1980s therefore has come largely from women doing less, rather than men doing more, house work.[504] And as things stand, for every hour a man puts in housework, a woman puts in about 1.7 hours.[505]

---

[503] Eagly and Carli, 2007, Figure 4-1: 50.
[504] Harkness (2003), quoted in Compton and Lyonette, 2007.
[505] Eagly and Carli, 2007: 50.

For the OECD as a whole, statistics show that on average women devote more than 2 extra hours per day to unpaid work than men do.[506] Furthermore, when men do undertake housework, they are more likely to carry out some tasks than others. Recent evidence suggests that men are more likely to participate in childcare, shopping and cooking and less likely to take on less creative and less interesting domestic work, particularly cleaning, laundry,[507]i.e. tasks than entail a lower status. Generally speaking, and as Craig's (2006) analyses of time use surveys demonstrate, men's contribution involves less multi tasking activities, less physical work, less responsibility for managing care and is more flexible than women's, even when mothers are working full time. A notable finding in the study is that when men undertake domestic work, it is more likely to involve pleasurable, higher status and enjoyable aspects such as play, which often involves greater emotional rewards from children along with the benefit of avoiding the more burdensome physical care.[508]

So there are two related issues to housework, one is the tasks themselves, and the other is the conditions of performing these tasks, with routine, repetitive, burdensome chores relegated to women.[509] It is precisely these routine chores over which one cannot exercise much control that are relevant to women's wellbeing, because their frequency and routine nature make them difficult to skip, which adds to women's burden.[510] Research indicates that performing larger amounts of these types of chores is associated with more depression in women (and sometimes in men). Conversely, it is primarily men's participation in these routine, repetitive chores that relieves women's domestic burden, contributes to

---

[506] OCED, 2011a: 4.
[507] Duyvendak and Stavenuiter (2004), quoted in Crompton and Lyonette, 2007:118.
[508] Quoted in Hanlon, 2012: 47.
[509] See Hanlon, 2012:136.
[510] Eagly and Carli, 2007: 51.

their sense of fairness and reduces their chances of depression.[511, 512] It won't escape the reader by now that in addition to the drudgery aspect of routine, repetitive housework, it is their association with low status that compels most men to avoid them at all cost.

A lop sided division of domestic labour, in men's favour, is at the crux of the power play between women and men in society. Men's ability to avoid routine, burdensome housework and care, which symbolises lower status, and women's inability to escape them makes evident the distribution of power within the household. An equitable distribution of routine housework and care can therefore be seen as the acid test of genuine equality in the home, paving the way for equitable outcomes in the outside world. This equitable distribution of domestic labour must by necessity include joint ownership of the responsibility for it, since managing the activities that fall within unpaid work can be as demanding as the actual doing of them.

IV.5.2 Factors affecting household division of labour

IV.5.2.1 Education, pay and occupational status

Most studies show that women who are employed longer hours, earn more money, have more education and endorse gender equality tend to do less housework; whereas men who are employed fewer hours, have more education, and endorse gender equity do more of the housework.[513] It is not surprising therefore that professional and managerial women tend to receive more assistance with domestic work than women in other occupational classes, since occupational class acts as a proxy for

---

[511] Coltrane, 2000.

[512] For their part, men often report some difficulty assuming more responsibility for work, although the initial frustration is typically short lived (Coltrane, 2000).

[513] Coltrane, 2000.

both higher educational levels and more liberal attitudes toward gender roles. Furthermore, professional and managerial women are more likely to be able to afford paid domestic help.[514]

In their investigation of occupational class and the domestic division of labour in Britain, France and Greece, Crompton and Lyonette (2007) found that managerial and professional women were more than three times as likely as those engaged in manual work to be in non-traditional domestic division of labour arrangements - but there were no significant differences in domestic traditionalism between intermediate and routine and manual working women.[515] Importantly, managerial and professional women get significantly more help with the less attractive domestic chores (cleaning, laundry, etc) although the majority of managerial and professional women still take the main responsibility for these chores.[516]

Crompton and Lyonette found that two more factors impact the domestic division of labour include: whether or not the woman works full time and whether or not there is a child in the household. Women employed full time are more than twice as likely as those employed part time to have a non traditional domestic division of labour arrangements, while having a child significantly reduces the likelihood of having a non traditional domestic division of labour. Surprisingly, the extent of the partner's working hours did not have an impact.[517]

---

[514] Ibid.
[515] Crompton and Lyonette, 2007: 123-4.
[516] Ibid.
[517] Crompton and Lyonette, 2007, also found that country was important: women living in Britain were significantly more likely than those in Portugal to have a non traditional domestic division of labour, as were women in Finland and Norway. However living in France was not significantly different from Portugal in terms of having a non traditional domestic division of labour arrangement (pp: 123-4).

IV.5.2.2 'Gender ideology'

Scholars have proposed that gender ideology (how a person identifies her/himself with regard to marital and family sex roles), provides a lens through which marital dynamics such as the allocation of housework, wives' economic independence, and spousal support are viewed. More specifically, it is argued that women's gender ideologies help to determine how they view equalities in housework and whether such inequalities impact their marital quality.[518] Women with egalitarian gender ideologies are expected to react more negatively to inequalities, including experiencing reduced marital happiness, compared to women with traditional gender ideologies. This was supported by research by Greenstein (2009) that used data covering 30 nations. The research found that perceived fairness in the division of household labour was more strongly related to family life satisfaction of women with egalitarian gender ideologies than women with traditional ideologies.[519]

Coltrane's (2000) meta study found that the fit between husbands' and wives' gender ideology is extremely important to marital satisfaction, as it entails congruence between spouses' attitudes and actions. In general, if spouses align their attitudes and the division of housework, their marital happiness is higher. Coltrane shows that because men continue to do substantially less housework than women, a sex-bifurcated pattern emerges: women who believe in sharing housework tend to have lower marital satisfaction than others, and men who believe in sharing tend to have higher marital satisfaction than others. Similarly, when husbands are more egalitarian than wives, marital disagreements are fewer, but when wives are more egalitarian than husbands (the more typical case) then marital disagreements are more common.

---

[518] See Minnotte et al., 2010, for a fuller discussion.
[519] Quoted in Minnotte et al., 2010.

Minnotte et al. (2010) went further by looking at the relationship between gender ideology, work-life conflict, and marital satisfaction in dual earner families, and found that gender ideology had a significant impact in mediating work-life conflict and martial satisfaction in those families, particularly that of the women: the more egalitarian the women's gender ideology, the more negatively marital satisfaction was affected by work-life conflict. They also found that the dependence of men's marital satisfaction on wives' gender ideologies varies according to men's own gender ideologies. The authors propose that dual earner couples who have similar gender ideologies, regardless of whether they are both more traditional or more egalitarian, will have higher levels of marital satisfaction. By contrast, similar gender ideologies may result in dual earner couples more readily agreeing on solutions to work-family issues, reducing marital conflict in the process. For example, a dual earner couple with both partners holding egalitarian gender ideologies might not think twice about the husband increasing his housework performance to reduce stress experienced by his wife. By contrast, a dual earner couple with differing gender ideologies might encounter difficulty agreeing on such a solution.

IV.5.3 Housework and career work: what does all this mean for women's career choices?

Scott Coltrane (2000) states that women tend to do more housework than men in part because most husbands are employed longer hours and earn higher income than their wives do. But, which way does the causation run? Baxter (2000) argues that one of the barriers to equity in dividing labour in the home is the rigid structure of the workplace that is organised around continuous, full time career paths with severe penalties for deviating from this norm - fewer promotion opportunities, loss of leave entitlements, superannuation benefits and other financial penalties. So, rigidity in the division of labour at home sustains inequality in the workplace and rigidity in the workplace sustains inequality at home. And both are reflections of the same system of belief that relegates women to a subordinated status and prioritises men's careers, because of their presumed superior competence.

A recurring theme in studies of differences in motivation and achievement between men and women is the latter's focus on their family life, whilst men's focus tends to be on themselves, their status and by extension achievements in the workplace. Furthermore, research shows that men believe that their achievements will contribute to their families, by providing a higher standard of living, while women believe that their achievement will detract from their contribution to family life.[520] Put differently, men still largely believe that working is caring while women still largely believe that working is uncaring. Linda Austin (2000) argues the psychological process underlying these choices is often the same: to the degree that a woman believes it is women's lot to be sacrificial, she perceives family-career choices in a narrow either or frame of reference, as entailing a painful threat to either her love relations or to her commitment to her work. "Such beliefs will unconsciously lead her to constrict the way she conceptualises her options; no matter what she chooses she will feel unhappy."[521]

So it appears that, at a deep unconscious level, a woman still constructs her identity in terms of being a mother, a wife, and a homemaker. To abrogate her domestic duties is to surrender her feminine identity, a failure of an existential proportion, or so it seems to her. Men know this too, at a deep unconscious level, and it is this knowledge that bolsters their choice to remain largely uninvolved in domesticity. Men also have their own set of constraints that stop them from equally sharing housework: domestic work's strong association with femininity makes it a dread. It signifies everything men know themselves not to be, and its low status is the epitome of failing to become masculine.

---

[520] Austin, 2000: 25.
[521] Ibid: 12.

In their book 'why women don't ask' Babcock and Laschever (2008) state that experiments show that women don't ask in the same way that men do, and when they do, they ask for less. Over time they accumulate disadvantages in both opportunities and resources. In addition, since women accept less, they are less valued and therefore their disadvantage accumulates to include regard and respect. The authors further argue that women make more sacrifices in their lives than men, prioritising the man's job over theirs, their children's needs over their own, and so on.[522] So here again, women's careers are hampered by both their reluctance to accumulate opportunities and resources as fast as men, *and* their readiness to de-accumulate these resources and opportunities when they have families, putting themselves at a further disadvantage.

The gender myth that women must put the needs of others ahead of theirs, otherwise known as the 'nurturant imperative', creates a powerful psychological drag on women's careers. Women's intense drive to connect, to nurture, and to support leads them to be more willing than men to sacrifice their time and energy for the welfare of the family, particularly if the alternative is an ongoing state of conflict and discord over these issues.[523] "All of this depletes the energy (women) could be putting toward career advancement, and may also result in having less power at home".[524] "Research shows that a husband's capacity to be nurturing and expressive is the most important indicator of marital satisfaction for working wives with young children."[525]

Halpern and Cheung (2008) interviewed 62 women in high powered jobs and found that these women have strategies that allow them to combine work and family in ways that protect their own mental and physical health. One of these strategies is "overthrowing the tyranny of the supermom syndrome" as it applies to housework: "Having it all

---

[522] Babcock and Laschever, 2008: chapter 3.
[523] Austin, 2000: 190.
[524] Ibid: 196.
[525] Ibid.

doesn't mean doing it all". The new home economics practiced by these executive women takes a more relaxed and creative approach to running a home. For them "homes are important but homemaking is not."[526]

Clearly then, success for women does entail shedding off the images, discourses and cultural messages of what it is to be a 'woman', often confounded with being a devoted mother and a faithful wife. What a woman is or, more accurately, should be is elaborately constructed in the media as someone who is totally dedicated to the happiness of her husband and children, which includes providing a meticulously organised home life.

IV.6   Conclusion: The Smokes and Mirrors of Changing Sex Roles

Considerable consciousness has been brought into the sexism of education since the early part of the last century, leading to a dramatic rise in females' educational attainment that currently overshoots that of males at secondary and tertiary levels. Yet, women's lives continue to be channelled toward childbearing and childrearing from a very young age, steering them away from fields of study that are men's traditional domains, namely science, technology, engineering and maths – STEM, and toward the arts and humanities. The higher up the educational ladder females and males go, the wider these disparities become, peaking in tertiary education.

There is nothing inherently better about STEM fields than humanities, but in androcentric societies, STEM fields are the more prestigious choice of study since, generally speaking, they are more conducive to higher pay and promotion that the arts or humanities. Furthermore, to the extent that girls and young women are shooed away from STEM

---

[526]   Halpern and Cheung, 2008: 54.

fields by negative stereotyping, they are not exercising a real but a false choice.

Gender stereotyping that sees men as superior to women in STEM fields creates a false consciousness in women, as they internalise society's inferior evaluation of their abilities. The resulting negative self-belief of incompetence in these fields translates into a behavioural reality of inferior results, either directly through epigenetic control mechanisms (that harmonise behaviour with perception), or indirectly through the cognitive mechanism of stereotype threat (where the fear of confirming a negative stereotype itself leads to inferior results through various cognitive processes). Critically, as a defence mechanism against the negative stereotype and in order to avoid embracement and shame, many women disidentify with STEM fields and move toward subjects where they have a neutral or a positive stereotype, such as the arts and humanities, perpetuating gender stereotypes in the process.

The same pattern of women arriving at academic institutions in large numbers but not showing up in STEM fields is repeated in the workplace: while female employment has risen phenomenally in the last fifty years, women still don't show up commensurately in prestigious professions or at executive levels. Instead, women are still highly concentrated in low paying, low ranking jobs, particularly in service and support positions. Again here, there is nothing inherently inferior about service and support, if anything they should be assigned a higher order because they touch our humanity, but in androcentric, capitalist societies care, service and support are subordinated in status and monetary value to intellectual fields such as science and law or the hard edged field of money and finance.

Women face real as well as imagined obstacles in advancing their careers. Sexism in the workplace is still a reality, albeit a far subtler reality than a few decades ago. Long are gone the days when overt sexism was tolerated in the workplace and when 'a woman's place is in the home' was believed to be a statement of fact. And yet, there is more than just a hint to committing women to communal spaces when it comes to employers' decisions of hiring and promoting. The expectation that women should exhibit communal attributes in the workplace, otherwise they are not liked or accepted, keeps their careers hamstrung. To be influential, women need to be accepted and therefore have to behave in a communal manner, but at the same time communal attributes are not considered congruent with leadership positions. Nor are communal attributes conducive to negotiating economic outcomes with employers that are at par with those of men. Finally, the principle of homophily, associating oneself only with those who are socially and culturally similar, which excludes women anyway, will have a double whammy effect when women behave in a communal manner.

Women are also constrained in their career choices by the invisible forces of gender stereotypes that tell them which professions are appropriate for women, namely those professions that give them the opportunity to fulfil the 'care imperative'. As a result, while women pile up in service and support professions, men populate the full range of professions. The care imperative, born out of society's assumption that childcare is a women's first and foremost priority in life, creates the false belief, and matching physiological changes, that compel women not only to care but to associate themselves very strongly with domestic spaces. The opposing image for men is the compulsion to work and associate themselves with public spaces, because of the breadwinning imperative. With these invisible forces at work, even in the twenty first century, men are still highly uncomfortable being in domestic spaces without playing the leadership role. The upshot is that men still refrain from the equal sharing of housework and childcare with women, and invariably opt out of repetitive, routine activities that are associated with lower status. Men's ability to avoid tedious domestic duties and women's inability to negotiate themselves out of them is a clear indication that men hold the reins of power in society.

It is important to note the full ramifications of taking on the majority of domestic work by women in hindering their advancement in the workplace, which takes place through many loops: *first*, the burden of the double shift stops the vast majority of working women from taking on demanding jobs that have the potential to advance their careers, in favour of a better quality family life. *Second*, women don't only support their own dependents but their male partners too when they take on household responsibilities, which allows men to advance their careers unencumbered. This simultaneously gives men a larger advantage, and women a larger disadvantage, in the labour market than would otherwise be the case. *Third*, the latter aspect allows employers to harden their stance with respect to offering flexible working arrangements, particularly for higher status jobs, as the majority of men are both willing and able to work not only full time, but also long and out of office hours and without any career interruptions, relieved as they are from family care.

V

THE WAY FORWARD: THE DISAPPEARING ACT OF SEXISM IN THE WORKPLACE

"You will wake up! You are waking up! The paradigm is shifting. The world is changing. It's happening right before your eyes." Neal Walsch (Spiritual teacher and author)[527]

When I first started writing this book, my intention was to find convincing arguments for women to pursue their careers wholeheartedly, in order for them to achieve equal outcomes to men in the workplace. The process of enlightenment that writing a book is showed me however that many women are simply not buying into that male model of work that deprives them of precious time with their children and impinges on the quality of their family life. Women are more constrained than willing in lagging behind men in the highly masculinised workplace. What women want instead is a new paradigm for their participation in paid work, which is long overdue.

---

[527] Walsch, 1998: 294.

V.1   Catapulting the Workplace from 20ᵗʰ to 21ˢᵗ Century

"Stepping out into the river of change, and being comfortable with that level of discomfort, means you're in the unknown. And when you're in the unknown that is the best place to create from." Joe Dispenza (Neuroscientist and author)[528]

The incompatibility of current work practices with family life, at a time when women have accumulated considerable human capital through educational attainment and work experiences, is manifested in a significant decline in fertility in many countries around the world. In 2005, the OECD countries with the highest female employment rates were also among those with the lowest birth rates.[529] In many of the OECD countries, difficulties with reconciling work and family life contribute to parents having fewer children than they may have desired.[530] Family supportive policies aimed at allowing parents back to work soon after childbirth can have a dramatic impact on this outcome: In Switzerland, where these policies are absent, on average 15-20% of women remain childless around age 40, but this figure rises to 40% for women with tertiary education. By contrast, in Sweden, with its longstanding policy emphasis on giving parents the opportunity to maintain employment relationships, at age 40 only 15% of the women born in 1961 remained childless, while this is around 20% for women with a university degree.[531]

These policies would have been redundant had work organisation and work practices been less rigid and more accommodating of family demands. CEOs are still largely in denial about the extent to which they

---

[528] Dispenza, 2013.
[529] OECD, 2007d: 8.
[530] Ibid.
[531] OECD, 2007a: 34; OCED, 2014: Chart SF2.5.A.

are squandering skill and talent by sticking to their old guns of command and control, face time and long working hours as a badge of honour in the workplace. Despite the stated objective of many of businesses to promote family-friendly policies, there is still a disconnection between how the workplace is organised and the demands of family life. The single most important point that CEOs, and society at large, need to come to terms with is the degree to which current work norms depend on the outdated paradigm that assumes the performance of considerable amounts of unpaid work by women in a home and/or a community context,[532] allowing them to continue premising their business on the assumption of the 'ideal worker' - a *notion* of a worker who functions in the workplace as if s/he either has no care responsibilities or, if s/he does, has a stay at home spouse who assumes these responsibilities.[533] "The flip side of this idealisation of the workplace worker is the marginalisation of the care giver, who continues to provide unpaid family care work."[534] These work norms allow businesses to demand that workers leave their personal affairs 'where they belong', since by assumption it is taken care of by someone else, invariably women. This paradigm also assumes that flexible working arrangements, when given, are an alteration in work norms given to those who do not fit this ideal worker image, which again is invariably a woman.

This idealisation is not a coincidence; it is born out of a wrong system of thought that attaches higher status to all things masculine, including achievement, and lower status to all things feminine, including care. It is an absolute necessity for the fulfilment of the masculine project. Without this idealisation, men would not have the advantage, and women the disadvantage, in the workplace that allows them to maintain their superior status in society. The upshot of this thought system is that 'life' is organised around work, and 'family life' has to adjust to work requirements rather than the other way round, which would have been

---

[532] Conaghan and Rittich, 2005:1.

[533] Appelbaum, 2002: 140.

[534] Ibid.

more logical had human welfare rather than achievement and success *per se* been society's top priority. In younger generations, more and more men are assuming primary care responsibilities, but given rigid last century work norms those men invariably have to slow down, take on part time work or abandon paid work altogether in order to manage family responsibilities. These young men opt out of full time work knowing fully that careers that deviate from the ideal worker model will be subject to severe financial and promotional penalties. Most of the so called dual earner families are one-and-a-half earner families, regardless of the sexual division of paid and unpaid work, curtsey of outmoded work norms.

V.2   The Masculine and the Feminine in the Workplace

"Wholeness is not achieved by cutting off a portion of one's being, but by the integration of the contraries." Carl Jung (Swiss psychiatrist and founder of the school of analytical psychology)

The workplace still favours the masculine traits and skills that are associated with being male and devalues those feminine traits that are associated with being female. At the heart of the issue is that people hold different beliefs about the *nature* of women and men and as a result assign the caregiver-family role to women, who are seen as feminine only, and the assertive-breadwinning role to men, who are seen as masculine only. This leads to having different perceptions and ensuing expectations of women's and men's behaviour, believing falsely that men are more competent than women (see false consciousness in section III.3.3). Crucially, these perceptions of fundamental sex differences that people hold about themselves and others lead to sex differentiated behaviour, through a plethora of psychological and physiological processes, giving credence to the beliefs that gave rise to the behaviour in the first place, in a perpetual cycle (see chapter III).

V.2.1   Sex differences in leadership style

A logical conclusion to the assignment of agency to men and communion to women, and putting men on a pedestal so to speak, is that agentic traits also define leadership roles, which means that men are seen as possessing more leadership traits than women. In the role congruity theory, Eagly and Karau (2002) state that the disparity between the communal female stereotype and the agentic leader stereotype leads to two forms of prejudice: *First*, women's potential for being endorsed as leaders is less than men's, because the male stereotype is closer to the leader stereotype. *Second*, women's actual leadership is evaluated less favourably than men's, because women's assertive behaviour is perceived as undesirable or threatening, particularly to men.[535]

The most prevalent style of leadership amongst men is an autocratic or directive one of command and control.[536] Women on the other hand tend to employ democratic leadership styles that allow subordinates to participate in decision making. Generally speaking, women leaders more than men leaders tend to be inclusive and aim for consensus-building. Research also shows that women are more interpersonally oriented than men – more concerned with the welfare of the people they work with and with maintaining good professional relationships.[537] In their in-depth survey of managers around the world, Maitland and Thomson (2011) found that women managers put a higher priority than men managers on giving people freedom to achieve results in their own way. In her book 'America's competitive secret: utilizing women as a management strategy,' Judy Rosener (1995) argues that women push for benefit programmes that are responsive to a wide range of employee needs, and share power and information in a way that is conducive to

---

[535] Reid et al., 2009.
[536] Eagly and Carli, 2007: 133.
[537] Babcock and Laschever, 2008: 197.

shared responsibility. Compared with men's directive style, therefore, women's leadership style can be described as collaborative.

As with all studies of sex differences, when women's and men's attributes and styles are examined, women tend to conform to stereotypically communal styles and men to agentic styles. Is this merely a self-fulfilling prophecy? an eye of the beholder phenomenon? a manifestation of the inseparability of the observer from the observed? or is there more to it?

V.2.2   Confounding sex with gender

What is often confused in writing about female and male differences, be it cognitive ability or in leadership styles, is the attribution of differences in behaviour to women and men instead of, more accurately, to women's femininity and men's masculinity. The confusion arises because we confound women with femininity, since girls are brought up to be feminine, and men with masculinity, since boys are brought up to be masculine. Masculinity in women is frowned upon, while femininity in men is rejected, denigrated and repressed.

Remember that the gender system is constructed in order for marriage to take place and be successful, i.e. for women to bear and rear children and for men to provide for their families (see section II.2). In order for the gender project to succeed, women are bred as feminine, i.e. other oriented, communal, intuitive and compassionate. Masculine behaviour in women does not serve the objectives of child bearing and rearing and is therefore discouraged. That said, as women increasingly combine paid with unpaid work, their masculinity has been rising, not least to compete with men in a man-made workplace. The same is not true for men, because the masculine project is two-prong: economic provision for the family and upholding male superiority in society. This double burden on men raises the bar on masculinity leading to the outright rejection of feminine attributes in men. Masculinity is heavily policed in society, particular by other men, with severe penalties for those who veer into feminine territory, symbolised by care and service.

Given this system of thought, or social indoctrination more accurately, it is easy to see why we confound men with masculinity and women with femininity, with masculinity and femininity being the two pillars of the gender system. Left to their own devices, society fears, and without the whip of gender proscriptions and prescriptions, individuals may make choices that don't serve the greater good, which in this case is society's reproduction of itself, both literally and culturally.

Prima facia, there is logic in the madness of the gender system: as female power rises and women become more and more agentic, many women across the world are now choosing to be childless. However, what is not understood is that rather than reflecting women's free choice, declining fertility more accurately reflects another of women's false choices: constrained by the rigidity of the gender system that precludes caring practices from men's lives and creates work practices that are incompatible with family life, many women avoid the double burden of paid and unpaid work by choosing to remain childless.

V.2.3   ... and confusing feminine and masculine attributes for sex differences

As a result of confounding sex with gender, we inevitably confuse differences between feminine attributes (dominant in women) and masculine attributes (dominant in men) as differences between women and men *per se*. In the vast literature on sex differences, rarely do scholars attribute observed differences to masculine and feminine traits. Rather, they invariably attribute differences to women and men themselves. Experiments of sex differences consistently show differences between women and men, because women are conditioned to be predominantly feminine and men are conditioned to be predominantly masculine. In effect, what is being observed is a conditioned state in women (the dominance of femininity and near absence of masculinity) and in men (the dominance of masculinity and near absence of femininity). The differences in behaviour observed would be more appropriately attributed to and explained by the feminine and masculine aspects of each individual, rather than by their sex *per se*.

One of the rare examples that rightly attribute difference to feminine and masculine traits is Cahill et al. (2004) who looked at sex differences in the recall of emotional information. The scholars did not find any differences between women and men. They did however find significant differences between those high on masculine and those high on feminine attributes, as measured by Bem's index (see section III.2.3 for details). The authors conclude that "sex-related traits, rather than actual sex *per se*, may be a more sensitive indicator of these influences."

Societies the world over raise boys to be masculine and girls to be feminine, but in the absence of any conditioning, both feminine and masculine attributes are present in both sexes in varying degrees. It is possible, in theory at least, to have males with predominantly feminine attributes and females with predominantly masculine attributes. Psychologists, like Lefkowitz and Zeldo's (2006) mentioned in section III.2.3, acknowledged that we all have both masculine and feminine attributes in various degrees, but folk wisdom is still in denial.

It is worth pausing here to make the distinction between the natural feminine and masculine attributes and aspects of our humanity and conditioned femininity and masculinity.

V.2.4   Natural masculine and feminine attributes *vs.* conditioned masculinity and femininity

Even in the 21st century we are still highly confused about the feminine and the masculine, and we live our lives as women and men out of the mythology that men are masculine and women are feminine, and that the masculine is all powerful and the feminine is ineffective. There are many layers of error that lead to and sustain this myth which aims to create difference and division between women and men.

The first error is that we do not distinguish between natural feminine and masculine attributes and conditioned feminine and masculine attributes. The conditioned feminine is symbolised in girls by the colour pink, as in 'pretty in pink', to convey the high value of girls' 'prettiness' to society, in order for them to be marketable for marriage as adult women or useful for sex for men more generally. Hence society's need to emphasise looks and appearance for women. Women's conditioned femininity is also symbolised by 'emotionality' - a kind word for 'irrationality'. By contrast, in men aggression is a highly conditioned masculine attribute, as Sapolsky and others have demonstrated (see section I.4.5). Men's addiction to paid work and their push for longer and longer working hours is also conditioned masculinity.

Natural feminine and masculine attributes by contrast are all positive. Masculinity expresses self-power, self-confidence and inner strength. It manifests in accomplishment, decisiveness, focus and reason. Femininity expresses love for others, compassion and nurturance. It manifest in doing other-focused good in life, in fluidity, creativity and intuition. Negativity associated with the feminine and the masculine is either conditioned directly, like aggressiveness in men and ineffectiveness in women, or created through the imbalance between the two sets of attributes, which is also a conditioned state. Male 'selfishness' for example is not a natural outcome of masculinity but of underdeveloped femininity that would have balance men's self-focused masculine attributes with the other-focused feminine attributes of inclusion and nurturance. Repressing feminine attributes leave men with considerable fear and doubt about their ability to connect with others and create community. Similarly, woman's lack of agency is not a natural outcome of their femininity but of the suppression of their masculine attributes that would have allowed them to take lead, to direct, and to trust themselves to move in the world with greater self-confidence. Women's underdeveloped masculine attributes leave them with considerable fear and doubt about their ability to operate in the world.

The second layer of error is that we create a rigid, unnatural divide between the feminine and the masculine, when they are intended to be integrated in all of us. Very little research has been undertaken in this area, but the research that exists supports the idea that we all have feminine and masculine aspects in ourselves in varying degrees, and that the combination of strong forms of the feminine with strong forms of the masculine is far more conducive to wellbeing than the presence of either of them in solitary form or the combination of both of them in weak forms (see section III.2.3).

The third layer of error, which arises from the second error, is that we attribute the masculine to men and the feminine to women. As explained above, the lack of balance between the two sets of attributes creates many ills, not least of which are the conditions that underpin sexism: seeing women as feminine only and men as masculine only is the foundation of the sexual division of labour, which was thought necessary to create a feminine-masculine unit of production and reproduction in society. The sexual division of labour in turn is the main underpinning of sexism.

This brings us to the forth and most toxic layer of error, which is the belief that the masculine is superior and the feminine is inferior, so much so that both women and men in contemporary societies are clamouring to become more masculine and to shun the feminine, with deleterious effects on our interpersonal relationships, on our wellbeing and on the stability of our societies' demographic structures.

Starting with Enlightenment that elevated rationality and debased emotions and intuition, and ending with capitalism that values production and devalues care, masculine strength and power is seen as superior to feminine love and compassion. Masculinity, with masculinity confounded with men, is held as the gold standard and femininity, with femininity confounded with women, is debased to a lower status. But where would our societies be without the power of love? Love in our contemporary societies is conditioned, gendered and caricatured as 'soft', 'sweet', 'romantic', and most certainly 'pink' or at least 'red'!, instead of the awesome power that love is in birthing and sustaining life. This is the real feminine that we are denigrating. And where would our societies be without the genius of intuition? Intuition too is often gendered and caricatured as 'inexplicable', and juxtaposed with the all powerful 'rational' mind, instead of the genius 'inner knowing' that intuition is, which allowed Einstein and others before him to help us fathom the otherwise unfathomable universe. We may be starting to see where contemporary societies are heading without compassion, as we witness the rise in narcissism and the eternal pursuit of self-development (see Twenge's studies in section III.2.4), leading the Dalai Lama XIV to assert: "Compassion is the radicalism of our time."[538]

Love, intuition and compassion, among other things, are the awesome feminine. These are the things that we 'swim in' as we go through life and therefore cannot see but without which life would desist. This is the feminine that men need to embrace if they want to come out of the cold of emotional disconnection, of having to do it all on their own, and of having to constantly prove themselves.

It is not only men who need to develop and strengthen their feminine, but women too need to honour and strengthen their feminine. With femininity in today's societies caricatured beyond recognition, it has been abandoned by many ambitions, high achieving women. But even those women who believe that they remained true to their femininity need to realise that what they have embraced is the gendered not the true feminine. In order for women to accomplish in life and to have self-fulfilment, neither of which is possible without authenticity, they

---

[538] http://www.goodreads.com/quotes/73528-compassion-is-the-radicalism-of-our-time.

need to restore the integrity of their femininity by, first, degendering it and, second, by fully embracing the truly powerful and empowering feminine.

Women also need to develop and empower their masculine. While self-reports from women portray them as more masculine now a days (see section III.2.2), I have shown throughout chapter III that compared to men, women still have a lower sense of entitlement in life than men and also still have an external sense of control over their lives, believing that someone other than themselves holds the reign to their fate. By embracing the masculine, women will be able to assert themselves in life as equal partners to men and internalise their sense of control.

A final word on the masculine and the feminine: the combination of the masculine and the feminine in each of us and the right proportion of the masculine to the feminine in women and men are all esoteric issues that remain part of the big mystery that is life. No one can answer these questions with any kind of certainty, and perhaps the reason is because these are issues of Free Will for each of us to resolve for ourselves. And perhaps the proportion of the masculine to the feminine is not meant to remain constant but to change throughout our lives. If this is true, it would be a real antidote to sexism.

V.2.5   Revisiting leadership styles

In her paper on female leadership advantage, Eagly (2007) points to a new style of leadership called 'transformational' leadership that is seen as most suited to contemporary organisations, since they reflect the cultural shift in leadership norms: "Gone is the 'Powerful Great Man' model of leadership, in favour of leadership styles that are modelled on great coaches or gurus and their ability to inspire and mentor."[539]

---

[539]   Eagly, 2007.

Transformational leaders establish themselves as a role model by gaining followers' trust and confidence. They mentor and empower their subordinates and encourage them to develop their potential in order to contribute more effectively to their organisation. Conventional leaders on the other hand appeal to subordinates' self-interest by establishing an exchange relationship with them. In terms of management of tasks, transactional leaders clarify subordinates responsibilities, reward them for meeting objectives and correct them when they fail to do so.[540]

Transformational leaders motivate their followers through a variety of mechanisms, including connecting followers' individual identity to the collective identity of the organisation; being a role model for followers and inspiring them; allowing followers to take greater ownership of their work; and aligning followers with tasks that match their skill set to enhance their performance.[541] The transforming approach involves a significant change in perceptions and values, in order to remould employees' expectations and aspirations: away from following instruction and 'give and take', typical of the transactional approach, toward a more inspired action, following in the footstep of their leader and her/his well articulated and energised vision, to meet their challenging goals.[542]

There are four pillars to transformational leadership. *First,* is the idealised influence of transformational leaders who gain the respect and trust of their followers. *Second,* articulating an inspiring vision to followers, in an understandable, precise, powerful and engaging way. *Third,* soliciting ideas form followers, stimulating their creativity and nurturing their independence. *Fourth,* individualised consideration where the leader attends to each follower's needs, acts as a mentor or coach and listens to the follower's concerns and needs. The leader gives empathy and support, keeps communication open and places challenges before the followers.[543]

---

[540]   Ibid.

[541]   Ibid.

[542]   Bass and Bass, 2008.

[543]   Bass and Riggio, 2006.

A meta analysis of female and male styles of leading done by Eagly, Johannesen-Schmidt and van Engen (2003) revealed that female leaders were more transformational than male leaders.[544] Women particularly exceeded men on individualised consideration, which encompasses a supportive and encouraging treatment of subordinates. A meta analysis of 87 studies done by Judge and Piccolo (2004), tested the relationship between leadership styles and measures of leaders' effectiveness and found that transformational leadership was associated with greater effectiveness.[545] Rohmann and Rowold (2009) also found female leaders to be more transformational, and men more transactional, leaders; and that female leaders were more effective than their male counterparts.

In essence, the exulted transformational leadership is leading through inspiring and empowering, with its focus on people and a commitment to unleashing their potential in order to fulfil the organisation's goals. A closer look at transformational leadership reveals that it bears the hallmark the feminine/masculine duality: leadership by its nature requires considerable masculine energy, to forge the way ahead, to make things happen, and to be self-focused enough to promote oneself to a position of leadership. On the other hand, communication skills, inclusion, and focusing on followers to tap into their potential all require the feminine attributes of nurturance and other-orientation.

Kark, Waismel-Manor, and Shamir (2012) studied the relationship between managers' perceived femininity, masculinity and androgyny (mixing femininity with masculinity) and their leadership effectiveness, in terms of the degree to which their leadership is considered transformational and the degree of personal identification between

---

[544]   See also Vinkenburg et al., 2011.

[545]   Some aspects of transactional leadership, such as rewarding subordinates for appropriate behaviour, were found to be almost as effective as transformational leadership, but other aspects, namely drawing followers' flaws to their attention and otherwise using punishment to shape their behaviour, showed a weak positive relationship to effectiveness (Eagly, 2007).

leaders and staff. They found that among both male and female leaders, androgyny was more strongly related to transformational leadership and followers' identification than non-androgyny, and that leaders' femininity was more strongly related to leadership effectiveness than masculinity. Furthermore, the results show that women paid a higher penalty for not being perceived as androgynous in comparison to men, with regard to followers' identification – this may be due to the perceived incongruity between femininity and leadership positions. in masculine workspaces (see section IV.4.3). When Kark, Waismel-Manor, and Shamir examined same- *vs.* cross-sex relationships, they found that non-androgynous male managers were rated higher by their male employees than by their female employees. These findings suggest that women and men who are interested in being perceived as effective leaders may be advised to blend feminine and masculine behaviours, particularly when they are in situations of non-congruency (i.e., women in leadership roles and leading in cross-sex relationships).

Blending the masculine and feminine aspects of personality has power for many reasons, not least of which is the power inherent in balance, as Bem (1975) demonstrated in her experiment (see section III.2.3). Furthermore, given the doctrine of homophily, or the tendency for individual to associate with others who are socially and culturally similar, a balanced masculine/feminine personality speaks to a larger audience than an overly masculine or an overly feminine one, as Kark et al.'s study clearly shows.

Another support for the superiority of combining the masculine with the feminine in leadership teams comes from studies that have linked higher representation of women in leadership to better performance. For example, a Catalyst study (2004) found that companies in the top quartile of representing women among their executives had substantially better financial performance than the companies in the bottom quartiles.[546] Another study related the percentage of women in the top

---

[546] Eagly 2007.

management teams of companies in fortune 1000 to their financial performance from 1998 to 2000. After controlling for company size and industry performance, they found that companies with a larger percentage of women had better financial performance.[547] Similar studies of large US companies have revealed a positive relationship between the percentage of women on boards of directors and financial performance in the 1990s.[548]

While studies like these are often taken as evidence of the superiority of women's leadership style, since a higher percentage of women in leadership teams lead to better results, a more accurate interpretation maybe relating improved results to the presence of a more balanced leadership team. Since women are invariably a minority in leadership teams, a higher percentage of women in these teams only means the teams are closer to parity than otherwise would be the case, rather than the teams are dominated by women. What is measured therefore is by no means a reflection of women's superior abilities, but rather of the superiority of more balanced leadership teams.

Since we are conditioned to be either or, when it comes to femininity and masculinity, balancing the number of women with that of men on boards is akin to combining feminine and masculine attributes. In time, when we have shed our prejudice against men being feminine as well as masculine and women being masculine as well as feminine, balance would be achieved within each of us. Leadership then becomes about finding the right set of skills for the job in hand, rather than assuming one sex or the other have those desired skills. When this is achieved, we know that we have abolished sexism.

It follows that while imposing quotas of the percentage of women on boards may appear too artificial to fight sexism, since they do not

---

[547]   Ibid.
[548]   Ibid.

address our wrong system of thought, they are nevertheless effective tools of bringing more success to the organisation, by bringing about a more effective form of leadership through balance. Quotas also play a role in fighting sexism by creating the external conditions that would trick our minds into believing that sexism has disappeared, giving us a chance to correct our beliefs, a subject that I will address in a later section.

V.2.6 The feminine-masculine workplace

If there is virtue in integrating the feminine and the masculine in each of us, does it follow that integrating the feminine with the masculine in the workplace itself is virtuous? The answer is unequivocally yes. It is precisely the masculinity of the workplace that disallows women from achieving equal labour market outcomes to men. From a pure equity point of view therefore, the feminine must be brought into the workplace in order to relinquish its prejudicial androcentricity. Benefits from the inclusion of the feminine with the masculine in the workplace go beyond sex equity to include the ability to move to a much higher plane of functioning. Remember from chapter III, Block (1984) presented the feminine as a move toward 'universal principles of justice and concern for human worth'. Bakan (1966) advocated the integration of the feminine with the masculine to move away from opportunism and fulfil social viability. Peter Drucker, a very influential figures in modern management, believed strongly that all institutions including private sector ones have a responsibility to the whole of society. In his book 'Management: tasks, responsibilities, practices', Drucker (1974) wrote: "The fact is that in modern society there is no other leadership group but managers. If the managers of our major institutions, and especially of business, do not take responsibility for the common good, no one else can or will."[549] It is the feminine that is always on the

---

[549]   Drucker, 1974: 325.

lookout for serving the common good, balancing out the masculine that is focused on the self.

Organisations acknowledge the need to widen their sphere of interest, but are pulled away from it by the fear of diluting their profit making abilities, hence the lip service to Corporate Social Responsibility manifestos. They, wrongly, believe that a 'soft' approach to making profit will make them less profitable. This fear and apprehension of anything that is not hard driving, competitive, and uncaring is the macrocosm of the 'fear of the feminine' microcosm, where the feminine is wrongly believed to dilute or weaken the masculine.

How does a workspace in which the feminine and the masculine are fully integrated look like? The masculine, which is already in place, is focused on the self, be is self-fulfilment, self-promotion, or self-expansion, can remain in place to fulfil the business' objectives of growth and expansion. What needs to be brought in is the feminine aspect of focus on 'others'; focusing on the employees; focusing on the community within which the business operates; and focusing on the economy at large. These aspects now exist in businesses in a highly diluted form called 'corporate social responsibility', which like its sister 'family-friendly policies' is more of a statement than a dedicated action or a deep commitment to 'others'.

V.3   Reversing Sexism

"Of all the evils for which man has made himself responsible, none is so degrading, so shocking or so brutal as his abuse of the better half of humanity; the female sex." Mahatma Gandhi (Indian nationalist leader)

I have shown in chapter III that conscious and unconscious beliefs can diverge widely, and that unconscious beliefs have far superior powers to conscious beliefs in running our lives. It follows that it is not enough to examine our stated views on sex equality issues to measure advances in sex equality. It also follows that, to the extent that our reality reflects our deeply held unconscious beliefs, testing observable reality can gives us guidance to the nature of these beliefs. The persistence of sex inequality therefore indicates strongly that our belief system is still one of inequality.

We know from epigenetic studies (section I.3.2) that harmony must always exist between perceptions of environmental signals and human behaviour. This entails that our sexist perceptions will, *via* epigenetic control mechanisms, translate into a sexist behavioural reality. Perceptions are shaped by systems of belief, the collection of ideas and discourses in our social culture and the tacit agreement we reach on the extent to which these ideas should guide our life. Consider for example a religiously zealot group that believes strongly in the tenets of their religion. Their minds will create a perception of 'us', those who adhere to their beliefs, *vs.* 'them', those who don't. Others are perceived as 'different' and not deserving of the same love from God as they are. If they further agree that they need to separate from others in order to preserve the purity of their beliefs, every aspect of their reality will manifest this belief: not only will they be segregated from others, but their behaviour, daily routines and rituals, institutions, the cultural heritage they create and pass on to their off springs will all manifest their belief of difference and separation from others.

Gender beliefs work in exactly the same way, including in the workplace, where our beliefs of fundamental differences and divisions between women and men that stem from assigning femininity to women and masculinity to men lead each sex to see the other sex in 'opposite' light. Given our conversation about the caring nature of women, as we confound women with femininity, and the agentic nature of men, as we confound men with masculinity, the workplace becomes a bastion of masculinity; the arena where the masculine project gets seriously underway; where work achievements validate men's masculinity; and where reaching the pinnacle of the organisation affords them the opportunity to dominate not only femininity (women) but other masculinities (men) too.

With gender being the vehicle for sexism, it follows that in order to achieve equality, the workplace needs to be de-gendered. Individuals need to be seen as simply 'people', 'human beings', rather than the caring, communal women and the assertive, agentic men who arrive at work every day, bringing with them expectations of certain behaviour. Because the workplace is a bastion of masculinity and a shrine of masculine achievement, women cannot but fail. They fail what is expected of them, namely communality, as they themselves become masculinised to meet the masculine standards of success, and are consequently disliked and discriminated against for violating gender norms. And they fail to meet the long hours and uninterrupted careers work norms, initially designed for care free men.

Sexism is a treacherous social phenomenon that has been with us for millennia, and fighting it is no mean task. My own humble attempt at eradicating sexism from the workplace is a two prong solution: the first is aimed at challenging our belief system at its very core, and the second, which stems from the urgency of fighting sexism, is a more pragmatic solution that aims at creating the conditions in the workplace that would have prevailed had sexism been absent.

V.3.1   Changing our minds!

> *"A belief is only a thought that you keep thinking. So why not think a thought that you don't believe long enough until you believe it?" Ester Hicks (Inspirational speaker and author)*[550]

To the extent that femininity as we know it is highly gendered, and that gender is the vehicle that delivers sexism, women need to give up their fear of being truly feminine and embrace the powerful attributes of femininity that uphold truth, beauty, justice and empowerment for

---

[550]   http://www.youtube.com/watch?v=_JgHVlcaQJ0.

all. To do that, women need to drop the wrong belief that man's way is a better way, simply because society upholds it as the gold standard. Those women with a strong desire to achieve, compelled by feminists' advocacy to equate outcomes in their lives to those of men, have felt it necessary to emulate man's way. This was perhaps inevitable in an androcentric world with androcentric standards for achievement and success; women were swimming in this soup and had no other way of defining success. Even today, most of us still cannot distinguish that success in public life is mostly androcentric, i.e. defined by men for men.

The apparent rise in women's masculinity however has not resulted in true empowerment for women, or not enough empowerment to elevate their status to that of men's. The reason for this shortfall is twofold. *First*, it is difficult to achieve results without being authentic. Authenticity entails that our thoughts, utterances and actions are all in line with who we truly are, and emulating men's way doesn't bring women into their authentic selves. *Second*, what is embraced by women in the workplace and in life in general is not the true and powerful masculine but merely the gendered version of masculinity: toughness, single mindedness, super competitiveness, and self-focus or perhaps even narcissism. This has had serious ramifications to women's relationship with men, just as men's disavowal of the feminine has had serious consequences to their intimate relationships with women.

As women embrace their truly feminine qualities, moving into their authentic selves, they will find it considerably easier to manifest their wishes and desires in life, including fulfilling careers and personal relationships. They will be helped in doing so by embracing those masculine qualities that energise them and guide them toward the right action. Women therefore have the double task of embracing the awesome feminine within themselves as well as those powerful masculine qualities of self-power and self-confidence that would, paradoxically, enable them to assert their feminine ways and manifest full self-expression.

Men have a more difficult choice to make, because any change in the *status quo* may occur to them as relinquishing power which would be automatically resisted. Higher status has considerable allure to all of us, and to willingly relinquish it goes against the grain of human ego. Male resistance to embracing the feminine, which is equated by men with loss of power, has been a major contributor for the delay in delivering equality in the workplace. But men need to put their choices in the right framework, which they have not done so far: they need to relinquish the mentality of 'lack' and 'scarcity' which lead them to believe that empowering women would diminish their power, when nothing could further from the truth. This kind of thinking is a logical conclusion to our misunderstanding of power: power is still seen in our societies as power over other, when real power is taking ownership of the power and strength within ourselves that enables us to function at considerably higher levels of consciousness.

With that in mind, the first thing for men to acknowledge is that their superior status in society has come at a very heavy price, namely the disavowal of those aspects of their humanity that would have allowed them to connect with others and experience full emotional expression. Since in our societies femininity is highly gendered and is equated with 'irrationality', 'emotionality', 'softness', 'ineffectiveness' and so on, it is excruciatingly difficult for men to embrace it, which is understandable. Many women find this kind of gendered femininity difficult to embrace, particularly high achieving women, which explains the rise in contemporary women's masculinisation. De-gendering femininity, and masculinity, is the first step to understanding the true nature of feminine and masculine qualities that are part and parcel of our humanity, and to know that denying them is denying certain aspects of ourselves with inevitable disconnection and self-alienation.

A real obstacle to embracing femininity in men and masculinity in women is the mental associations we have because we confound sex with gender, as a consequence of which we associate femininity with women and masculinity with men. When women are invited to embrace masculinity, therefore, they imagine themselves becoming 'like a man': less attractive, less sexually appealing, and unwanted by men. The same is true of men, when they are asked to embrace femininity, the automatic association between gendered femininity and women leads men to imagine themselves becoming 'like a woman': less competent, unsuited for success, and unable to succeed in a heterosexual relationship.

It is critical to reversing sexism therefore that femininity and masculinity are decoupled from women and men, respectively. Instead, they need to be seen as universal qualities that help us manifest certain realities in our lives. They are not opposing but complementary sets of qualities that are not intended to exist in isolation. Nor are they intended to be fixed in nature, but rather to be subject to our free will: just as we have chosen to be feminine as women and masculine as men up till now, we can equally chose to be both feminine and masculine at the same time. We can be equally feminine and masculine or predominantly feminine, which is true for men as it is for women, or predominantly masculine, which is true for women as it is for men.

V.3.1.1   The how of changing our minds

> *"Change the way you look at things, and the things you look at change." Wayne Dyer (Spiritual teacher and author)*[551]

With sexist gender beliefs lodged deep in our subconscious mind, changing our mind can be a slow process. It unfolds through constantly raising our consciousness and challenging the assumptions that underlie our deeply held beliefs, or as Devine (1989) suggests, engaging in conscious, stereotype-inhibiting thought processes. Recall from section III.4.2 that low-prejudice individuals, those whose value system uphold equality and for whom prejudice is anathema, consciously censor

---

[551]   Dyer, 2004: chapter 10, para. 1.

negative and inappropriate thoughts that detract from their goals of achieving a non prejudiced identity; this requires *intention, attention* and, as always, *time*.[552]

The mental constructions we have of ourselves as women and men are ones of difference and division: division of labour, division of life between home sphere and work sphere, and even division of the visions we have for our lives. For too long now we have seen ourselves as either caring women or leading men, but never the two at the same time, despite our utterances to the contrary. And this is the reality that has manifested in our lives thus far: our reality always reflects our inner world, because we consciously and unconsciously line up events in our lives to fulfil our inner most thoughts, wishes and desires (see section I.4). As a first step to changing our mind about sex equality therefore we need to declare our *intention* of seeing similarity and unity.

Similarity here is not meant in a literal sense, but merely in opposition to difference which has been highly divisive and on which sexism has been founded. Women and men will always be different at some level and the extent of that difference is constantly being examined. It is not difference *per se* that is relevant to sexism, but rather what we make this difference mean. I have discussed in chapter I that similarity is not a prerequisite for sex equality, any more than it is for race, class or religious equality. The negation of similarity therefore is no proof that women and men are unequal. What has been relevant to sexism in the study of sex differences is that the ways in which men are found to differ from women has invariably pointed to their superior fitness to success in public life. This is accurate to the extent that success in public life is defined in an andocentric manner and therefore by definition men are more suited for that kind of success than women. Androcentricity itself is founded on the premise that men are masculine only, and therefore success and all that qualifies for it must also be masculine. The mental

---

[552] Devine, 1989.

construction of success and its prerequisites therefore excludes women, and women attempting to achieve success thus defined can only lag behind.

In order for change to happen, including moving away from androcentric standards of success, new ideas need to emerge to inspire people into moving to a new paradigm. New ideas about how women can succeed on their own terms are emerging slowly, but are not yet coherent enough to replace the old androcentric paradigm. Mostly, this is taking the shape of self-employment and starting a business, the vast majority of which remains small scale since, as primary carers, women tend to wrap the business around their family commitments. A more effective way for society as a whole to fully utilise women's talents and give them a sense of fulfilment is to alter work norms away from androcentric standards and assumptions to ones that are equally accommodating of both sexes.

The corner stone of the androcentric definition of success in public life is the ideal worker who has no care responsibilities. Changing the way we look at workers is therefore a necessary condition to removing the androcentric bias built in our view of success. Instead of care free, workers need to be thought of as people with care and other responsibilities and business organisations need to declare their intention of accepting these responsibilities as unalienable parts of workers' lives, regardless of their sex.

This may look like a simple solution but it has profound implications to sex equality. The assumption that women care and men are care free is the single most important manifestation of sex decimation in work spaces. We don't necessarily associate care with sex discrimination, since for the majority of us it is a fact of life that women care more than men. However, it is precisely this blind spot that is behind treating men's careers as sacrosanct and women's careers as secondary. And since this is the way we look at things, this is also the way things appear in reality.

Once we declared our *intention* of assuming that all workers have care and other non-work related responsibilities, *attention* is paramount. Wayne Dyer (2004) states that "the secret to manifesting anything that you desire is your willingness and ability to realign yourself so that your inner world is in harmony with the power of (your) intention,"[553] "and to continuously contemplate yourself as being surrounded by the conditions you wish to produce."[554] Dyer (2004) gives these examples: the Wright brothers didn't contemplate 'staying on the ground', nor did Alexander Graham Bell contemplate 'non-communication' any more than Thomas Edison contemplated 'darkness'. "In order to float an idea into your reality, you must be willing to do (mental) somersault into the inconceivable (reality) and land on your feet, contemplating what you want instead of what you don't have."[555] Dwelling on sex differences and sex inequality amounts to constantly contemplating what we don't want, which leaves us 'on the ground', in 'non-communication' and in the 'darkness'. Instead, it's time to contemplate equality and pay considerable attention to how we want an equal world to look like.

V.3.1.2   Intention and attention at work

Business managers, particularly at executive level who are still largely men, are accustomed to seeing things from a command and control mindset, which is pivotal to the construction of dominant masculinity; outside control, in dominant men's minds, there is only chaos and disintegration. They underestimate the power of their own 'intent' in creating order in a way other than the old way of 'power over other', which no longer works in the changing world of work of the 21st century.

Intent is a powerful concept that can unleash enormous hidden energies within the business, from both employers and employees. This is

---

[553] Dyer, 2004: chapter 3, para. 2.

[554] Ibid: para. 4.

[555] Ibid.

vaguely recognised by businesses that declare their 'mission statement'. Alignment to mission statement is not always solicited at employee level, nor is it rigorously adhered to by the business. But those businesses that do adhere, and commit their employees, to mission statements tend to be more successful. Research shows that the mere practice of writing a mission statement itself is directly linked to greater returns on investment in the same companies, and those businesses that have mission statements have double the return on equity than those who do not.[556]

It is paramount that business owners and managers get clear on their desire to achieve a work environment that is free of prejudice, and to declare this intent to their employees to get their alignment on achieving the same goal. Businesses that have openly adhered to promoting women have achieved great success in increasing the proportion of women at executive level, as Deloitte and Touche have set a good example of (see section IV.4.1).

We no longer mention the S word in a work environment, we sugar coat our deeply ingrained sexist assumptions and behaviours with the more palatable talk of 'sex differences' and, the more fashionable subject, of how to bring more women to the top of organisations. As laudable as these efforts are, they give us a way out of tackling the core issue of sexism, that of wrong beliefs about women and men and their abilities, and it provides the smoke screen that we have actually changed our sexist beliefs, when nothing could be further from the truth. Businesses need to get clear and align their employees on the idea that it is sexist thoughts and behaviours that are responsible for keeping women's careers on a separate track from that of men's.

---

[556] http://www.thinkbigpartners.com/start-a-business/202-the-importance-of-a-mission-statement.html.

V.3.1.3　The hidden gender conversation

"For as he thinketh in his heart, so is he." Hebrew Bible[557]

Dyer (2004) states that one of the main obstacles to connecting to our intent is our inner speech or dialogue. Despite 'gender equality' rhetoric and 'family friendly' policies, managers' underlying assumptions about how women and men fit in the organisation, and who should take care of children is invariably prejudiced. In depth interviews by Smithson and Stokoe (2005) of accountancy and banking sector employees revealed almost without exception that work-life balance practices are discursively constructed as issues relevant to women only, particularly those with childcare responsibilities, but not to men. These background normative assumptions are made by managers and employees alike and by both sexes. There is further the assumption that women with young children who take maternity and other family related leaves are not seriously committed 'core' employees.

Similarly, in Pini and McDonal's (2008) survey of employees working flexible hours at a local authority in Australia, the narrative of participants including women betrayed the prevalence of gendered assumptions about care and work. These included: "flexible work is thought of as something for women with children"; flexible work would be different for men as they would "worry about perceptions if they took it"; and male flexi workers would have to deal with people who "think there's something wrong with them"; all three opinions were stated by women. One male flexible worker found working flexibly difficult: "it's not the blokey thing to work part time. If you are a real man you work full time they still have this image that men are breadwinners and that if he is not working the whole time then what is he doing?" The researchers state that women attempt to conform to this view by working long hours; "in other words they too do the masculine thing."

---

[557] A verse from the Hebrew Bible the Book of Proverbs: chapter 23, verse 7.

Of the 13 men interviewed by Pini and McDonal's (2008), only two worked flexibly for family reasons. By contrast, the rest of interviewees unequivocally distanced themselves from female flexible workers who were viewed as doing so for familial reasons. For those men, the conflation between hegemonic masculinity and full time work remained unquestioned. They justified working flexibly by their need for study (particularly younger men), for doing private business, or for life style purposes (particularly men over 60 years of age). One man stated that he didn't believe working flexibly to study would hinder his career, since studying would upgrade his skills and knowledge - for use in the world of paid work later on - and since it was only temporary, therefore emphasising his commitment to the masculine path of full time employment. Another emphasised that if he did flexi work for childcare purposes he "would be looked down upon". The researchers conclude that although these men were working flexibly, they were still keen to demonstrate "their work commitment, capacity for career success, ambition and singularity of purpose." The older male group that worked flexibly showed similar legitimisation. Like the younger men, they saw themselves as 'different' from women but also from young male workers. They were able to work flexibly because their hegemonic masculine identity has been fulfilled – through working most of their adult life. They didn't believe that younger males would get away with working flexibly, part time or doing job share, which are all thought of as relating to women with young children.

The two males who worked flexibly for family reasons considered themselves progressive and aligned with sex equality. They both confessed to having had difficulty at work requesting flexible work. Critically, both men believed working flexibly would harm their careers and that their commitment to their families is holding them back. "Employer sponsored flexibility is seen as *quid pro quo* for forfeiting promotion or development prospects."

I mention these two studies at length because they reveal the unspoken rules in work organisations that betray their hidden beliefs about career

213

success and progression: contrary to publically stated family friendly policies, professional success is still predicated on working long hours, full time and without interruption, all of which are the domain of male workers.

Society is more open about the conversation that 'it is only women who care' and that 'real' men don't. Juxtaposing these two conversations, one out in the open and one hidden and buried under family friendly rhetoric, we can see where the confusion, tension and incongruity lie and that without restoring integrity to the conversation about women and men, care and work, women's chances of succeeding in public life on equal footing with men are minimal.

V.3.1.4   The culture of long hours and dominant masculinities

Assigning breadwinning to men in the gender system entails that working full time and long hours is the modality for establishing dominant masculinity in the workplace. This explains why working long hours has become a badge of honour for those who value status above all. Given the, wrong, perception that higher status individuals are more competent (see section IV.4.4), working long hours is by extension associated with competence too. Seen like this, it is easy to understand, although not excuse, management reluctance to relinquish the culture of face time, the only way to visibly account for the long hours.

A study by Hewlett and Luce (2006) found that 62% of high earning individuals work more than 50 hours a week, 35% more than 60 hours and 10% more than 80 hours. Importantly, the researchers found that managerial and professional men worked significantly more hours per week than did their equivalent women, who worked 5 hours less on average; more men than women had the support of a stay at home spouse or partner; and more men than women had children.[558] Burke and Fiksenbaum's (2009) study of Canadian MBA graduate students also found that fewer females than males in their sample worked 56 hours or more per week. This was the case even though females were less likely to be married or have partners; were less likely to have children; and if they did, had fewer children and were less well established in their careers (had less job and organisation tenure and were younger). The scholars conclude that "men are more likely to work harder and longer to establish themselves in their career". The upshot is that if organisations saw working extreme hours to be a prerequisite for career advancement, managerial and professional women would be at a career disadvantage.[559]

A corollary of the culture of long hours is that the higher people get on the corporate ladder the more time seems demanded of them; hence the failure of women in arriving to executive positions in proportionate numbers. Furthermore, Halpern and Cheung (2008) point to the demographic implications of this work culture: "Given these work hour norms, it is understandable that among the relatively few women who make it to the top, approximately half do not have children. It is hard to see how anyone can fit children and a family life into such punishing work schedule."[560]

V.3.2   The pragmatic approach: imagining sexism away

Another approach to resolving the complex issues that underpin sexism is to imagine sexism away! We can then ask ourselves, how would societies look like in the total absence of sexism? What kind of a workplace would we have in the total presence of sex equality? If gender was to disappear, and we were merely women and men with families, hopes and dreams

---

[558]   Quoted in Halpern and Cheung, 2008: 52.
[559]   Burke and Fiksenbaum, 2009
[560]   Halpern and Cheung 2008: 52.

that go well beyond work, what kind of work practices would be present in the workplace?

If we consciously create a reality and adopt practices that ongoingly affirm sex equality, reality will reflect equality back onto our minds, changing our perceptions of women's and men's competencies and entitlements. Epigenetic control mechanisms would translate these 'no difference' perceptions into 'no difference' genetic expression, in order to maintain harmony between brain and body, mind and environment. So in effect, this is imagining sex equality into existence.

But does this make sense? Will it work?

V.3.2.1   Changing our environment to change our minds

The two aspects of our biological reality that I discussed in chapter I, namely neuroplasticity and epigenetics, both point unequivocally to our ability to create a new reality for ourselves, including a sex equality reality. Neuroplasticity entails that our brains are not hardwired, but are constantly changing in structure and function in response to our environment and our experiences. Epigenetics entail that we are not doomed by our genes but can change our genetic expression by changing our environment. The inseparability of our behaviour from our environment points to another powerful way of reversing sexism, namely changing our environment from a sex biased to a sex equal one.

We are just beginning to grasp the awesome powers of the mind and how these powers can be harnessed to affect our behaviour in desirable ways, for example in fighting disease. Equally, and no less importantly, the power of the mind can be harnessed to counter cultural diseases, like sexism, racism, and many other isms. In his book 'How your mind can heal your body', David Hamilton (2010) says what we believe and what we think about physically change the chemistry of the brain and impact systems all around the body, giving rise to different gene expressions.

Even imagining something repetitively, without doing it in reality, can cause changes to the physical structure of the brain. Hamilton quotes a study by Harvard Medical School in 1994 where they had two groups of volunteers playing a simple combination of notes on the piano for two hours every day for five consecutive days. The first group physically played the piano but the second group imagined themselves playing the same piano notes for the same amount of time. The scientists scanned the volunteers' brains after five days, and they found that those areas of the brain connected to the finger muscles have grown to the same extent in both the two groups, meaning that the brain structure had changed just through imagining playing the piano as it had through physically playing the piano.[561]

It's not only the brain that changes with imagined exercise, but the imagined muscles too since they are connected to the brain by nerves. In other words, simply imagining things leads to real physiological changes. A 2004 study at the Department of Biomedical Engineering at the Lerner Research Institute in Cleveland was able to measure a substantial increase in muscle strength through imagined exercise. Taking thirty volunteers, some physically trained their little finger, while others imagined doing the same. In each session, the participants did 15 contractions at a time, real or imagined, followed by a 20-second rest period. Each session lasted 15 minutes and took place five days a week over twelve weeks. At the end of the experiment, scientists tested the strength of each volunteer's little finger and found that the muscle strength of the group that did the physical training increased by 53%, and that of the group that did the mental training increased by 35%, even though, as Hamilton (2010) puts it, "they hadn't actually lifted a finger."[562] Hamilton concludes that: "in many ways we understand from science now that the brain doesn't really distinguish whether

---

[561] Hamilton, 2010: 56.
[562] Ibid: 55-56.

something's actually happening or whether you're just imagining that thing is happening".[563]

The key to successfully imagining something into reality is repetition, repetition, repetition, in a fashion not dissimilar to athletic training – it is worth mentioning here that in addition to physical training, all top athletes use an extraordinary amount of mental training to achieve their desired results. Repetition of thought consolidates the change in gene expression, which manifests as change in behaviour.[564] Another key factor to harnessing the ability of the mind to impact behaviour is attention to detail of the actual process of achieving the result, and not just the end result itself.

The inseparability of our behaviour from the environment through epigenetic control mechanism entails that our behaviour is in consonant with the environmental signals we receive. The link between environment and behaviour that kicks off epigenetic control mechanisms is perception. Our perception of environmental signals sends certain messages to the brain, changes the brain chemistry unleashing a myriad of physiological changes and giving rise to the gene expression that allows behaviour to be in line with perception. To reverse sexism therefore we can intentionally reverse the environmental conditions that keep re-creating sex biased behaviour, letting the mind do the rest in creating the behaviour that is in consonant with our bias free environment sex biased.

The question to ask now is what are the conditions of a sex equal work environment?

[563] Hamilton, 2013.
[564] Ibid.

V.3.2.2 Equalising family leave

As discussed in previous chapters, the single most important manifestation of sex inequality in general and in the workplace in particular is men's superior status to women. This hierarchy of status is not achieved in vacuum, but is founded on a number of practices that underpin inequality, the single most important of which is relegating care to women while allowing men to be care free. In the home, this manifests in assigning the lion's share of housework and care to women, and in the workplace it manifests in giving relatively generous maternity leaves to women and puny paternity leaves to men, if any at all. Rectifying this aspect, by equalising family leave between women and men, is therefore pivotal to reversing sexism.

The positive effects of equalising family leave goes far beyond levelling the playing fields for women and men, to include demolishing one of the main pillars of the gender system, namely the assumption that women take care and men take charge. This aspect of reversing sexism requires great diligence from management, to counter the bias of associating family leave with women which is a significant factor is creating divergent career paths for women and men. Businesses need to declare the ethos of equal family leave for women and men, to remove any doubt from men's mind that taking a family leave will be perceived by their employer as lack of commitment. Upholding equality publically in this way may even give businesses an edge in the overly competitive global markets.

V.3.2.3 Integrating home life with work life

From the microcosm of separate and oppositional existence of the masculine and the feminine within us, follows the macrocosm of a dichotomous existence of a domestic sphere and a public sphere. Given this rigid construction of our social life, equality between women and men is not only difficult but impossible to achieve, as I have elucidated throughout this book. To reverse sexism at the macro level therefore the principle of disappearing difference entails abolishing the home/work life dichotomy by removing the artificial boundaries between the two domains. Getting to this point requires a radical shift in businesses' thinking and in work norms. Businesses need to acknowledge that employees don't only have care responsibilities, but also need fulfilment outside work in order for their productive energies to be unleashed at work. Work is a means to an end and not an end in itself. Of course for business owners profits are all important, but they too can wake up to the fact that their own fulfilment might come from elsewhere, and that pursuing this non work related fulfilment might unleash their own genius at work.

The big wobbles we are seeing in the world economy are a reflection of how old methods of creating the economy are no longer working. Businesses still adhere to obsolete work practices because they fear change and the uncertainty that comes with it. They forget that employees too need certainty and control over their lives. By working full time under face time conditions, employees are robbed of exercising control over their personal lives, leading to considerable stress and absenteeism.

These two guiding principles, equalisation of family leave between women and men and integrating home and work lives, can be the main pillars in designing the new workspace with the intention of reversing sexism. The common denominator in the two principles is integrating feminine and masculine qualities: in sharing care and work equally, men are embracing their feminine qualities of care and compassion and women are embracing their masculine qualities of self-expression and assertion. In relinquishing separation between the masculine work space and the feminine domestic space, care and compassion are integrated with achievement and self-fulfilment, relieving in the process considerable stress and consternation from people's lives.

V.4   Requirements of the New Workspace

"There is something in the nature of CEOs – pride, vanity, a primal need for control, an obsession with success, good old-fashioned idealism - that makes many smart, well-regarded chief executives into idiots when the world turns against them." 'CEOs in Denial', Fortune, June, 1999[565]

V.4.1   The empowerment principle

"Empowerment really is ....releasing the power within people to achieve astonishing results." Blanchard et al.[566]

"If people were given the option, do you think they'd choose to be magnificent or ordinary at work?" Blanchard et al.[567]

"We are conditioned to be ordinary."
Wayne Dyre (Spiritual teacher and author)

Work organisation still relies on outdated practices that have not fully taken into account changes in technology, flow of information, complexity of networks, rising workforce diversity;[568] and the globalised nature of many aspects of work. These changes mean that command and control methods of managing are not only outdated but outright obstructionist, both in terms of the efficient flow of information and in terms of personnel's ability to respond to and deal with complex networks in a timely manner. These changes also mean that the physical location of work is less relevant that it used to be during the industrial revolution, when these work practices were put in place.

---

[565]   Quoted in Tedlow, 2011: Introduction.
[566]   Blanchard et al. 1999: 2.
[567]   Ibid.
[568]   Eagly, 2007.

An important organisational change that would accommodate both the imperatives of family care and changes in technology and globalisation of work is personnel empowerment. Empowering others is a feminine attribute and a half a century old concept that is yet to be implemented whole heartedly and on business-wide scale. Douglas McGregor introduced the juxtaposition of authority *vs.* autonomy in his Theory Y (direction and control) *vs.* Theory X (integration and self-control). Acknowledging the limitation of management through authority, as opposed to empowerment, he wrote: "Many managers would agree that the effectiveness of their organizations would be at least doubled if they could discover how to tap the unrealized potential present in their human resources."[569]

Empowering personnel has been rising very slowly in the last half century. Gone are the days when employees are be called 'subordinates'. Yet, full empowerment is still an alien concept in the workplace, except in few enlightened pockets. Although the *modus operandi* of manager in control and employees under control is no longer effective,[570] it is still widely practiced. Empowerment would turn common concepts of personnel management on its head: instead of directing and supervising people, managers would aim to find out what would unleash people's creativity to obtain the results the business needs. Creativity is a feminine attribute and direction and control is a masculine one. To combine the two, direction and control can be targeted at end results, aiming to keep them on track, while support and nurturance can be the *modus operandi* in dealing with the people aspect of the business. To get to this point however would take a gigantic leap of faith in people's ability to focus on the business and in their willingness to contribute to its success, which entails a conscious shift from mistrust to mutual trust. Maitland and Thomson (2011) put it this way: "Too many leaders still need to get over

---

[569] McGregor, 2005: 6.
[570] Blanchard et al. 2001: ix.

the notion that their employees head off to work every morning asking themselves how they can get by with doing as little as possible."[571]

Empowerment starts with the belief system of top management.[572] The current system of belief in work organisations is built on lack of trust between employer and employees: businesses lack trust in their employees' commitment to the business and to furthering its objectives, and employees lack trust that their employer has their welfare at heart, and there is probably a grain of truth in both these sets of beliefs. This mutual mistrust is created by a mentality of 'lack' and 'scarcity'. Employers wrongly believe that if they focused on their employees' welfare this would amount to 'taking their eyes off the ball', off 'what is really important' and 'what really counts' for the bottom line.

In an environment where trust is lacking, people are afraid to go the extra mile and do their absolute best believing, perhaps rightly, that the starting premise of their managers is to catch them out when they make mistakes, rather than support them to thrive. In an untrusting environment, leaders too fear losing their jobs if they empowered others, in addition to losing power and control, given their underlying belief that others are not trustworthy.[573] Lack of trust is often a projection of our own mind: managers' distrust in the employees' commitment to business objectives can be a projection of their own lack of commitment to their employees' welfare. Employees, sensing their employer's lack of interest in their welfare, feel they need to fend for themselves. Concern for the self and for unmet personal needs creates a distraction away from business objectives and, at the same time, removes a critical condition for loyalty, that of fulfilling mutual interests.

Research shows that increasingly pay is no longer the main motivator for work but that success is being redefined to include wider benefits from

---

[571]   Ibid: 13.
[572]   Ibid.
[573]   Blanchard et al., 2001: 22.

working life, and that employees are actively seeking organisations that can deliver on this front.'[574] If businesses ask their employees to commit to serving their business objectives, they need to commit in return to serving the wider aspects of their employees' welfare. When employees know their own needs and demands are met, they are more able to focus on the job in hand. Trust and the mutual fulfilment of needs can be a potent mix to further businesses' ends, leading to higher performance.

There are companies around the world that successfully operate from the principle of mutual trust, which I will discuss in detail in the last section of this chapter. But as a quick example, Maitland and Thomson (2011) mention Syd Nadim, founder and chief executive of Clock, an award-winning UK-based digital marketing agency, who acknowledges the principle of mutual trust: "If you really trust people and really rely on them, they are more reliable and trustworthy".... "The approach has to be genuine otherwise people will see through it. If they know you don't really trust them and you've got a 'plan B', it's easier for them to let you down. Let go and watch how well other people can deliver and perform."[575]

A great way to motivate employees is to trust them enough by granting them full autonomy over how they achieve agreed upon results. Countless surveys have shown significant improvements in output when people have greater autonomy over *how*, *where* and *when* they carry out their work to meet their objectives.[576] Research in the Centre for Organizational Effectiveness at the University of Southern California reports that when people are given more control and responsibility over their jobs, companies achieve a 10.3% more return on sales than those companies that don't involve people.

---

[574] Maitland and Thomson, 2011: 21.
[575] Quoted by Maitland and Thomson, 2011: 114-116.
[576] Maitland and Thomson, 2011: 2.

Blanchard et al. (1999) state that when leaders empower people, they are placing additional responsibly for results on team members. Team members in turn embrace empowerment because it leads to the joys of involvement, ownership and growth.[577] In their view, giving people authority and responsibility to make important business decision is a key structural aspect of empowerment, but it is not the whole picture. The real essence of empowerment comes from releasing the knowledge, experience and motivational power that is already present in people but is severely underutilised: command and control management practices use 25-30% of the human resource capacity.[578] Blanchard et al. describe empowerment as a cutting-edge "technology" that provides both the strategic advantage that companies are after and the opportunity people are seeking too. It is the means for involving team members as business partners in determining company success or failure - which today is defined as being simultaneously customer driven, cost effective, fast and flexible and continuously improving.[579]

One key aspect of empowerment is sharing information relating to business performance, including profits, costs, budgets, market share, and productivity. Sharing accurate information empowers employees to make good business decisions in a timely manner.[580] In effect, managers and employees will have the same set of information to base decisions on, which is an anathema to current managerial practices and belief systems that are built on mistrusting employees' ability and willingness to focus on the business', and on the suspicion that information shared will be leaked to the competition. But without information sharing the empowerment process is hamstrung, as timely decisions at employee level will not be possible.

---

[577] Blanchard et al. 1999: 5-6.
[578] Ibid: 6.
[579] Ibid: 5.
[580] Blanchard et al., 2001: 27.

The underlying principle of equal sharing of information between management and employees is equality in status. Blanchard et al. (2001) state that the perceived difference in people's positions hangs over from the old hierarchical mind-set and its assumptions of the need for division between 'superior' and 'subordinate'. This division however has not only outlived its purpose, but it directly counters success in today's business organisations that can only succeed through team effort. Team work is now supported by unprecedented advances in technology that enable people to fully engage in the business, hampered in doing so by obsolete systems of belief. Sharing performance information like margins, profitability, costs of losing customers and so on sends a strong signal of trust to employees, who are asked to use the information and their own talents to help the business succeed.[581] It follows that leaders who are unwilling to share accurate and detailed performance information with their employees will forfeit the chance to have their employees as partners, which is a prerequisite to having an empowered organisation.[582]

The main obstacle to achieving an empowered organisation is strikingly similar to that of achieving sex equality in the workplace, namely a conditioned masculinity that is apprehensive about losing control and with it status and power. This prevents men from sharing equally with employees/women, be it information, decision making or care responsibilities. But this situation only arises because men for a long time have taken the wrong perspective on power, be it in their personal relationships or at work, and because they have not made themselves fully aware of the positive outcomes of change. Blanchard et al. (2001) explain that an empowering manager does not lose her/his job as a manger but gets a different one. Rather than directing, controlling, and supervising their people as they did in the past, they serve as a linking pin between people and the rest of the organisation. Their

---

[581] Ibid: 31.
[582] Ibid: 28-29.

role becomes more vital and engaging as their activities now focus on coordination, resources acquisition, strategic planning, working with customer, coaching people and so on. Managers' roles also become more focused on helping people to be more effective in developing and using their talents and energy to achieve company's goals.[583] This new way of managing is far more engaging and fulfilling than directing, controlling and catching people out when they make mistakes.

The crowning principle of empowerment is autonomy, which at the same time helps demolish the conditions that lead to unequal outcomes in the workplace. Autonomy not only allows people to make the right business decision at the opportune time without recourse to top management's approval, but it also allows them to manage their business and personal affairs simultaneously, i.e. to integrate home and work life fully.

Autonomy is such a powerful and effective tool in raising the roof on business performance that businesses must guard it jealously, by putting in place all the conditions necessary for its success. Paramount amongst these is creating boundaries, which *prima facia* is counterproductive, but on closer inspection is vital to its success. Boundaries, particularly in the earlier stages of moving toward empowerment, generate clarity around people's rights and responsibilities allowing them to use their initiative and creative energies to fulfil business goals within their own specified roles. As Blanchard et al. (2001) put it: boundaries provide the playing field on, and the rules by, which people are free to play their own outstanding game, since within certain guidelines they know which aspects of the work they have full control over, when autonomy is concerned. As people become more empowered, these boundaries naturally expand.[584]

---

[583]   Ibid: 22.
[584]   Ibid: 86.

The true abolishment of hierarchy, and with it status, comes from managing work through teams, rather than through chains of command. Without this condition and even in the presence of full information sharing and autonomy the organisation remains hierarchical and therefore underpowered, since decision making is still concentrated at the top. Self-managed teams on the other hand empower each individual within the team with decision making. Moving from chains of command to self-managed teams is perhaps the most challenging step in the empowerment process, as it takes a giant leap in suspending the disbelief that every individual is capable of being fully engaged in the decision making process. This inevitably takes trial and error and the willingness to make mistakes, both individually and collectively, and to accept this as part of the learning process; not for the faint heart in other words. But the results vouch for the process, as Blanchard et al. (2001) catalogue the benefits of self-managed teams that range from increased job satisfaction, to greater employee commitment, more efficient decision making process, improved quality and, the crowing result, a more profitable organisation.[585]

As in any process of change, fear of uncertainty and the distinct possibility of failure are major inhibitors to embarking on and persevering with the process of empowerment. Business leaders and managers must be prepared to cross a 'river of change' and live with the discomfort of doubt which is inevitable during any change, until the reach the shores of safety when they start to reap the benefits of the new system.

V.4.2   Broadening the perspective

The assumption of the 'ideal worker' expired at least thirty years ago. Its survival is a testament to the institutional power businesses have over individuals. If businesses chose to align themselves with contemporary

---

[585]   Ibid: 103.

values, and maybe even contribute to raising social consciousness, they can not only drop the ideal worker assumption but also turn themselves into leaders of change, which may after all give them a much needed competitive edge in the globalised economy.

The first step toward abolishing the home-work dichotomy is acknowledging that employees are 'people' and not 'ant workers', they have broad interests that go beyond work or even family responsibilities, to include health, leisure, self-development or contribution to community. Anderson, Vinnicombe and Singh (2010) looked at 31 women partners who had left an international management consulting firm.[586] About half of the women had children under 18, and yet the issue of motherhood for them was not about coordinating childcare arrangement or dividing time between parenting and partner work. Rather, motherhood to them meant spending real time and being with their children at varying stages of their lives. Several women without children or with grown up children, talked about their desire to acquire broader experiences in their lives that go beyond work.

In a study by Catalyst (1998) of women who left their employers to start their own businesses, 51% of the women from the private sector (and 44% from other employment backgrounds) gave flexibility as a primary reason for leaving their companies. The women cited the following reasons for needing flexibility: child care obligations; participation in community affairs; personal health concerns; elderly care and other family obligations. Understandably, since 82% of the women had dependent children staying at home, the greatest percentage (30% from private, and 34% from non private, sector) gave child care obligations as the reason for leaving the private sector. However, nearly a fifth of the women from non private sector (and 14% of private sector) gave community involvement or community care as a reason for needing

---

[586] The women were aged 37-60; two-third of whom were married or with a partner; 52% had children under 18 and 48% had no children or had grown up children; and 16% of women were at home full time with their children.

more flexibility in their lives. Another 10-15% of the women needed flexibility to care for elderly relatives.

A survey done by ACCA (the global professional accountants' body) and Mercer (a consulting firm) of over 3,200 Generation Y finance professionals across 122 countries found that lifestyle factors outweighed contractual ones in their choice of job. "Perhaps the preference toward lifestyle factors is in part due to a changing definition of success," said their report. "Our survey suggests the historical view of career success being defined by more money probably rings less true for this generation. This is a generation that seeks a much broader range of benefits from working life, and actively seeks out organizations that can deliver this."[587]

V.4.3   Starting to care!

These broader but critical aspects of our lives that involve family and community care are generally excluded from work discourses, because care is highly devalued in capitalist societies. The single minded pursuit of achievement in these societies leads to the appreciation of all things masculine and the depreciation of all things feminine (as Hanlon's (2012) and Twenge's (1997a) studies have shown - see chapter IV). Elderly care in particular is approached in contemporary Western societies as a problem to solve, rather than an integral aspect of our humanness. This is the result of failing to temper the masculine drive for achievement and self-expansion with feminine compassion, and is at the heart of declining fertility and the ageing population problem. And yet, the lesson is all but lost on governments and societies who focus squarely on the symptom, namely closing the pension gap, rather than open up the conversation about the cause, namely deficiency of care. The combination of failure of public policy to provide affordable and adequate care, of businesses'

---

[587]   Quoted in Maitland and Thomson, 2011: 22.

intransigence in offering genuine flexibility to working parents and caring employees and of men's refusal to fully embrace care has convinced many working women to either remain childless or have less children than they would have desired had these conditions been reversed.

V.4.4   The highly prized flexibility

A study by Minnotte (2012) found that when parents, particularly single parents, have low levels of control over their work hours, they report the highest levels of work-family conflict which decreases as they have more control over their working time. Conversely, as Hayman (2009) found, employees operating under flexitime work schedules display significantly higher levels of work-life balance than their counterparts utilising traditional fixed-hour schedules. On the other hand, Hayman's study found no significant differences in the levels of work-life balance between employees operating under flexiplace (and job share) and fixed-hour work schedules. So, time seems to be the more significant factor in relieving work-life stress. Similar results were found by Shockley and Allen (2007).

Anderson, Vinnicombe and Singh (2010) study mentioned above found that women partners who had left their firm tended to see their choices as clearly defined in terms of either their roles within the firm or a life outside the firm. Despite being partners, or rather because they are partners, these women were not granted any flexibility to manage their personal lives. Any measures of flexibility offered by the firm tended mainly to be given to *women* lower down the hierarchy. The discourse presented by these women was one of forced choice, since they perceived the firm to expect all or nothing. The resulting loss of control over their personal lives, at a time when they had an increasing desire to attend to demands outside the work domain, was the primary driver for these women partners to leave the firm.[588]

---

[588]   Anderson, Vinnicombe and Singh, 2010.

Maitland and Thomson's (2011) book 'Future work' catalogues studies and surveys that demonstrate the high value employees attach to flexibility. According to a survey carried out by PricewaterhouseCoopers in early 2010, the top benefit sought by professionals across the UK was flexible working, with almost half putting it top of their list. Interestingly, flexibility was given fairly equal priority by men and women.[589] Other countries are seeing similar trends. A survey of hourly paid workers in the US in 2009 found that flexibility was an important factor in deciding to take the job for 83% of workers who had joined in the last two years.[590] A survey by Corporate Voices for Working Families reported that 60% of the workers said they are likely to leave the company if they did not have the opportunity to work flexibly.[591]

A study in the UK that questioned fathers and mothers about what would be most helpful in achieving a better balance in their lives found that 'a wider range of flexible job opportunities in all types of jobs' was the most desired aspect. The Shriver Report, 'A Woman's Nation', mirrored these findings in the US.[592] It is not only young people with families who are looking for flexible work. Research indicates that both baby boomers and the young workers of Gen Y, particularly in advanced economies, place at least as much importance on having flexible work as they do on financial rewards – in addition to high-quality colleagues, recognition and access to new challenges.[593]

A report by the Chartered Institute of Personnel and Development in the UK found that fewer than one in ten employees looked forward to going to work all of the time, and just over a quarter rarely or never looked forward to going to work. Younger employees were more disengaged than their older colleagues. Perhaps the most interesting

---

[589]   Maitland and Thomson, 2011: 21.
[590]   Ibid.
[591]   Ibid.
[592]   Ibid: 3.
[593]   Ibid: 6.

finding was that people on flexible contracts felt much more positive about their managers than did non-flexible workers 'most probably because managers who take the trouble to find ways of helping their staff manage their work– life balance are also those who have better general management skills'.[594]

V.4.5   What kind of flexibility?

In its broadest sense, flexible work is working outside the confines of specified time and place.[595] In its most advanced state, flexible work is working from anywhere at any time, enabled by communication technologies. Employers often grant flexible working arrangements grudgingly, as many mangers regard them as a business inconvenience to accommodate workers' circumstances at best, and an impediment to achieving their business objectives at worst. Premising flexible working arrangements on 'accommodating employees' circumstance, by altering 'normal' or 'ideal' working patterns, prejudices these provisions, both in legislation and in practice.[596] Employees are particularly ambivalent about giving flexible working arrangements to men because, despite their public relations rhetoric, most employers assume that 'work-family' programs are designed only for working mothers,[597] as Smithson and Stokoe's (2005) and Pini and McDonal's (2008) surveys have clearly demonstrated (see section V.3.1.3). Men who might want to take a leave after the birth of a child know that management will see such behaviour as lack of career commitment.

Maitland and Thomson (2011) quote Laura, a young worker aged 29, describing her flexible working arraignments and their benefits: "Instead of working 9–5 in an office or designated cube, I may work from home,

---

[594] Ibid: 22.
[595] Ibid: 22.
[596] Ibid: 24.
[597] Coltrane 1996: 26.

a coffee shop, a park with Wi-Fi, or have a cube-share with another employee. I work the amount of hours needed to get the job done by the deadline instead of doing the job between certain hours on certain days. It's just a different way of looking at time."[598] Laura adds: "There is flexibility that allows you to work in your most productive way. You may work better late at night or be working with business partners in another time zone. In my experience, more work gets done in a flexible workspace environment because I can take care of things like getting my car registered. I can work hours at home when I would normally be travelling to and from work. I can do focused work without the distractions that come with sitting at my cube, and I can be completely accessible for tasks that can be handled over email."[599]

Maitland and Thomson (2011) state that what makes this working arrangement possible is trust: Laura works in a trusting culture, where she is expected to meet objectives without needing to be micro-managed. The authors compare this to a low-trust environment where people are assumed to be inherently unreliable and prone to abuse 'the system' unless the boss keeps a close eye on their every move. They further state that it is not difficult to see which of these environments is more likely to encourage initiative, creativity and a willingness to put in extra effort, rather than simply counting down the hours to going-home time. Nor is it difficult to see which environment is more likely to attract and keep good employees.[600]

If Laura's example sounds too extreme that it cannot be applied to manufacturing settings, Maitland and Thomson give the example of Stuart Fell, owner of Metal Assemblies, a medium-sized engineering firm in the West Midlands in the UK, (the traditional heart of England's manufacturing industry), who believes in two-way flexibility based on trust. "The needs of the business can frequently be met better by people

---

[598] Maitland and Thomson, 2011: 110.
[599] Ibid.
[600] Ibid: 117.

who also are having their needs met," he says. "I could name employees who would not work for us were it not for the flexibility we offer. I also know there is business we have won because we have been able to respond quickly to a customer demand… The organizations that don't adapt will end up the dinosaurs. They won't be able to move fast enough or recruit people to work for them."[601]

V.4.6   The productivity myth

The main obstacle to genuine flexibility is managers' attachment to counting working hours, for which presenteeism is important, and their constant push for longer and longer hours believing wrongly that this is the way to beat the competition beast. Their pitfall is that they collapse hours worked with productivity, and while hours worked are a factor in increasing productivity, they only lead to more output if they are well used. Motivation, enthusiasm and high energy are significant factors in raising productivity that cannot be measured by time. To see employees working, therefore, works more as a psychological pacifier for mangers, dispelling the fear that their employees are 'not working'. This psychological need and the corporate culture that equates long hours with commitment are deeply engrained and continue to this day, despite advances in technology that make physical presence in many instances superfluous, and overwhelming evidence that employees are more productive when they have greater autonomy over where, when and how they work.[602]

We can easily imagine an employee who meets face time requirements, and may even put in extra time to assuage managers' psychological comfort factor, but is still highly demotivated because s/he is unable to meet their non work commitments. Face time will be counterproductive

---

[601]   Ibid.

[602]   Ibid: 2.

235

in this case, since not only is the employee distracted and distressed, but s/he is further disempowered by the mangers' message of distrust. By contrast, a happy, self-fulfilled employee who knows s/he will leave work early enough to collect the children from school or visit an elderly parent, or have Friday off to do voluntary work is likely to be happier and more productive for every hour s/he spends working.

Productivity is the amount of output produced over a specific period of time, given a certain set of resources – labour, capital and a given level of technology. Common sense entails that businesses would convince their employees to produce more output in the same amount of time, or the same output in less time, in order to maximise their productivity, instead of insisting on 'putting in the hours'. In makes far more sense therefore to focus on measuring results more rigorously. Maitland and Thomson (2011) argue that "people who are paid by results have every incentive to think up smarter ways of getting the work done. Their reward is more 'spare' time for them to use as leisure or to generate more income."[603] At Google, one of the hyper successful global businesses, people are judged on their results, not the time they put into their work. Matt Brittin, head of the internet group's operations in the UK and Ireland, says: "I can't remember having a conversation with anybody about their hours. All employees have quarterly objectives, and their manager reviews their performance, scores them and measures their scores against their peer group. Performance scores feed into pay and quarterly and annual bonuses. Objectives are set for the next quarter and coaching is given for areas that need improvement."[604] Vodafone UK is another leader who believes in managing by output, Guy Laurence says managing by output means trusting people to manage themselves and use common sense: "If you move to team-based objectives and measure on output, it's mostly self-regulating. If one person lets the side down, someone else picks them up on it."[605]

---

[603] Ibid: 115.
[604] Ibid: 116.
[605] Ibid.

V.4.7   Flexible work and productivity

Shockley and Allen (2012) examined employees' motivation in using flexible work arrangements, in terms of both flexitime and flexiplace. They looked at two types of motivation, life-related (management) and work-related (increasing productivity) considerations, and studied how these motives varied according to sex, family responsibility, marital status, and preference for separating work and non-work aspects of their life. They found that overall employees are more driven to use flexibility for work-related, than for life management motives. Those with greater family responsibilities and those married/living with a partner were more likely to endorse life management motives, whereas individuals with greater separation preferences were more motivated to use flexibility for work-related motives. Contrary to expectations there were no differences in life management motives between women and men. The main implication of these findings is that individuals recognise flexibility as not only a work-family policy, but also as a potential means to increasing productivity.

V.4.8   The new work requirements in a nutshell

Hierarchical organisations that operate *via* lines of authority and manage through command and control are obsolete. Horizontal, or more accurately matrix style, organisations that are run by self-managed teams produce superior results in today's highly competitive globalised work organisations. In these types of organisations, employees have maximum exposure to clients, and clients have continuous access to employees empowered with the ability to make decisions. Vast hidden energies in the business are unleashed as performance information is shared freely with all employees, and the business mission, and each employee's role in its fulfilment, is made crystal clear. Employee are trusted to find the best way to achieve well defined results within agreed upon time frame using whatever processes they see fit.

The modern worker has aspirations that go well beyond money, to include fulfilling non work related roles that have a very broad spectrum, much broader than family care. For those workers, to reach peak performance they need to be given maximum flexibility in order to align their work and non work priorities. Such alignment can bring huge gains in emotional and physical energy, not to mention greater clarity and focus at work, all of which is bound to yield substantial gains in productivity.[606] What really matters is the business' output, not the time input, and mangers need to wean themselves of the psychological comforter called 'face time' and 'long hours'. Defining and achieving business results and specific outcomes matter far more than the process of achieving these results.[607]

It follows that clear communication is required both ways: the business mission and the specific results required of each employee should be communicated to, and agreed with, each employee. Each employee needs to communicate their personal interests and non work obligations to their mangers. Both parties, managers and employees, stand to benefit from this two way communication and from, crucially, delineating where work falls in the spectrum of overall life priorities for each employee.[608]

V.5   Pioneers of The New Work

"Although the world is full of suffering, it is full also of the overcoming of it," Helen Keller (American author)

"It is well known that the most radical revolutionary will become a conservative on the day after the revolution," Hannah Arendt (Political scientist and philosopher)

---

[606] See Riordan, 2013.
[607] See Friedman, Christenssen and Degroot, 2000: 5.
[608] Ibid: 4.

Friedman, Christenssen and Degroot (2000) studied a small but growing number of businesses, of varying sizes and from different industries, who organise work practices in a way that meet the requirements for the new workspace mentioned above. The authors state that in the cases they have studied, the new approach has yielded tangible payoffs, both for organisations and for individual employees. While sex equality is not the agenda for these businesses, their examples do provide a good template for organising work in such a way that equalises conditions for women and men, by siphoning off prejudicial practices such as granting more family leaves to women and separating home and work life.

The work in these pioneering businesses is organised by three mutually reinforcing principles. *First,* starting from the premise that employees are 'whole people' with roles outside the office that are to be celebrated rather than swept under the carpet. There is an understanding that skills and knowledge can be transferred from one role to another, and that boundaries are needed to establish where these roles overlap and where they must be kept separate. *Second,* managers clarify what is important in terms of business priorities, which are defined in terms of outputs and specific results. Employees are encouraged to clarify their personal interests and concerns, and to identify where work falls in the spectrum of their overall life priorities. *Third,* mangers continually experiment with how work is done, seeking approaches that enhance the organisations' performance while creating time and energy for employees' personal pursuits. A road map is drawn toward the simultaneous achievement of business success and individuals' fulfilment at the same time. This leads to a virtuous cycle of mangers helping employees balance their work and non-work lives, and employees feeling a stronger commitment to the organisation, giving a boost to their trust, loyalty and the energy they dedicate to work and improving their performance in the process. Strong results allow mangers to continue practicing the principles that help employees strike a work-life balance.[609]

---

[609] Ibid: 4-5.

The key to success in this style of management is defining business results and placing all the importance on the outcomes not the process. To that end, managers give their employees specific goals but also greater autonomy over how to achieve those goals. Simultaneously, they ask employees to identify their personal goals, concerns and demands that require time and energy outside the office. One person might be responsible for his elderly mother's health care, which involves three trips to the hospital each month. Another might be in the process of qualifying for a Gold Star in figure skating. Still another may feel strongly that, at this point in her career, none of her priorities is more important than success at work.[610]

The scholars report that these managers' understanding of the employees' life is 'deep and detailed' and they support the full range of their employees' life roles, not just parent or caretaker but volunteer, aspiring musicians or passionate golfer. "Tuning into their employees' roles outside office creates a bond and with it trust, which brings organisational benefits familiar to any manager."[611] The managers help their employees establish clear boundaries between the different aspects of their lives to allow them to concentrate on the task in hand, by removing distractions.[612]

At face value, delving into every employee's priorities and designing an individualised action plan may seem impractical, complicated and time consuming. But the scholars state this method doesn't necessarily involve much more time and energy than the traditional way of managing. "Virtually all mangers today are held accountable for developing their employees professionally, i.e. they already engage in discussions about what people want and need from work and what they are expected to contribute. To bring personal life priorities and gaols into the conversation really only involves asking two or three

---

[610] Ibid.
[611] Ibid.
[612] Ibid.

more questions."[613] Furthermore, working from these principles can be delegated to the employees themselves, who can apply them personally and to their dealings with one another. The scholars report that they have seen people become quickly engaged in the process as they realise how the solutions they develop benefit both the business and their own personal lives. The researchers state that increasingly this integrated work-life approach in becoming common as more companies use life-friendly policies as a strategy to attract and retain talented people.[614]

The benefits to the organisation are incalculable, not least in terms of the loyalty the employees feel toward their mangers, which shows up in more commitment to work. One of the less obvious benefits is that experimenting with different work processes is an opportunity to improve the organisation's performance and the lives of its people at the same time. The managers discovered that conflicts between work and personal priorities can actually be a catalyst for identifying work inefficiencies that might otherwise remain hidden or intractable. Taking a new set of parameters into account can allow people to question old ways of doing business that are so ingrained that no one would think to consider changing them otherwise. The managers encourage employees to question basic assumptions, such as the common sales mantra: real commitment means total availability. They also encourage employees to learn, through trial and error, about new ways to organise work that might well challenge the legitimacy of exiting practices; "valuing productivity over face time is a crucial element in experimenting with work processes."[615] Employees involved in these experiments report feeling that their lives are more predictable and they are able to relax when are at home and plan more personal projects and events.

Given its resounding success, why are these methods of organising work not widely spread? In addition to listing the usual objections

---

[613]   Ibid.
[614]   Ibid: 26.
[615]   Ibid: 11-12.

of complexity, the high requirements of time and energy, and the assumption that only women need life-work balance policies, the scholars conjecture that it is "fear of finding out how many of their practices are dysfunctional that prevent businesses from digging deeper and allowing change to come in."[616]

We can take this statement word for word, put it in a gender beliefs context and it will remain truthful: it is fear of finding out how many of our gender practices are dysfunctional that stops us from digging deeper into our gender belief system and allowing social change to come in. This fear is also a major driver in holding managers back from challenging the *status quo* of work norms and practices.

Working long hours under face time conditions has become the symbol of masculinity in the workplace. It is proof positive that the employee is an ideal one, i.e. without care responsibilities. Employees that do care are seen as either feminine or not masculine enough, and have therefore abrogated their right to the masculine work space. They are marked as 'uncommitted', not one of the 'core employees', and are relegated to a lower trajectory of pay and promotion. This is why many women feel the need to masculinise themselves to be able to stay on the same employment trajectory as men. Children and family life are subjects to avoid; maternity leave is as short as possible and the word maternity is avoided, 'when the baby arrives' is a more palatable statement because men too have babies, but they don't have 'maternity' leaves; and many women avoid having children altogether while others have less children than they would have desired. By abandoning the masculine project, but not the masculine, and embracing care for their employees and their lives, i.e. bringing in the feminine, these managers are bringing forth the demise of an institutional devise that has been instrumental to sustaining the gender system, the vehicle for sexism.

---

[616]   Ibid: 1-29.

V.6   Conclusions: The Genderless Workplace

"It always seems impossible until it is done." Nelson Mandela
(A South African anti-apartheid revolutionary)

There are work practices that have long been suggested in a different genre of literature, namely management and workplace organisation, which have within them the capacity to eliminate sexist practices from the workplace and bring about sex equality; paramount amongst those is empowerment practices. Empowering others is a feminine trait, which explains resistance to this half a century old concept in the overtly masculine workplace. Men have been conditioned for millennia to be masculine only, and the prospect of diluting their masculinity with femininity throws them into panic and confusion. This strict conception of what it is to be a man resides deep in men's psyche such that 'fear of the feminine' is not a mere psychoanalytic artifact but a reality that is yet to be unconcealed and embraced by most men. The higher the status in society, the greater the stakes attached to embracing femininity, and so it is the case with most CEOs that they see empowerment as a threat to everything they have achieved through 'striving', 'competing', 'commanding and controlling', through the sheer power of their conditioned masculinity.

The error in our thinking of the need to separate masculinity from femininity arose from our attachment to dichotomies; an otherwise useful analytical tool. As artificial mental constructions, dichotomies lead us astray by giving us the illusion that what they are projected upon is truly separable and contrasting: namely, if something or someone is one thing, they cannot be the other, when in reality they are both at the same time. And so it is with the dichotomy that men are masculine and women are feminine, when in reality they are both at the same time. As is the separation between home life and work like and the sexual division of labour that amounts to "a taboo against the sameness of men and women, a taboo driving the sexes into two mutually exclusive

243

categories, a taboo which exacerbates the biological differences between the sexes and thereby *creates* gender."[617]

I have shown in this book that dichotomies further create the *illusion* of choice in women's lives which, given the nature of a dichotomy, becomes an either/or choice. The dichotomy of femininity and masculinity, which obligates women to, and frees men from, care combined with the dichotomy of work life and home life, with women assigned to home and men to work, create the illusion of free choice for women to pursue their careers unhindered. Obligated to care and assigned the responsibility of managing the domestic realm, most women make highly constrained life-career choices that push their careers on a downward trajectory compared to men, whose careers are given an artificial boost since they are not only freed from care, but are cared for by women.

Giving up our attachment to dichotomies would bring about sex equality. This is particularly true for the dichotomy of the masculine and the feminine: as we juxtapose them next to, and pit them against, each other we have the illusion that we can only be one or the other, when the reality of human nature is both at the same time. This is the single most important aspect in resorting balance not only within ourselves as individuals but in the home, the workplace and the world at large. The dichotomous conceptualisation of home life and work life has pitted businesses against families, work against care, and women against men.

Embracing unity and harmony and eschewing division and difference at every level seem to offer a way out: *1)* if women and men were both feminine and masculine; *2)* if we had one integrated life, rather than a work life and a home life; *3)* if both women and men were to care, and *4)* if the workplace had feminine and masculine, rather than

---

[617] Rubin, 1975: 178. Rubin also suggests that the division of labour can be seen as a taboo against sexual arrangements other than those containing at least one man and one woman, 'thereby enjoining heterosexual marriage.'

androcentric, standards of work, the status of women and men in society would equalise, leading to the disappearance of sexism.

Empowerment principles seem to create the conditions necessary (but not sufficient) for the abandonment of dichotomies in work spaces. The most important aspect of leading through empowering is the fundamental change in the belief system of top management about their employees. Instead of the top-down approach of command and control, based on suspicion and mistrust, empowerment aims to unleash the creative powers of employees allowing them to have ownership of the business and its objectives. The main pillar of empowerment is agreeing on the results to be achieved and granting employees full autonomy over *how, where and when* they achieve these results. This entails a sea of change in the work culture, away from manager knows best toward a genuine belief in people's ability to come up with creative solutions. Inherent in empowerment is the equalisation of status between managers and employees, as information is shared by all equally and as employees are empowered with decision making abilities Achieving higher status is the *raison d'être* of dominant masculinities, empowerment principles therefore seem to remove many of the underpinnings of sexism in the workplace, leaving considerable room for achieving sex equality.

The two remaining pieces in the jigsaw of de-gendering the workplace are the equalisation of family-related career breaks and the full integration of work and family lives. The simultaneous implementation of these mechanisms would relinquish androcentricity as the norm in the workplace since, combined, they establish a vanishing point of the dichotomous existence of femininity and masculinity, as care is shared between women and men, and as work life and home life are fully integrated. And as these dichotomies disappear, so does the hierarchical status of women and men.

In this new work environment, the idealised worker, the lynchpin of sexism in the workplace, is redefined: no longer is it the person who works the longest hours, has no care responsibilities and has someone at home caring for them. Instead, it is the person who is energised enough to come up with the most creative solutions that directly feed into meeting business objectives. Gone is the need for both women and men to be as masculine as they can possibly be in order to succeed, for success measures are no longer androcentric. Employees have to draw on their creativity and intuition, and to put as much trust in those as they do in their intellect, to make decisions that would not only solve immediate problems but would also advance the business and allow it to grow.

VI

WHAT DO WOMEN WANT?: WOMEN AND REAL CHOICE

"Women don't want to hear what you think. Women want to hear what they think...." Bill Cosby (Comedian)

"It is our choices that show what we truly are, far more than our abilities." J.K. Rowling (Author)

"Define success on your own terms, achieve it by your own rules, and build a life you're proud to live." Anne Sweeney (American businesswoman and Co-Chair of Disney Media)

"And yet, underneath the make-up and fashion, women possess a natural and subtle power that remains hidden from most men's awareness in our modern society." Kevin and Donna Philippe-Johnson (Bloggers)

"The stereotypical male is portrayed as a warrior, gladiator, muscular athlete, stiff-shirt CEO with a gigantic portfolio. It isn't popular or fashionable to be gentle and wise like Jesus, Buddha or Gandhi....the cost of such folly has been the closing of the masculine heart, the uprising of patriarchal religious oppression, the suppression of the feminine aspect of life and the commonplace chaos and violence in the world today." Kevin and Donna Philippe-Johnson (Bloggers)

We often underestimate the power of myths, primarily because we do not see them as such. There was a time when the earth was flat, and other times when the sun revolved around the earth. We need to stop and ponder where our life on planet earth would be today if we still held these myths as truths. The first lesson here is that myths appear to be the absolute truth at a given level of consciousness. The second lesson is that our consciousness is constantly evolving, and therefore instead of believing that we have 'arrived' at the truth, it is more fruitful to keep 'inquiring' into the truth. It follows that we must acknowledge the myth that we do know the truth about the nature of reality, including our reality as women and men.

The biggest myth of our times is that women and men are *by nature* fundamentally different, and that women are feminine and men are masculine, with hardly any cross over between them. This simple 'truth' has created sexist societies and allowed sexism to flourish for millennia. It has also lead to the repression of many of our natural attributes and tendencies that are thought to belong to the 'opposite' sex, leading to much unhappiness and alienation. Since women and men see each other as distinctly different, they live their lives in different ways, with women's lives primarily focused on care and service of others, even when they work, and men's lives primarily focused on work and achievement, even when they care. In this universe of difference and division, women collectively excel in the home sphere, and men collectively excel in the public sphere.

Because human beings are born female and male we misunderstood the intent of their creation in this way to be one of separating the feminine from the masculine and assigning each to one sex but not the other, creating unbridgeable difference and division between the two sexes in the process. It's far more conducive to human happiness to think of the feminine and the masculine as a collection of traits, attributes and qualities that are present in all of us in combination rather than in separate form. Allowing the masculine to integrate with the feminine removes the need for repressing any kind of natural attributes that we might have, leaving us feeling freer and far more fulfilled as human beings.

There is very little research in this area, but psychologists implicitly acknowledge that we all have both masculine and feminine attributes in various combinations. Some psychologists, like Bakan (1966) and Block (1984) go further by asserting the need for feminine and masculine attributes to coexist in each of us as a prerequisite to living in harmony both individually and as a society (see section III.2.3); without the feminine, the masculine is lopsided and emotionally dysfunctional and without the masculine, the feminine is weakened and ineffective. The integration of masculine and feminine qualities in each of us increases our adaptability to different life situations, gives us more power in life and allows us to function at a higher plane of consciousness. By allowing the feminine to integrate with the masculine in men and the masculine to integrate with the feminine in women we are abandoning centuries of social conditioning that repress many of our most natural reflexes, in favour of gendered attributes. The suppression of relatedness, social connection and emotional expression in men and assertion and full self-expression in women are particularly toxic.

We know from epigenetic studies that the environment, including cultural beliefs, has a profound impact on behaviour and genetic expression, and that changes happen in the brain as well as in the body. The role of the mind is to maintain coherence between environmental signals and behaviour. The brain therefore unconsciously generates behavioural responses that are in line with the programmed perceptions that are the outcome of social conditioning.[618] As boys and girls and women and men perceive themselves to be different, brain plasticity and epigenetic control mechanisms create behavioural differences along stereotypical lines, which are inherited generation after generation. To the extent that cultural beliefs grant leadership to men and nurturance to women, women's and men's behavioural realities will reflect male supremacy and female subservience.

---

[618] Lipton and Bhaerman, 2009: chapter 2, section 4, para. 5.

What shapes neural circuits is *attention* and hence the transcendental/ ontological saying '*what you focus on increases.*' Our attention has been for too long on sex differences and divisions, on the 'either/or' of the masculine and the feminine and the hierarchical relationship between the two sexes. This is what we have created in our minds and what has as a consequence shaped our understanding of ourselves and the world. And this is reflected back to us in a social world where women and men *are* different and men have a higher status than women.

This is the gender framework that is still operating in the world, with varying degrees of strength. While the gender structures are coming loose in the Western world, in many parts of the world they still have a firm hold, and in some are extreme with severe consequences for girls and women. In many countries around the world, young girls are still being forced into arranged marriages, where they serve a life of physical hardship and of mental, emotional and sexual abuse. These are the extremes of a gender system that is still in place that puts women in second place. The conditions that these girls and women live under are far removed from those in Western societies, but not so the seed of the thought that allowed them to arise in the first place. Even in the Nordic countries where gender equality discourses are most advanced, the seed of the thought about who women and men are is still one of difference and hierarchy, and of repressing similarly. Men's control of and violence against women in the West is also widely prevalent, an open secret that is spoken of only in academic and specialised circles, but not in conversations amongst ordinary people, at least not commensurately with its prevalence. The reason for being taciturn is our shame of what is really going on in our minds about women and men: that we still believe that men are more important and more deserving than women, and by extension deserving of their control over women.

Gender dictates lead men to genuinely believe that they are rational and unemotional. Men deny, suppress and denigrate their feelings, emotions and intuitions as 'womanly' and therefore undeserving of recognition in themselves. The cost to men, women and society is incalculable.

As Einstein rightly said "the intuitive mind is a sacred gift and the rational mind is a faithful servant. We have created a society that honours the servant and has forgotten the gift." At a conscious level, men are forfeiting a sublime quality in human beings, that of intuition, mistakenly thinking it will lead them to become 'like a woman', and to losing their edge in business and public life. Unconsciously though, men are fighting against losing their status, power and prestige in society. What men don't acknowledge however is that intuition will not only raise their performance, as it did Einstein's, to considerably higher planes of consciousness, but it can give them access to emotional openness which is necessary for social connectedness and emotional freedom, and without which men's alienation and the outsider looking on the inside quality to their life continues.

Also as a result of gender dictates, women genuinely believe that they are innately focused on others and that their lives are about service, not realising that they are socially constructed and conditioned to do so. Society denies and represses in women those masculine attributes of self-focus that allow them to flourish in their own right, without male patronage. Women genuinely believe that to focus on the self and serve its wants, needs, and desires is selfish and out of society's order; only men are allowed to behave in this way. The lack of emotional expression in men is only paralleled by the lack of self-expression in women. Pursuing careers and other self-focused endeavours leave most mothers feeling guilty; a conditioned behaviour born out of seeing the self only in relation, and of service, to others.

The gender project is underpinned by the need to create a viable unit of economic production and social re-production. Having been spurred by the agricultural revolution and strengthened during the industrial revolution, the gender project reigns supreme in hard driving capitalist societies where the need to maximise economic production creates the need for dedicated care. The capitalist project and the gender project are therefore mutually reinforcing and have much in common, not least of which is setting untenable ideals. In the capitalist project, human

251

consumption is the holly grail and economic production enables its pursuit. Those who have access to economic means matter and those who don't matter less. Out of these tenets is born the ideal worker: someone whose productive capacity is maximised by being relieved of care responsibilities. This dichotomous separation between those engaged in economic production and those engaged in care is the foundation of the gender project. To enable the fulfilment of this design, those assigned economic production, i.e. men, are also exclusively assigned masculinity to maximise production, and those assigned care, i.e. women, are also exclusively assigned femininity to maximise care. The culmination of both the capitalist and the gender projects is the creation of a dominant masculinity whose very existence is predicated not only on being care free, to dominate femininities, but also on being able to amass such power and prestige that they can dominate other masculinities too.

As men's identities are shaped by the pursuit of a highly illusive dominant masculinity, they lose more than a chance to care. To dominate in society in this way, men have to abandon any recognition of those aspects of themselves that might jeopardise the fulfilment of the masculine ideal, namely loving tenderness, compassion, intuition and emotional connection. Even when men choose to recognise these aspects of themselves and/or to care, society comes down hard on them because of their 'betrayal' to and 'violation' of the masculine code. Helped by mythology, symbolism and folk wisdom that malign the feminine in men's psyche, men feel compelled in repressing any feelings that are associated with femininity, such as fear, uncertainty and vulnerability. Men are also socialised to pay less attention to relationships, particularly attachments to others, and are conditioned to be less interested in affectionate bonds than women. The suppression of emotions and detachment from others are interrelated: the more emotions are suppressed, the more difficult others have in relating to us; but the more isolated we feel, the easier it is to suppress emotions. Suppressing emotions and distancing from relationship allow men to become 'mobile' and seek accomplishments outside the home. Such mobility however comes at a high price: alienation from self-and others, and a propensity for aggression and violence.[619]

In the famous film American Psycho, an investment banker for whom happiness only comes from status, experiences a total emotional shut down. The anti-hero's inability to connect with people around him at any emotional level is acted out in extreme violence that was at first hidden from the world but eventually bursts out into the open. A satire of course, but can be thought of as the exaggeration that elucidates the point. On the surface, the anti hero would qualify as an exemplar of dominant masculinity: ultra rational, successful, super fit and never betrays an emotion. His alienation however is so absolute than it creates uncontrollable amounts of anger and aggression that manifest in endless gruesome crimes.

Sexism and sex inequality is only one aspect of sex division and difference. We need to understand the full ramifications of denying the feminine in men and the masculine in women in order to become conscious of the consequences of our decision to divide and separate in this way. To begin with, any disconnection from our true self leads to alienation and unhappiness, and so it is my contention that the gender system is a major culprit in the ingrained unhappiness in contemporary societies. Not only are we lying to ourselves about being fundamentally different as women and men, but we are also lying to ourselves about being unequal. This reason alone should prompt us to think differently, to change our 'truth' about who we are as women and men.

But there are other ills in our lives that relate to the myth that we are either feminine or masculine but never both at the same time. Our belief that men's 'gendered' masculinity, with its drive for domination, should remain untempered with femininity, with its attentiveness, care and compassion, creates toxicity in men's bodies, minds, lives and the

---

[619]   See Scheff, 2003, for references.

life of the planet. The destructive powers of wars for example, are a powerful manifestation of the unbridled 'conditioned' masculine. Financial market crashes are another significant example of how when in overdrive, conditioned masculinity can destroys lives. At a personal level too, men's suppression of the feminine aspects of their personalities drives them to avoid not only care for others but care for themselves too. It is strongly believed that men's shorter life span compared to women is not only genetic, but is also due to their avoidance of self-care,[620] especially during illness which brings men closer to vulnerability and feeling 'like a woman'.

The cost to women from adhering to rigid gender constructs goes well beyond the subordination of their status in society, which is built into the gender structure. Assigning care to women and work to men creates the false consciousness in women of their relative incompetence, of having inferior abilities to men. False consciousness, a negative or misleading state of self-awareness that is built on a faulty system of thought, is a very powerful aspect of the human psyche that can rob people of fulfilment in life. Those with false consciousness are unaware of their real merits and they, as a consequence, devalue themselves in society.

False consciousness is a term developed by Marxist theorists (particularly Engels) to describe how material, ideological and institutional processes in capitalism mislead members of the proletariat as to the true nature of relations between classes. Similarly, gender ideology and institutions mislead women as to the true nature of the relations between them and men. Instead of seeing their abilities in a true light, as equal to those of men, gender beliefs create the false consciousness in women of having inferior abilities to men and of being, as a consequence, deserving of their lower status in society.

---

[620]   Kirby et al., 2011.

From a psychosocial point of view, false consciousness develops in order for our psyche to make sense of an otherwise incomprehensible situation, namely a situation that lacks justice. In a sense, the false beliefs that we develop about ourselves in that situation are a protective device that allows us to comprehend the situation: to make sense of child abuse, children grow up believing they are 'bad' and deserving of the punishment they received; to make sense of slavery, slaves believe they are 'helpless' and 'childlike', a different group of people to their masters, and deserving of being enslaved; to make sense of sexism, women believe they are less competent and therefore less worthy of an equal status to men.

Since our bodies obey our minds and their perceptions, right or wrong, through epigenetic control mechanisms, in male dominated societies women's and men's behaviours differ in line with gender beliefs and stereotypic expectations, making sex differences a reality. Scientists who observe these differences invariably conclude that the two sexes' behaviours *are* different. There are three layers to this erroneous conclusion. The first, which is unravelling slowly but surely, is that we cannot distinguish between behaviour and environment in a one way manner, since the two systems continuously feed into each other. Behaviour mirrors the environment, through brain plasticity and epigenetic imperatives that ensure our minds and bodies are in synchronicity with our perceptions of environmental signals. The environment is shaped and changed by our minds that process environmental inputs and move toward adapting the environment to suit our new ways of thinking. As we change the environment, our minds change accordingly, and so continues the process of evolution.

The second layer of error, which is intimately related to the first, is the relentless conditioning of girls and women to be feminine and boys and men to be masculine. Social conditioning can take place simply by mirroring the environment. However, given society's deep commitment to the gender system, conditioning tends to go further by rewarding behaviours that are in line with gender norms and punishing those that deviate from these norms. Over the centuries, masculinity became indistinguishable from men and femininity from women, leading us to confound sex with gender.

The third layer of error, which follows directly from the second error and which remains obscure to most, is that we attribute behaviours observed in women and men to their sex rather than, more accurately, to their gendered femininity and masculinity. Given gender indoctrination that women are feminine and men are masculine and the relentless conditioning of women to be feminine and men to be masculine, it is not surprising that experiments of sex differences consistently show those differences to exist along gendered lines. However, social scientists invariably misinterpret these results as differences between women and men *per se*, when they merely reflect differences between femininity, which is dominant in women, and masculinity, which is dominant in men.

Because half a revolution of liberating women from subordination has started half a century ago, women have been attempting to reclaim their masculine, but only half heartedly. They are stopped in doing so by the total and utter confusion surrounding masculinity and femininity. The confusion doesn't only come from assuming that women are only feminine, otherwise they are not *real* women, and men are only masculine, otherwise they are not *real* men. But also from seeing the masculine as all powerful, effective, and authoritative, and ignoring its underside of overdrive, violence, not least against women, and even death and destruction when left untempered with the feminine. And from seeing the feminine as powerless, weak and ineffective, and ignoring its power of birthing life into this world, of the amazing strength of its compassion and the genius of its intuition.

Built into this confusion is mistaking the conditioned, gendered feminine for the real feminine. The conditioned feminine is 'pretty', 'sexy', 'emotional', 'weak', 'ineffective', and so on, all of which attributes are necessary for the gender project to succeed in convincing women to seek men's protection, to find husbands and to look after their children. The real life birthing feminine on the other hand is extremely powerful, with its power derived mainly from its ability to give and receive love, the highest and most sought after emotion in all humans and without which life would desist.

In order for women to be powerful, therefore, they need first to reclaim the power inherit in their life giving and life sustaining femininity, as well as embrace and strengthen the masculine of self-assertion and self-expression. Compassion is made all the more powerful when combined with assertiveness, because it "helps you feel comfortable giving compassion, since you know your needs will be met."[621] For men to be more powerful, they need to relinquish their pseudo power that comes without, power over others, and embrace their power within: the feminine powers of love, compassion and care for others, as well as embracing the masculine powers of self-confidence, inner strength and accomplishment.

None of these things are achievable if society doesn't change its mind about collapsing the masculine with men and success and holding it as the gold standard, and collapsing the feminine with women and care and denigrating it to a lower status. Contemporary societies assign a higher value to competition and drive, and a lower value to compassion and care. They believe in the supremacy of rationality over intuition and of paid work over unpaid care. This hierarchy of values makes it difficult for men to embrace anything feminine, fearing the loss of their status, power and prestige. Given these societal values, men believe the 'weak' and 'ineffective' feminine will stop them from fulfilling the masculine project: winning wars, cornering stock markets, rising to the top of organisations, and so on.

---

[621] Hanson Mendius, 2009: 137.

Women too have been misguided about the feminine. As androcentricity remains the norm in the workplace, career oriented women, particularly high achieving women, have thought it necessary to abandon or neglect their femininity. They are encouraged in doing so by the negative images of the gendered feminine, which are highly incompatible with success and which are a mere shadow of the all powerful feminine. Instead, many women have fully embraced the gendered masculine, in order to strive hard, compete and succeed in public life.

So it seems that owning and honouring the awesome feminine by both women and men is a key first step in fighting sexism. A necessary condition to embracing the feminine is de-gendering femininity, and seeing its highly conditioned version for what it is: a vehicle to denigrate women and care and sustain their lower status in society; a vehicle, in other words, for sexism.

The road back to womanhood, to remember what it is to be a woman, is therefore quiet tricky. Women need first to recognise that they have been emulating men's way in order to succeed, and to acknowledge that this is part and parcel of our conditioning and is therefore not the only way to succeed. Women need to change their mind about what does it mean to be feminine. Femininity has been gendered beyond recognition, therefore it takes considerable courage for woman to cut through the fog and recognise their femininity in their own way. Embracing the awesome feminine will allow women to embrace the power they already have, the power within. They may find as they do so that their life purpose goes well beyond raising a family or supporting their husbands. It may include being an artist, a teacher or a surgeon. It may be writing a novel or becoming politically active. It may very well include serving humanity, and maybe even on a large scale. Women need to find a way in their own hearts to remember who they are as women and what their real life purpose is, in order for them to feel fulfilled.

Importantly, women will not be able to fulfil their life purpose without embracing the masculine of accomplishment, action, focus, and making things happen. Masculinity too has been gendered beyond recognition, to suit the ethos of capitalist production. In our contemporary societies, masculinity has become hard driving and uncompassionate. Excluding femininity from men's personalities is part and parcel of gender conditioning, and has pushed men to adopt highly uncaring masculinities in order to succeed. The real masculine on the other hand, has powers that go beyond command and control, and beyond naked greed and competition. The masculine is intended to be a real force of creation in life, rather than a force of domination, violence and cruelty that has destroyed rather than created life on our planet, including the planet itself. Women will do well in life to embrace the masculine that was never intended to exist on its own without the feminine. It is only the gender system that imposed this prohibition, in order to create male dominated societies.

So it seems that masculinity too needs to be de-conditioned in order to abolish the gender system. The high achieving, super competitive, even ruthless and certainly 'uncaring' masculinity is born out of our drive to achieve. These are the masculine attributes that are needed in order for the capitalist project to succeed. What is in common between all these attributers is excess, which is born out of eliminating the socialising, humanising feminine. The true masculine does espouse accomplishment, initiative, steadfastness, perseverance, leadership, intellect and so on, all of which are highly conducive to success, but perhaps not cut throat success, not the kind of success that comes at a price to others, such as relegating women to a lower status.

The feminine traits of compassion, intuition, introspection and inclusion need to be embraced not only in ourselves but also by institutions, businesses and governments and by society at large. These attributes need to be consciously brought into every public decision making process, to avoid unnecessary wars and stock market crashes. Our current deep discontent is partly due to disowning this significant aspect of our humanity, which is why life is increasingly experienced as hard. We have exulted the capitalist version of the masculine and espoused it in all aspects of our personalities and our lives; we have become so hard driving that life has become hard.

By acknowledging that the gender system we created is not only dysfunctional, as it has not kept pace with the change in our *stated* social values of equality, it is totally unnecessary. Put differently, there is no need to fix the gender system, but there is an urgent need to abandon it. The gender system is a mere construction of the mind that was intended to guide us through the *apparently* complex issues of love, commitment, sex and babies. But we mistook the map for the real territory. We live our lives as if the gendered self that we created in our minds is the truth, instead of the myth, of who we are. We believed the roles created within the gender system are those that women and men are meant to fulfil on this earth. And like the good actors we are, we whole heartedly embraced the traits, attributes, behaviour, dispositions and even emotionality of the characters we are merely acting out. We constructed ourselves as highly gendered beings and we believed that is the entirety of who we are. Our minds and bodies fulfilled the myth by creating the physiology, the emotionality and the behaviour that are congruent with our mental constructions, but not with who we truly are.

Inevitably, our unbounded human nature yearns for the truth and our now endemic unhappiness is the sign that it is time to free ourselves of these mental shackles and to awaken ourselves out of this gender nightmare. Breaking away from the bondage of mental construction is already happening in some areas of our gendered lives, most notably marriage and sexuality. Abandoning heterosexuality as the norm is probably the most advanced rebellion against the gender system, although total liberation is by no means achieved. Similarly, abandoning the highly gendered way in which we constructed marriage as the only valid template for family life is well on its way. So our enlightenment is going piecemeal about deconstructing those areas of our lives that are most restrictive of true self expression and personal power. It is time now to see the gender system as the artefact that it is and abolish it at once. This will not lead to chaos, but to more order. Instead of a mother spending her life being a 'good mother' and fearing social condemnation when she veers away from the prescriptions of idealised mothering, she can simply mother her children in any way she finds fulfilling, joyous and fun which are the telltale signs of being true to oneself. Similarly, instead of a man spending his life being a 'good provider', working long hours and hardly spending any family time, he can simply ask himself what kind of work would be in line with his authentic self? What would fulfil him as a person? What is his passion in life? It is been said often enough, 'follow your passion and money/success will follow you.'

We are conditioned to reject the feminine in men and the masculine in women. However, men who embrace femininity don't become 'effeminate', allowing love and compassion instead gives men an awakened heart: they are neither afraid to give or receive love. They become wonderful fathers, compassionate husbands and attentive lovers. Their personal relationships become rich and fulfilling. Women who embrace the masculine don't become 'butch', allowing self-focus and taking action gives women an edge in life. They are no longer afraid to succeed and accomplish big things. Allowing the masculine to balance the feminine makes women's personal relationships rich and fulfilling, as they are not only giving but are now allowing themselves to receive love and attention.

What women, and men, want is fulfilment through life accomplishments, the route to which is not only different for women from men but for every individual. Sex has nothing to do with it. Fulfilment or self-actualisation is a very personal project, but when we live our lives as if the personal is political, when we wait for governments, thinkers, religious leaders, feminists, gay liberation activists to tell us how to live our lives, we lose touch with who we are and what our personal project is.

The truth about sexism is that the feminine has been silenced in all of us, women and men, for far too long. With women deemed feminine and men masculine, this has been akin to silencing women's truth. Women have been attempting for quite some time to find their truth, the truth of who they really are and what they really want but we have gone astray, thinking that their truth may lie in being masculine and succeeding in life like a man, or, at the other extreme, it may lie in being 'feminine' and dancing in men's laps. But with the real feminine still silenced, women have not yet spoken their truth. With the real feminine still silent, androcentricity rules our life.

Succeeding in public life by eschewing quality family life is androcentric. Dancing in men's laps is the ultimate androcentric standard, it is the epitome of success of the gender project, where women are nothing without men, without their money and without their patronage.

It is time for each woman to find her real feminine, to unearth the power that lies dormant within her, and to unleash it on the world to do much needed good: to feed the hungry, to stop wars and civil strife, to stop domestic violence and so on. It is time for every woman to speak Her own truth, the truth of what She wants, the truth of who She is; it is for no one else to say.

BIBLIOGRAPHY

Allport, G. W., 1954, *The Nature of Prejudice*. Cambridge, MA: Addison-Wesley.

Anderson, D., Vinnicombe, S., and Singh, V., 2010, Women partners leaving the firm: choice, what choice?, *Gender in Management: An International Journal*, 25 (3), 170-183.

Apelbaum, E. et al., 2002, *Shared Work/Valued Care: New Norms for Organising Market Work and Unpaid Care Work*, Institute of Economic Policy.

Archer, J., and Lloyd, B., 2002. *Sex and Gender*, Cambridge: Cambridge University Press.

Aronson, J. et al., 1999, When white men can't do math: necessary and sufficient factors in stereotype threat, *Journal of Experimental Social Psychology*, 35 (1), 29–46.

Aronson, J., Fried, C. B., and Good, C., 2002, Reducing the effects of stereotype threat on African American college students by shaping theories of intelligence, *Journal of Experimental Social Psychology*, 38 (2), 113-125.

Arulampalam, W., Booth, A. L. and Bryan, M. L., 2004, *Are there asymmetries in the effects of training on the conditional male wage distribution?*, London: Centre for Economic Policy Research.

Austin, L., 2000, *What Is Holding You Back? 8 Critical Choices for Women's Success*, New York: Basic books.

Ayers, M. Y., 2011, *Masculine Shame: From Succubus to the Eternal Feminine*, London and New York: Routledge.

Babcock, L, and Laschever, S., 2008, *Why Women Don't Ask: The High Cost of Avoiding Negotiations - and Positive Strategies For Change*, London: Piatkus.

Baggini, J., 2011, *The Ego Trick*, London: Granta.

Bakan D., 1966, *The Duality of Human Existence: An Essay on Psychology and Religion*, Boston: Beacon Press.

Ballou, M. and Brown, L. S., (ed.), 2002, *Rethinking Mental Health and Disorder, Feminist Perspective*, New York; London: Guilford Press.

Baron-Cohen, S., 2004, *The Essential Difference: Male and Female Brains and the Truth About Autism*, New York: Basic Books.

Barron, L. A. 2003, Ask and you shall receive? Gender differences in negotiators' beliefs about requests for a higher salary, *Human Relations*, 56 (6), 635-662.

Bassanini, A. and Duval, R., 2006, *Employment patterns in OECD countries: reassessing the roles of policies and institutions*, OECD Economics Department Working Paper No. 486.

Bass, B. M., and Bass, R., 2008, *The Bass Handbook of Leadership: Theory, Research, and Managerial Applications*, New York; London: Free Press.

Bass, B. M., and Riggio, R. E., 2006, *Transformational Leadership*, Mahwah, N.J.; London: Lawrence Erlbaum Associates.

Baxter, J., 2000, Barriers to equality, men's and women's attitudes to workplace entitlements in Australia, *Journal of Sociology*, 36 (1), 12-29.

Baxter, J., and Wright, E. O., 2000, The glass ceiling hypothesis: a comparative study of the United States, Sweden and Australia, *Gender and Society*, 14 (2) 275-294.

Bem, S. L., 1974, The measurement of psychological androgyny, *Journal of Consulting and Clinical Psychology*, 42 (2), 155-162.

Bern, S. L., 1975, Sex role adaptability: one consequence of psychological androgyny, *Journal of Personality and Social Psychology*, 31(4), 634-43.

Benko, C., and Weisberg, A., 2007, *Mass Career Customization*, Boston, Massachusetts: Harvard Business School Press.

Bennett, K. M., 2007, No sissy stuff: toward a theory of masculinity and emotional expression in older widowed men, *Journal of Aging Studies*, 21 (4), 347-356.

Berger, J. et al., 1966, characteristic and expectations states, in Berger, J., Zelditch, Jr. M. and Anderson, B., (ed.) *Sociological Theories in Progress*, Boston: Houghton Mifflin.

Birksted-breen, D., (ed.), 1993, *The Gender Conundrum: Contemporary Psychoanalytic Perspectives on Femininity and Masculinity*, Hove and New York: Brunner and Routledge.

Blanchard, K., Carlos, J. P., and Randolph, A., 2001, *Empowerment Takes More Than a Minute*, San Francisco, California, [Great Britain]: Berrett-Koehler.

Blanchard, K., Carlos, J. P., and Randolph, A., 1999, *The 3 Keys to Empowerment: Release the Power Within People for Astonishing Results*, San Fransico: Berrett-Koehler Publishers; London: McGraw-Hill (distributor).

Blazina, C., 1997, "The fear of the feminine in the western psyche and the masculine task of dissidentification: their effect on the development of masculine gender role conflict", *Journal of mens studies*, 6 (1), 55-68.

Block, H. J., 1984, *Sex Role Identity and Ego Development*, San Francisco: Jossey-Bass.

Blyton, P., and Dastmalchian, A., 2006, Work-life integration and the changing context of work, in Blyton, P. et al. (ed.), *Work-life Integration: International Perspectives on The Balancing of Multiple Roles*, Basingstoke: Palgrave Macmillan.

Booth, A. et al., 2006, The linking of sociology and biology testosterone and social behavior, *Social Forces*, 85(1), 166-192.

Booth, A., Johnson, D. R., and Granger, D. A., 2005, Testosterone, marital quality, and role overload, *Journal of Marriage and the Family*, 67 (2), 483-498.

Borysenko, J., 1996, *The Woman's Book of Life: The Biology, Psychology and Spirituality of the Feminine Life Cycle*, New York: Riverhead Books.

Borysenko, J., 2013, Interviewing Bruce Lipton for Hay House World Summit, 2013, http://hhfiles.edgesuite.net/hhus/audio/worldsummit2013/060913/11_Bruce_H._Lipton_Ph.D._interviewed_by_Joan_Borysenko.mp3?_token_=1396993679_72f95632f8a7b444afab9d06925adf62.

Brandth, B., and Kvande, E., 1998, Masculinity and child care: the reconstruction of fathering, *The Sociological Review*, 46 (2), 293-313.

Brown, B., 2011, *The Power of Vulnerability*, http://www.youtube.com/watch?v=iCvmsMzlF7o; accessed on May 15, 2013.

Burke, R. J., and Fiksenbaum, L., 2009, Are managerial women in "extreme jobs" disadvantaged? *Gender in Management: An International Journal*, 24 (1), 5-13.

Burke, R., and Vinnicombe, S., 2005, Advancing women's careers, *Career Development International*, 10 (3): 165-167.

Burnett, S. B. et al., 2010, Well-balanced families?: a gendered analysis of work-life balance policies and work family practices, *Gender in Management*, 25 (7), 534-549.

Byron, K., 2008, Differential effect of male and female managers' non-verbal emotional skills on employees' ratings, *Journal of Managerial Psychology*, 23 (2), 118-134.

Cahill, L. et al., 2004, The influence of sex versus sex-related traits on long-term memory for gist and detail from an emotional story, *Consciousness and Cognition*, 13 (2), 391-400.

Catalyst, 1998, *Women Entrepreneurs: Why Companies Lose Female Talent and What They Can Do About It*, New York.

Catalyst, 2004, *The Bottom Line Connecting Corporate Performance and Gender Diversity*, New York.

Catalyst, 2006, *Different Cultures, Similar Perceptions: Stereotypes of West European Business Leaders*, New York.

Chodorow, J. N., 1994, *Femininities, Masculinities, Sexualities: Freud and Beyond*, London: Free Association Books.

Chodorow, J. N., 1999, *The Reproduction of Mothering: Psychoanalysis and the Sociology of Gender*, London: University of California Press.

Clausen, J. A., (ed.), 1968, *Socialization and Society*, Boston: Little, Brown & Co.

Cohany, S. R., and Sok, E., 2007, Trends in labor force participation of married mothers of infants, Monthly labor review, U.S. Department of Labor, Bureau of Labor Statistics, 130 (2), 9-16.

Coltrane, S., 1996, *Family Man: Fatherhood, Housework, and Gender*, Oxford: Oxford University Press.

Coltrane, S., 2000, Research on household labour: modelling and measuring the social embeddedness of routine family work, *Journal of Marriage and Family*, 62 (4) 1208-1233.

Conahghan, J., and Rittich, K., (ed.), 2005, *Labour Law Work and Family, Critical and Comparative Perspective*, Oxford: Oxford University Press.

Connell, R. W., 1987, *Gender and Power: Society, The Person and Sexual Politics*, Cambridge: Polity in association with Blackwell.

Connell, R. W., 1995, *Masculinities*, Cambridge: Polity Press.

Connell, R. W., 2002, *Gender*, Oxford: Polity: Blackwell Publishers.

Connell, R. W., 2005, *Masculinities*, 2nd edition, Cambridge: Polity Press.

Connell, R. W., 2009, *Gender: In World Perspective*, Cambridge: Polity Press.

Crompton, R., and Lyonette, C., 2007, Occupational class, country and the domestic division of labour, in Crompton, R., Lewis, S., and Lyonette, C., (ed.), *Women, Men, Work and Family in Europe*, Basingstoke: Palgrave Macmillan.

Cross, S. E., and Madson, L., 1997, Models of the self: self-construals and Gender, *Psychological bulletin*, 122 (1), 5-37.

Damasio, A. R., 2008, *Descartes' Error : Emotion, Reason and the Human Brain*, London: Random House (Kindle Edition).

Damasio, A. R. et al., 2004, Emotions and feelings: a neurobiological perspective, *Feelings and emotions: The Amsterdam Symposium; Amsterdam, The Netherlands*, June, 49-57, Cambridge: Cambridge University Press.

Davison, H. K., and Burke, M. J., 2000, Sex discrimination in simulated employment contexts: a meta-analytic investigation, *Journal of Vocational Behaviour*, 56 (2), 225-248.

David, M. and Starzec, C., 1992, Women and part time work: France and Great Britain compared, in Folbre, N. et al., (ed.), *Women's Work in the World Economy*, New York: New York University Press.

Deacon, T., 2012, http://www.dnafiles.org/chimp-chat/day-four.

DeHenau, J., 2007, *Investigating the Desperate Housewives: Using Gender-Role Attitudes to Explain Women's Employment Decisions in Twenty Three European Countries*, Milton Keynes: Open University.

Denmark, F. L. et al., 1996, Women, work, and family: mental health issues, *Annals of the New York Academy of Sciences*, 789 (1): 101-118.

Desmarais, S. and Curtis, J., 1997, Gender and perceived pay entitlement: testing for effects of experience with income, *Journal of Personality and Social Psychology*, 72 (1), 141-150.

Devine, P., G., 1989, Stereotypes and prejudice: their automatic and controlled components, *Journal of Personality and Social Psychology*, 56 (1), 5-18.

Dex, S., 1986, *Women's Occupational Mobility: A Lifetime Perspective*, London: Macmillan.

Dex, S., and Bukodi, E., 2010, *The Effects of Part-time Work on Women's Occupational Mobility in Britain: Evidence from the 1958 Birth Cohort Study*, Centre for Longitudinal Studies, Institute of Education, University of London.

Dispenza, J., 2012, *Breaking the Habit of Being Yourself: How to Lose Your Mind and Create a New One*, London; New York: Hay House (Kindle Edition).

Dispenza, J., 2013, interview for Hay House World Summit 2013: http://hhfiles.edgesuite.net/hhus/audio/worldsummit2013/060813/48_Joe_Dispenza_interviewed_by_Michael_Neill.mp3?_token_=1398610075_14c223672461122b8313fb4f545e8c39.

Doucet, A., and Merla, L., 2007, Stay-at-home fathering, *Community, Work and Family*, 10 (4), 455-473.

Drucker, P. F., 1974, *Management: Tasks, Responsibilities, Practices*, New York: Harper & Row.

Dyer, W. W., 2004, *The Power of Intention*, Carlsbad, Ca; London; Sydney: Hay House Inc. (Kindle Edition).

Eagly, A. H., 1987, *Sex Differences in Social Behavior: A Social Role Interpretation*, Hillsdale, N. J.: Lawrence Erlbaum.

Eagly, A. H., 1995, The science and politics of comparing women and men, *American Psychologist*, 50 (3), 145-58.

Eagly, A. H., 1997, Sex differences in social behaviour: comparing social roles theory and evolutionary psychology, *American Psychologist*, 52 (1), 1380-1383.

Eagly, A. H., 2007, Female leadership advantage and disadvantage: resolving the contradictions, *Psychology of Women Quarterly*, 31 (1), 1-12.

Eagly, A. H., and Carli, L. L., 2007, *Through the Labyrinth: the Truth about How Women Become Leaders*, Boston: Harvard Business School Press.

Eagly, A. H., Johannesen-Schmidt M. C., and van Engen, M. L., 2003, Transformational, transnational and laissez-faire leadership styles: A meta-analysis comparing women and men, *Psychological Bulletin*, 129 (4), 569-591.

Eagly, A. H. and Karau, S. J., 1991, Gender and the emergence of leaders: a meta-analysis, *Journal of Personality and Social Psychology*, 60 (5), 685-7 10.

Eagly A. H., and Wood, W., 2009, Sexual selection does not provide an adequate theory of sex differences in aggression, *Behavioural and Brain Science*, 32 (3/4), 276-277.

Eagly, A. H., Wood, W., and Diekman, A. B., 2000, Social role theory of sex differences and similarities: a current appraisal, in Eckes, T., and Trautner, H. M., (ed.), *The Developmental Social Psychology of Gender*, Mahwah, N.J.; London: Erlbaum.

Eisenegger, C. et al., 2010, Prejudice and truth about the effect of testosterone on human bargaining behaviour, *Nature*, 463 (7279), 356-359.

Eliot, L., 2009, *Pink Brain, Blue Brain: How Small Differences Grow Into Troublesome Gaps and What we Can do About it*, Boston; New York: Houghton Mifflin Harcourt.

Elliot, J. R., and Smith, R. A., 2004, Race, gender and workplace power, *American Sociological Review*, 69 (3), 365-386.

Elster, J., 2009, *Reason and Rationality*, Princeton; oxford: Princeton University Press.

Epstein, M., and Ward, M. L., 2011, Exploring parent-adolescent communication about gender: results from adolescent and emerging adult samples, *Sex Roles*, 65 (1/2), 108-118.

Estes, Z., and Felker, S., 2012, Confidence mediates the sex difference in mental rotation performance, *Archives of Sexual Behaviour*, 41 (3), 557-570.

Federal Glass Ceiling Commission, 1995, *Good for Business: Making Full Use of the Nation's Human Capital*, Washington, D.C.: U.S. Department of Labor.

Feingold, A., 1988, Cognitive gender differences are disappearing, *American Psychologist*, 43 (2), 95-103.

Fine, B., 1992, *Women's Employment and the Capitalist Family*, London: Routledge.

Fine, C., 2010, *Delusions of Gender: The Real Science behind Sex Differences*, London: Icon Books.

Fine-Davis, M. et al., 2004, *Fathers and Mothers: Dilemmas of the Work-Life Balance: A Comparative Study in Four European Countries*, Dordrecht; London: Kluwer Academic.

Ford, D., 2011, *The Dark Side of the Light Chasers: Reclaiming Your Power, Creativity, Brilliance and Dreams*, London: Hodder & Stoughton.

Frenette, M., 2011, How does the stork delegate work? childbearing and the gender division of paid and unpaid labour, *Journal of Population Economics*, 24 (3), 895-910.

Folbre, N. et al., 1992, *Women's Work in the World Economy*, New York: New York University Press.

Friedman, S. D., Christenssen, P. and Degroot, J., 2000, Work and Life: the end of the zero sum game, in *Harvard Business Review on Work and Life Balance*, Harvard: Harvard Business School Press.

Friedman, S. D., and Greenhaus, J. H., 2000, *Work and Family-Allies or Enemies? What Happens When Business Professionals Confront Life Choices*, Oxford: University Press.

Geis, F., 1993, Self-fulfilling perspectives: a social psychological view of gender, in Beall, E. A., and Sternberg, J., R., (ed.), *The Psychology of Gender*, New York; London: Guilford press.

Gilgun, J. F., 2012, *Neurobiology, Trauma, and Child Development*, Jane Gilgun Books (Kindle Edition).

Glenn, N., Chang, G., and Rennie Forcey, L., (ed.), 1994, *Mothering: Ideology, Experience, and Agency (Perspectives on Gender)*, New York; London: Routledge.

Goldin, C., and Rouse, C., 2000, Orchestrating impartiality: the impact of "blind" auditions on female musicians, *The American Economic Review*, 90 (4), 715-741.

Good, C., Aronson, J., and Harder, J. A., 2008, Problems in the pipeline: Stereotype threat and women's achievement in high-level math courses, *Journal of Applied Developmental Psychology*, 29 (1), 17-28.

Gorman, E.H., and Kmec, J. A., 2009, Hierarchical rank and women's organizational mobility: glass ceilings in corporate law firms, *The American Journal of Sociology*, 114 (5), 1428-1474.

Graddy, D. B., 2006, Gender salience and the use of linguistic qualifiers and intensifiers in online course discussions, *American Journal of Distance Education*, 20 (4), 211-229.

Graham, D., and Cullen, C., (ed.), 1988, *Human Operant Conditioning and Behavior Modification*, Chischester: Wiley.

Greenwald, A. G., and Banaji, M. R., 1995, Implicit social cognition: Attitudes, self-esteem, and stereotypes, *Psychological Review*, 102 (1), 4 – APA.

Gregg, P., and Wadsworth, J., 2011, (ed.), *Labour Market in Winter: The State of Working Britain*, Oxford: Oxford University Press.

Grossman, M., and Wood, W., 1993, Sex differences in intensity of emotional experience: a social role interpretation, *Journal of Personality and Social Psychology*, 65 (5), 1010-1022.

Haas, L., 1992, *Equal Parenthood and Social Policy: A Study of Parental Leave in Sweden*, Albany, New York: State University of New York Press.

Hakim, C., 1998, *Social Change and Innovation in the Labour Market*, Oxford: Oxford University Press.

Halpern, D. F., and Cheung, F. M., 2008, *Women at the Top: Powerful Leaders Tell Us How To C Work and Family*, Oxford: Wiley-Blackwell.

Halpern, D. F., and Murphy, S. M., (ed.), 2005, *From Work-Family Balance to Work-Family Integration: Changing the Metaphor*, Kravis-deRoulet Leadership Conference (13th: 2002: Claremont McKenna College) Mahwah, N.J.; London: Lawrence Erlbaum.

Halpern, D. F., 2011, *Sex Differences in Cognitive Abilities*, New York, NY; Hove: Taylor & Francis (Kindle Edition).

Hamilton, D. R., 2010, *How Your Mind Can Heal Your Body*, London; New York: Hay House (Kindle Edition).

Hamilton, D. R., 2013, Interview with Michael Neil for Hay House World Summit, 2013, http://hhfiles.edgesuite.net/hhus/audio/worldsummit2013/060713/19_David_R._Hamilton,_Ph.D._interviewed_by_Michael_Neill.mp3?_token_=1377340228_f887989625568d99b2bdc0844c656ce3.

Hanson, R., and Mendius, R., 2009, *Buddha's Brain: The Practical Neuroscience of Happiness, Love and Wisdom*, Oakland, Ca: New Harbinger Publication (Kindle Edition).

Harris, M. J. et al., 1994, Mediation of interpersonal expectancy effects: expectancies about the elderly, *Social Psychology Quarterly*, 57 (1), 36-48.

Haas, L., 1992, *Equal Parenthood and Social Policy: A Study of Parental Leave in Sweden*, Albany, NY: State University of New York Press.

Hayman, J., 2009, Flexible work arrangements: exploring the linkages between perceived usability of flexible work schedules and work/life balance, *Community, Work and Family*, 12 (3), 327-338.

Heilman, M. E., and Eagly, A. H., 2008, Gender Stereotypes Are Alive, Well, and Busy Producing Workplace Discrimination, *Industrial and Organizational Psychology : Perspectives on Science and Practice*, 1 (4), 393-398.

Hekman, D. R. et al., 2010, An examination of whether and how racial and gender biases influence customer satisfaction, *Academy of Management Journal*, 53 (2), 238-264.

Hilliard, L. J., and Liben, L. S., 2010, Differing levels of gender salience in preschool classrooms: effects on children's gender attitudes and intergroup bias, *Child Development*, 81 (6), 1787-1798.

Hindin, M. J., 2007, Role theory, in Ritzer, G., (ed.), *The Blackwell Encyclopaedia of Sociology*, Blackwell Publishing.

Hogue, M., and Yoder, J. D., 2003, The role of status in producing depressed entitlement in women's and men's pay allocations, *Psychology of Women Quarterly*, 27 (4), 330-337.

Holstein, J. A., and Gubrium, J., F., 1999, *The Self We Live By: Narrative Identity in a Postmodern World*, New York, NY; Oxford: Oxford University Press, USA.

Hood, B., 2012, *The self Illusion*, London: Constable.

Hugkah, K., Berardi, A., Thomoins, W. L., Kosslyn, S. M., Alpert, N. M. And leDoux J. E., 1995, Brain mechanisms in human classical conditioning: a PET blood flow study, N*euroeport*, 6 (13), 1723-1728.

Institute for Women's Policy Research, 2011, *The Gender Wage Gap: 2009*, http://www.iwpr.org/search?submit.x=27&sort_order=ascending&b_start:int=90&SearchableText=gender%20wage%20gap&submit.y=13 (retrieved March 3rd, 2012).

Iversen, T., and Rosenbluth, F., 2010, *Women, Work and Politics, The Political Economy of Gender Inequality*, New Haven and London: Yale University Press (Kindle Edition).

Jackson, C., 2003, Motives for 'laddishness' at school: fear of failure and fear of the 'feminine', *British Educational Research Journal*, 29 (4), 583-598.

Jenkins, S., 2004, *Gender, Place and the Labour Market*, Aldershot: Ashgate.

Jost, J. T., 1997, An experimental replication of the depressed-entitlement effect among women, *Psychology of Women Quarterly*, 21 (3): 387-394.

Jost, J. T., and Banaji, M. R., 1994, The role of stereotyping in system justification and the production of false consciousness, *British Journal of Social Psychology*, 33 (1): 1-7.

Judge, T. A. and Piccolo, R. F., 2004, Transformational and transactional leadership, a meta analytic test of their relative validity, *The Journal of Applied Psychology*, 89 (5): 755-768.

Kamerman, S. B., and Moss, P., (ed.), 2009, *The Politics of Parental Leave Policies, Children, Parenting, Gender and the Labour Market*, Bristol: The Policy Press.

Kark, R., Waismel-Manor, R., and Shamir, B., 2012, Does valuing androgyny and femininity lead to a female advantage? The relationship between gender-role, transformational leadership and identification, *The Leadership Quarterly*, 23 (3), 620-640.

Katz, D., and Braly, K. W., 1935, Racial prejudice and racial stereotypes, *Journal of* Abnormal and Social Psychology, 30 (2), 175-193.

Kierski, W., 2007, Men and the fear of the feminine, self-*and Society*, 34 (5), 27-33.

Kirby, R. et al., 2011, First word: the trouble with men, *Trends in Urology and Men's Health*, 2 (1), 4-4.

Kolb, D. M., 2004, *Her Place at the Table: A Woman's Guide to Negotiating Five Key Challenges to Leadership Success*, San Francisco, Ca; [Great Britain]: Jossey-Bass.

Kupper, B., and Zick, A., 2011, Inverse gender gap in Germany: social dominance orientation among men and women, *International Journal of Psychology*, 46 (1), 33-45.

Lazarus, R. S. 1991, *Emotion and Adaptation*, New York; Oxford: Oxford University Press.

Lazarus, R. S., and Lazarus, B. N., 1994, *Passion and Reason*, New York; Oxford: Oxford University Press.

Le Feuvre, N., 2010, Feminising professions in Britain and France: how countries differ, in Scott, J., Crompton, R. and Lyonette, C., (ed.), *Gender Inequalities In The 21ˢᵗ Century: New Barriers and Continuing Constraints*, Cheltenham: Edward Elgar.

Lefkowitz, E. S., and Zeldo, P. B., 2006, Masculinity and femininity predict optimal mental health: a belated test of the androgyny hypothesis, *Journal of Personality Assessment*, 87 (1), 95-101.

Lenton, A. P., Bruder, M., and Sedikides, C., 2009, Meta-analysis on the malleability of automatic gender stereotypes, *Psychology of Women Quarterly*, 33 (2), 183-196.

Lewis, S., and Smithson, J., 2006, *Final Report on the Project "Gender, Parenthood and the Changing European Workplace: Young Adults Negotiating the Work-Family Boundary"*, Manchester: RIHSC: The Research Institute for Health and Social Change.

Lippa, R. A., Collaer, M. L., and Peters, M., 2010, Sex differences in mental rotation and line angle judgments are positively associated with gender equality and economic development across 53 nations, *Archives of Sexual Behavior*, 39 (4), 990-997.

Lipton, B. H., 2008, *The Biology of Beliefs: Unleashing the Power of Consciousness, Matter, and Miracles*, London; New York: Hay House (Kindle Edition).

Lipton, B. H., 2013, Interview with Joan Borysenko for Hay House World Summit, 2013, http://hhfiles.edgesuite.net/hhus/audio/worldsummit2013/060913/11_Bruce_H._Lipton_Ph.D._interviewed_by_Joan_Borysenko.mp3?_token_=1396993679_72f95632f8a7b444afab9d06925adf62.

Lipton, B. H., and Bhaerman, S., 2009, *Spontaneous Evolution: Our Positive Future (and a Way to Get There from Here*, London; New York: Hay House (Kindle Edition).

Lyness, K. S. and Heilman, M. E., 2006, When fit is fundamental: performance evaluations and promotions of upper-level female and male managers, *The Journal of Applied Psychology*, 91 (4), 777-785.

Lyonette, C., and Crompton, R., 2008, The only way is up? An examination of women's "under-achievement" in the accountancy profession in the UK, *Gender In Management: An International Issue*, 23 (7), 506-521.

Madsen, S. R., 2005, *Work and Family Conflict: Does Home-Based Telework Make a Difference?* Utah Valley State College.

Major, B., 1994, From social inequality to personal entitlement: the role of social comparisons, legitimacy appraisal and group membership, in Berkowitz, L., (ed.), *Advances in Experimental and Social Psychology, Volume 26*, 293--New York: Academic Press Inc.

Maitland, A., and Thomson, P., 2011, *Future Work: How Businesses Can Adapt and Thrive In The New World Of Work*, Basingstoke: Palgrave, McMillan (Kindle Edition).

Marx, D. M., and Stapel, D. A., 2006, It's all in the timing: Measuring emotional reactions to stereotype threat before and after taking a test, *European Journal of Social Psychology*, 36 (5), 687-698.

Marx, D. M., Stapel, D. A., and Muller, D., 2005, We can do it: The interplay of construal orientation and social comparison under threat, *Journal of Personality and Social Psychology*, 88 (3), 432-446.

McCall, C. and Dasgupta, N., 2007, The malleability of men's gender self-concept, self-*and identity: the Journal of the International Society for self-and Identity*, 6 (2/3), 173-188.

McDowell, J. M., Singell, L. D., and Ziliak, J. P., 2001, Gender and promotion in the economics profession, *Industrial and Labor Relations Review*, 54 (2), 224-244.

McDowell, L., 1997, Capital Culture: Gender at Work in the City, Oxford: Blackwell.

McDowell, L. 2010, Capital culture revisited: sex, testosterone and the city, *International Journal of Urban and Regional Research*, 34 (3), 652-658.

McClelland, D. C. et al., 1976, *The Achievement Motive*, New York: Irvington; New York; London: Distributed by Wiley.

McGregor, D., 2005, *The Human Side of Enterprise*, Annotated Edition, New York; London: McGraw-Hill.

Melkas, H., and Anker, R., 1997, Occupational segregation by sex in Nordic countries: an empirical investigation, *International Labour Review*, 136 (3), 341-364.

Metz, I., 2005, Advancing the careers of women with children, *Career Development International*, 10 (3), 228-245.

Miles, E. W., and Clenney, E. F., 2010, Gender differences in negotiation: a status characteristics theory view, *Negotiation and Conflict Management Research*, 3 (2): 130-144.

Miller, J. B., 1986, *Toward a New Psychology of Woman*, Boston: Beacon Press.

Minnotte, K. L., 2012, Family structure, gender and the work-family interface: work-to-family conflict among single and partnered parents, *Journal of Family and Economic Issues*, 33 (1), 95-107.

Minnotte, K. L. et al., 2010, His and her perspectives: gender ideology, work-to-family conflict, and marital satisfaction, *Sex Roles*, 63 (5/6), 425 438.

Minsky, R., 1996, *Psychoanalysis and gender: an introductory reader*, London, New York: Routledge.

Moã, A., and Pazzaglia, F., 2006, Following in mental rotation, *Learning and individual differences*, 16 (4), 369-377.

Moore, D. P., and Buttner, E. H., 1997, Women's organizational exodus to entrepreneurship: self-reported motivations and correlates with success, *Journal of Small Business Management*, 35 (1), 34-46.

Morgan, D. H. J., 1992, *Discovering Men*, London: Routledge.

Morgan, E., 1972, *The Descent of Woman*, London: Corgi.

Mosley, H., O'Reilly, J., and Schömannand, K., edited, 2002, *Labour Markets, Gender and Institutional Change: Essays in Honour of Günther Schmid*, Cheltenham: Elgar.

Mowbray, C. T., Lanir, S., and Hulce, M., (ed.), 1985, *Women and Mental Health: New Directions for Change*, New York: Harrington Park Press.

Neumann, E., 1994, *The Fear of the Feminine and Other Essays on Feminine Psychology*, Princeton, N.J., Chichester: Princeton University Press.

Niederle, M. and Vesterlund, L., 2005, *Do women Shy Away From Competition? Do Men Compete Too Much?*, Working Paper Series No. 11474, National Bureau of Economic Research.

Oatley, K., Keltner, D. and Jenkins, J. M., 2006, *Understanding Emotions*, Cambridge, Mass.; Oxford: Blackwell publishing.

O'Brien, M., Brandth, B., and Kvande, E., 2007, Fathers, work and family life: global perspectives and new insights, *Community, Work and Family*, 10 (4), 375-386.

O'Brien, M. et al. 2007, Fathers, work and family life: global perspectives and new insights, *Community, Work and Family*, 10 (4), 375-386.

OECD, 2001, *Employment Outlook*, Paris: OECD Publication.

OECD, 2002, *Employment Outlook, Chapter 2, Women at work: who are they and how are they faring?*, Paris: OECD Publication.

OECD, 2006, *Social Indicators*, Paris: OECD Publication.

OECD, 2007a, *Babies and Bosses - Reconciling Work and Family Life, A Synthesis of Findings for OECD Countries*, Paris: OECD Publication.

OECD, 2007b, Mothers in Paid Employment, in *Society at a Glance, 2006: OECD Social Indicators*, Paris: OECD Publication.

OECD 2007c, *Employment Outlook*, Paris: OECD Publication.

OECD, 2007d: *Women And Men In OECD Countries*, Paris: OECD Publication.

OECD, (2008), *OECD Employment Outlook. Chapter 3: The Price of Prejudice: Labour Market Discrimination on the Grounds of Gender and Ethnicity*, Paris: OECD Publication.

OECD, 2011a, *Report on the Gender Initiative: Gender Equality in Education, Employment and Entrepreneurship*, Paris: OECD Publication.

OECD, 2011b, OECD *Family Database, LMF1.6 Gender differences in employment outcomes*, Paris: OECD Publication.

OECD, 2012a, *Labour Force Statistics by Sex and Age: indicators, OECD employment and labour Market Statistics (databases)*, Paris: OECD Publication.

OECD, 2012b, *OECD Family Database, LMF1.2: Maternal Employment rates*, Paris: OECD Publication.

OECD, 2014, *OECD Family Database*, Paris: OECD (www.oecd.org/social/family/database).

Olmstead, S., Futris, T. G., and Pasley, K., 2009, An exploration of married and divorced, nonresident men's perceptions and organisation of their father role identity, *Fathering: a Journal of Theory, Research, and Practice About Men as Fathers*, 7 (3), 249-268.

Olson, J. E., Frieze, I. H. and Good, D. C., 1987, The effects of job type and industry on the income of male and female MBAs, *Journal of Human Resources*, 22 (1), 532–41.

Osborne, J. W., 1995, Academics, self-esteem, and race: A look at the assumptions underlying the Disindentification hypothesis, *Personality and Social Psychology Bulletin*, 21 (5), 449-455.

Pagnan, C., Lero, D., and Macdermid Wadsworth, S., 2011, It doesn't always add up: examining dual-earner couples' decision to off shift, *Community, Work and Family*, 14 (3), 297-316.

Phelps, E. A., O'Connor K. J., Cunningham W. A., Funayama, E. S., Gatenby J. C., Gore J. C., and Banaji, M., R., 2000, Performance on indirect measures of race evaluation predicts amygdala activation, *Journal of Cognitive Neuroscience*, 12 (5), 729-738.

Pini, B., and McDonal, P., 2008, Men, masculinities and flexible work in local government, *Gender in Management*, 23 (8), 598-612.

Pissarides, C., Garibaldi, P., Olivetti, C., Petrongolo, B., and Wasmer, E., 2005, *Women in the Labour Force: How Well is Europe Doing?*, Conference paper, http://people.bu.edu/olivetti/papers/women.pdf.

Pizzagalli, D. A., Greischar, L. L., and Davidson, R. J., 2003, Spatio-temporal dynamics of brain mechanisms in aversive classical conditioning: high-density event-related potential and brain electrical tomography analyses, *Neuropsychologia*, 41 (2), 184-194.

Polity, 2004, *The Polity Reader in Gender Studies*, Cambridge: Polity Press.

Povinelli, D., 2012, *The DNA Files*, www.dnafiles.org/chimp-chat/day-four.

Prentice, D. A., and Carranza, E., 2002, What women should be, shouldn't be, are allowed to be, and don't have to be: the contents of prescriptive gender stereotypes. *Psychology of Women Quarterly*, 26 (4): 269–281.

Purcell, D., MacArther K. R., and Samblanet, S., 2010, Gender and the glass ceiling at work, *Sociology Compass*, 4 (9), 705-717.

Reeser, T. W., 2010, *Masculinities in Theory: An Introduction*, Chichester: Wiley-Blackwell.

Reid, S. A. et al., 2009, Gender, language, and social influence: a test of expectation states, role congruity, and self-categorization theories, *Human Communication Research*, 35 (4), 465-490.

Ridgeway, C. L., and Diekman, D., 1992, Are gender differences status differences?, in Ridgeway, C. L., (ed), *Gender, Interaction and Inequality*, New York; London: Springer-Verlag.

Riordan, C. M, 2013, Work-life "Balance" isn't the point, *HBR Blog Network*, http://blogs.hbr.org/cs/2013/06/work-life_balance_isnt_the_poi.html, 1:00 PM, June 4.

Robert, K., 2007, Work-life balance – the sources of the contemporary problem and the probable outcomes: a review and interpretation of the evidence, *Employee Relations*, 29 (4), 334-351.

Rohmann, A., and Rowold, J., 2009, Gender and leadership style: a field study in different organizational contexts in Germany, *Equal Opportunities International*, 28 (7), 545-560.

Rosenberg, M., 1989, *Society and The Adolescent Self-image*, Princeton: Princeton University Press.

Rosener, J. B., 1995, *America's Competitive Secret: Utilizing Women As A Management Strategy*, New York, Oxford: Oxford University Press.

Rosenthal, R. and Jacobosn, L., 1968, *Pygmalion in The Classroom*, New York: Holt, Rinehart and Winston.

Rowland, S., 2012, Book review, Ayers, M. Y. Masculine shame: from succubus to the eternal feminine, *Journal of Jungian Scholarly Studies* 7 (5).

Rubin, G., 1975, The traffic in women: notes on the 'political economy ' of sex, in Reiter, R. R., (ed.), *Toward An Anthropology of Women*, New York; London: Monthly Review Press.

Rudman, L., A., and Glick, P., 2008, *The social Psychology of Gender: How Power and Intimacy Shape Gender Relations*, New York, London: Guilford.

Rudman, L., and Greenwald, A., 2001, Implicit self-concept and evaluative implicit gender stereotypes: self-and in group share desirable traits, *Personality and Social Psychology Bulletin* 27 (9), 1164-78.

Sapolsky, R., 2011, The trouble with testosterone, in Spade, J. Z. and Valentine C., G. (ed.), *The Kaleidoscope of Gender, Prisms, Patterns and Possibilities*, Thousand Oaks, Ca: Sage Publication, Inc.

Scheff, T., 2003, Male emotions/relationships and violence: a case study, *Human Relations*, 56 (6), 635-62.

Schmader, T., and Johns, M., 2003, Converging evidence that stereotype threat reduces working memory capacity, *Journal of Personality and Social Psychology*, 85 (3), 440-452.

Schmader, T., Johns, M., and Barquissau, M., 2004, The costs of accepting gender differences: The role of stereotype endorsement in women's experience in the math domain, *Sex Roles*, 50 (11/12), 835-850.

Schucman, H., 2007, *A Course in Miracles: Foundation for Inner Peace*.

Schwartz, S. H., and Rubel, T., 2005, Sex differences in value priorities: cross-cultural and multimethod studies, *Journal of Personality and Social Psychology*. 89 (6), 1010-1028.

Schwartz, S. H., and Rubel, T., 2009, Cross-national variation in the size of sex differences in values: effects of gender equality, *Journal of Personality and Social Psychology*, 97 (1), 171-185.

Scott, J., Dex, S., and Joshi, H., (ed.), 2008, *Women and Employment: Changing Lives and New Challenges*, Cheltenham : Edward Elgar.

Scott, J. Dex, S. and Plagnol. A., 2012, (ed.), *Gendered Lives: Gender Inequalities in Production and Reproduction*, Cheltenham: Edward Elgar.

Seabright, P., 2012, *War of the Sexes: How Conflict and Cooperation have Shaped Men and Women from Prehistory to the Present*, Princeton, New Jersey; Woodstock: Princeton University Press.

Segal, L., 1990, *Slow Motion: Changing Masculinities, Changing Men*, London: Virago.

Seidler, V., 2003, *Rediscovering Masculinity: Reason, Language and Sexuality*, London: Routledge.

Seidler, V., 2006, *Transforming Masculinity, Men, Culture, Bodies, Power, sex and Love*, London: Routledge.

Sharon, R., C., and Sok, E., February 2007, Married mothers in the labour force, *Monthly Labour Review*, http://www.bls.gov/opub/mlr/2007/02/art2full.pdf.

Shockley, K., and Allen, T., 2012, Motives for flexible work arrangement use, *Community, Work and Family*. 15 (2), 217-231.

Shockley, K. M., and Allen, T. D., 2007, When flexibility helps: another look at the availability of flexible work arrangements and work-family conflict, *Journal of Vocational Behaviour*, 71 (3), 479-493.

Smithson, J., and Stokoe, E. H., 2005, Discourses of work-life balance: negotiating 'genderblind' terms in organizations, *Gender, Work and Organization*, 12 (2), 147-168.

Smith P. B., and Dugan, S., 1997, Locus of control and affectivity by gender and occupational status: a 14 nation study, *Sex Roles*, 36 (1/2), 51-78.

Spencer, S. J., Steele, C. M., and Quinn, D. M., 1999, Stereotype threat and women's math performance, *Journal of Experimental Social Psychology*, 35 (1), 4-28.

Steele, C. M., 1997, A threat in the air: How stereotypes shape intellectual identity and performance, *American Psychologist*, 52 (6), 613-629.

Steele, C. M., and Aronson, J., 1995, Stereotype threat and the intellectual test performance of African Americans, *Journal of Personality and Social Psychology*, 69 (5), 797 --.

Spence, J. T., and Helmreich, R. L., 1972, The attitudes toward women scale. *JSAS Catalog of Selected Documents in Psychology*, 2: MS 153.

Spence, J. T., and Helmreich, R. L, 1979, Comparison of masculine and feminine personality attributes and sex role attitudes across age groups, *Developmental Psychology*, 15 (5), 583-4.

Spence, J. T., Helmreich, R., and Stapp, J., 1974, The Personal Attributes questionnaire: a measure of sex role stereotypes and masculinity-femininity, *JSAS Catalog of Selected Documents in Psychology*, 4: 43 (MS 617).

Spence, J. T., Helmreich, R., and Stapp, J., 1975, Ratings of self- and peers on sex role attributes and their relation to self-esteem and conceptions of masculinity and femininity, *Journal of Personality and Social Psychology*, 32 (1), 29-39.

Stone, J., 2002, Battling doubt by avoiding practice: The Effect of stereotype threat on self-handicapping in white athletes, *Personality and Social Psychology Bulletin*, 28 (12), 1667-1678.

Strober, M. H., 1982, The MBA: same passport to success for men and women? In Wallace, P. A., (ed.), *Women In The Workplace*, Boston: Auburn House.

Swaffield, J. K., 2011, Gender and the labour market, in Gregg, P., and Wadsworth, J., (ed.), *The Labour Market in Winter, The State of Working Britain*, Oxford: Oxford University Press.

Taylor, S., A., 2006, *Quantum Success: The Astounding Science of Wealth*, Carlsbad, Ca; London: Hay House.

Tedlow, R., S. 2011, *Denial: Why Business Leaders Fail to Look Facts in The Face and What to Do About it*, London: Portfolio.

Thistle, S., 2006, *From Marriage to The Market: The Transformation of Women's Lives and Work*, Berkeley, Ca; London: University of California Press.

Thompson, E., and Varela, F. J., 2001,, *Trends in Cognitive Sciences*, 5 (10), 418-425.

Tolle, E., 2010, *The Power of Now, A Guide to Spiritual Enlightenment*, Novato, Ca: Namaste Publishing and New World Library (Kindle Edition).

Tolle, E., 2009, *A New Earth: Create a Better Life*, Penguin Books (Kindle Edition).

Tong, J., 2008, Barriers to networking for women in a UK professional service, *Gender in Management*, 23 (7), 484-505.

Twenge, J. M., 1997a, Changes in masculine and feminine traits over time: a meta-analysis, *Sex Roles*, 36 (5/6), 305-326.

Twenge, J. M., 1997b, Attitudes toward women, 1970-1995, A meta-analysis, *Psychology of Women Quarterly*, 21 (1), 35-52.

Twenge, J. M., 2009, Status and gender: the paradox of progress in an age of narcissism, *Sex Roles*, 61 (5/6), 338-340.

Twenge, J. M., and Campbell, S. M., 2008, Generational differences in psychological traits and their impact on the workplace, *Journal of Managerial Psychology*, 23 (8), 862-877.

Twenge, J. M., Campbell, W. K., and Gentile, B., 2012, Male and female pronoun use in U.S. books reflects women's status, 1900–2008, *Sex Roles*, 67 (9/10), 488-493.

Vanderbroeck, P., 2009, The traps that keep women from reaching the top and how to avoid them, *Journal of Management Development*, 29 (9), 764-770.

Vidhya, A., 2012, *The Price of Motherhood: Women and Part-Time Work*, Resolution Foundation, http://www.resolutionfoundation.org/media/media/downloads/The_price_of_motherhood_-_women_and_part-time_work.pdf.

Vinkenburg, C. J. et al., 2011, An exploration of stereotypical beliefs about leadership styles: is transformational leadership a route to women's promotion?, *The Leadership Quarterly*, 22 (1),10-21.

Wai, J. et al., 2010, Sex differences in the right tail of cognitive abilities: a 30 year examination, *Intelligence: A Multidisciplinary Journal*, 38 (4), 412-423.

Waldfogel, J., 2011, Family-friendly policies, in Gregg, P., and Wadsworth, J., (ed.), *Labour Market In Winter: The State of Working Britain*, Oxford: Oxford University Press.

Wallis, K. C. and Poulton, J. L., 2001, *Internalization: The Origins and Construction of Internal Reality*, Buckingham; Philadelphia: Open University Press.

Walsch, N. D., 1995, *Conversations with God, An Uncommon Dialogue, Book One*, London: Hodder & Stoughton.

Walsch, N. D., 1997, *Conversations with God, An Uncommon Dialogue Book Two*, London: Hodder & Stoughton.

Walsch, N. D., 1998, *Conversations With God, An Uncommon Dialogue, Book Three*, London: Hodder & Stoughton.

Warren, T., 2010, Penalties of part-time work across Europe, in Scott, J., Crompton, R., and Lyonette, C., (ed.), *Gender Inequalities in the 21st Century: New Barriers and Continuing Constraints*, Cheltenham, Edward Elgar.

Walter, N., 2010, *Living Dolls, The Return of Sexism*, London: Virago.

Wexler, B. 2006, *Brain and Culture: Neurobiology, Ideology and Social Change*, Cambridge, Mass.; London: MIT Press.

White, M. J., and White, G. B., 2006, *Sex Roles: A Journal of Research*, 55 (3/4), 259-266.

Williams, J. E., and Best, D. L., 1982, *Measuring Sex Stereotypes: A Thirty-nation Study*, Beverly Hills; London: Sage.

White, K., Bagilhole, B., and Riordan, S., 2012, The gendered shaping of university leadership in Australia, South Africa and the United Kingdom, *Higher Education Quarterly*, 66 (3), 293-307.

Wood, J., 2009, *Gendered Lives: Communication, Gender and Culture*, Australia, United Kingdom: Thomson/Wadsworth.

Wood, R. G., Corcoran, M. E. and Courant, P. N., 1993, Pay differences among the highly

paid: the male-female earnings gap in lawyers' salaries, *Journal of Labor Economics*, 11 (3): 417–441.

Young, K., Wolkowitz, C., and McCullagh, R., (ed.), 1984, *Of Marriage and the Market: Women's Subordination in Internationally Perspective*, London: CSE.

Websites:

http://www.ayncatessullivan.com/how-to-awaken-a-mans-heart-keys-to-the-divine-masculine/

http://www.deloitte.com/view/en_US/us/About/Inclusion/Womens-Initiative/index.htm.

http://www.blog.gaiam.com/quotes/topics/blind-spot.

http://www.dnafiles.org/chimp-chat/day-four.

http://www.earthstar.newlibertyvillage.com/awakening.htm.

http://www.ec.europa.eu/social/main.jsp?catId=777&langId=en.

http://www.europeanpwn.net/index.php?article_id=29.

http://www.glassdoor.co.uk/Salaries/hr-manager-salary-SRCH_KO0, 10.htm.

http://www.goodreads.com/quotes/73528-compassion-is-the-radicalism-of-our-time.

http://www.healthcareers.about.com/od/compensationinformation/tp/Doctor-Salaries.htm

http://www.indeed.com/salary?q1=personnel+Manager&l1=United+States

http://www.mitchellteachers.org/WorldHistory/MrMEarlyHumans Project/PDFs/PaleolithictoNeolithicDescriptions.pdf.

http://www.reducingstereotypethreat.com

http://www.religioustolerance.org/femquote.htm.

http://www.startupdonut.co.uk/blog/tag/Hilary-Devey.

http://www.ted.com/talks/brene_brown_on_vulnerability.html.

http://www.thinkbigpartners.com/start-a-business/202-the-importance-of-a-mission-statement.html.

http://www.zeepedia.com/read.php?theories_of_gender_development_ 2_the_behavioral_approach_gender_issues_in_psychology&b= 88&c=10.

INDEX

alienation xx, 52, 74, 206, 248, 251, 253
ambitions xvii, 195
androcentric 105, 116, 148, 181, 182, 205, 209, 245, 246, 262
androcentricity 4, 13, 128, 201, 208, 245, 258, 262
androgynous
    construal of leadership 164
    non 199
    people 100, 101
    perceived as 199
androgyny 99, 101, 102, 198
anxiety 42, 67, 95, 101, 119, 121, 139
appreciation 92, 230
Archer and Lloyd xxii, xxiii, 4, 9, 10, 11, 100, 101, 112
a socially constructed identity xx, 74
assertive 41, 95, 100, 101, 105, 106, 107, 163, 164, 165, 166, 188, 189, 204
assertiveness 6, 105, 140, 257
associate the feminine with lack of power 86
attention 22, 51, 54, 74, 88, 126, 127, 132, 160, 198, 208, 210, 218, 250, 252, 261
attributes 140
    caring 71
    communal 183
    feminine 89, 101, 190, 191, 198
    feminine and masculine 102, 191, 192, 193, 200, 249
    gender 32, 249
    masculine 90, 105, 191, 193, 251, 259
    stereotyped 111, 112, 123
    two sets (feminine and masculine) of 193, 194
    women and men don't have access to the full range of 75, 99

authentic 205, 261
autocratic 189
autonomy 41, 222, 224, 227, 228, 235, 240, 245
awareness 4, 22, 59, 82, 109, 117, 123, 124, 131, 247

B

Babcock and Laschever 76, 93, 114, 115, 117, 119, 159, 160, 167, 180, 189
babies 33, 75, 130, 157, 242, 260
balance 103, 160, 193, 199, 200, 201, 231, 232, 239, 244, 261
barriers to women's advancement 140, 158, 178
behaviour
    aggressive 26, 96
    assertive 164, 166
    communal 167
    conditioned 92, 132, 251
    differences in 15, 190, 192, 249, 255
    expectations in the workplace 204
    females encouraged to engage in care and service oriented 29
    gender and xx, 60, 61, 76, 78, 90, 93, 131, 255
    harmony between environment and xxiv, 19, 20, 29, 133, 203, 216, 218, 249, 255
    impact of expectations on 82, 83, 84, 85, 119
    influence of stereotypes on 25, 26, 96, 117, 139
    learned 76, 93
    males encouraged to engage in achievement oriented 29, 93
    masculine 39, 190
    mind and 129, 216

equal sharing of housework
and 183
integral to a woman's role
172, 183
men unsuited for 41
mothers' over involvement in 70
participate in 174
responsibility for 72, 107
sharing housework and 106
women fulfil their gendered
identity through 46
women more suited for xxi, 2, 40
childless 142, 162, 186, 191, 231
Chodorow, Nancy 38, 41, 42, 46, 48,
56, 57, 60, 86, 87, 95, 96, 148
cognition 89, 90, 128
cognitive ability 8, 10, 126, 129, 190
Coltrane, Scott 56, 63, 66, 172, 175,
177, 178, 233, 268
command and control 187, 189, 210,
221, 225, 237, 245, 259
communal 14, 95, 97, 98, 105,
107, 108, 111, 138, 148, 163,
164, 165, 166, 168, 183, 189,
190, 204
communication 54, 139, 169, 197, 198,
210, 233, 238
communion 97, 103, 138, 148,
163, 189
community 46, 153, 187, 193, 202,
229, 230
companies 159, 199, 211, 224, 225,
229, 241
company 133, 159, 200, 225, 227, 232
compassion 17, 97, 104, 193, 194, 195,
230, 252, 256, 257, 259, 261
competence 8, 12, 67, 71, 97, 105, 115,
117, 165, 167, 179, 214
competitive 14, 26, 30, 41, 93,
122, 165, 189, 202, 219, 229,
237, 259

competitiveness 7, 14, 29, 40, 41, 76,
130, 131, 205
conditioned femininity xxiii, xxv, 37,
38, 39, 40, 45, 46, 47, 52, 55,
56, 63, 64, 67, 74, 78, 90, 101,
104, 105, 140, 190, 191, 192,
193, 194, 195, 196, 198, 199,
200, 203, 204, 206, 244, 245,
253, 256, 258, 259
conditioned masculinity 192, 193,
226, 243, 254, 256, 259
confidence xvi, 4, 12, 13, 57, 97, 112,
138, 167, 197
conformity 59, 91, 93, 96, 98, 168, 170
confound 190, 191, 203
confounding sex with gender 191, 206
congruent 30, 126, 183, 260
Connell, Raewyn 34, 35, 36, 38, 39,
45, 52, 63, 141
conscious 123, 124, 126, 128, 129,
158, 160, 202, 207, 222,
251, 253
consciousness 61, 109, 110, 111, 113,
117, 127, 135, 181, 206, 207,
229, 248, 249, 251
consensus-building 189
constrained xv, 5, 7, 93, 106, 172, 183,
185, 191, 244
contemporary societies xvii, 194, 195,
253, 259
continuous work 6, 155, 156
contradictions 37, 64, 79
control 18, 21, 24, 29, 36, 43, 44, 50,
52, 60, 67, 69, 97, 101, 106, 112,
115, 121, 123, 133, 158, 170,
174, 196, 220, 221, 222, 224,
226, 227, 231, 250
controlling 98, 116, 133, 150, 161,
200, 226, 243
control over genes. *See* epigenetics

conversation xv, 3, 32, 36, 57, 127, 148, 156, 203, 212, 214, 230, 236, 240
corporate social responsibility 202
corporation 168, 169
creativity 193, 197, 222, 234, 246
Cross and Madson 84, 85, 88

D

Damasio, Antonio 22, 55
decision making xxi, 55, 189, 226, 228, 259
Deloitte and Touche 159, 160, 211
Denmark 97, 105, 141, 142, 145, 153, 154, 156
depressed entitlement. *See* beliefs, women's gender beliefs and depressed entitlement
depression xxi, 61, 174
descriptions 33, 39, 40, 90
desirable 56, 83, 99, 100, 140
Devine, Patricia 126, 129, 207, 208, 269
dichotomies 7, 135, 243, 244, 245
dichotomous 36, 219, 244, 245, 252
dichotomy 25, 28, 35, 220, 243, 244
differences
    and divisions between women and men xix, xx, 78, 81, 93, 193, 203, 208, 244, 248, 253
    between women and men 1, 2, 5, 6, 8, 28, 95, 115, 150, 191, 192, 256
    disappearing 220
    gender 41, 118
    in cognitive abilities 10
    in entitlement 116
    innate 3, 4, 138
    justify power and status 111, 114
    no 3, 8, 216

psychological 12, 36
sex xxiv, 4, 9, 10, 11, 12, 13, 14, 17, 25, 28, 39, 40, 80, 81, 83, 95, 105, 113, 144, 150, 152, 188, 190, 191, 192, 208, 210, 211, 250, 255, 256
the illusion of 77
the persistence of 152
wage 115, 116
discourses xxiii, xxiv, xxv, 34, 36, 44, 68, 70, 72, 79, 89, 110, 128, 152, 155, 157, 181, 203, 230, 250
discrimination 3, 110, 124, 129, 150, 151, 161, 164, 209
Dispenza, Jo 19, 20, 79, 132, 186
dispositions 31, 78, 86, 98, 130, 132
distribution 9, 10, 11, 14, 151, 175
division of labour 36, 37, 46, 75, 135, 175, 177, 208, 243, 244
DNA 19, 20
dogma xxi, xxii, 81, 89, 108
domain 88, 118, 139, 140, 155, 181, 220, 231
domestic
    division of labour 181
    duties 40, 46, 63, 75, 122, 179, 183
    spaces 63, 106, 183, 220
    sphere 46, 219, 244
    violence 262
    work 173, 174, 175, 179, 183
dominance 6, 37, 40, 52, 53, 95, 97, 192
dominant 45, 49, 50, 55, 58, 64, 65, 67, 69, 80, 88, 95, 107, 172, 191, 210, 214, 245
domination 25, 44, 50, 52, 253, 259
Drucker, Peter 201
Dyer, Wayne 207, 210, 212
dysfunctional 68, 160, 242, 260

E

Eagly, Alice 81, 83, 85, 91, 97, 140, 196, 198, 199, 221
Eagly and Karau 164, 189
economic production 7, 95, 105, 251
economic resources 46
education 107, 110, 136, 137, 138, 140, 153, 156, 175, 181
    and gendered expectations 141
    attainment 1, 6, 136, 143, 144, 158, 181, 186
    caring through providing 68
    choices xxv, 146
    females avoiding STEM fields of 136
    gender and 45, 166
    higher xvi, xvii, 8, 136, 143, 165
    secondary 136, 143, 144
    tertiary 136, 143, 144, 181, 186
egalitarian 56, 121, 124, 128, 177, 178
Einstein, Albert 195, 251
embracing xxiii, xxv, 64, 196, 205, 220, 242, 243, 257
emotional
    competence xxi, 50, 74, 99
    connection xxi, 65, 75, 252
    control in men 51
    dependency 61, 75
    disconnection 195
    expression 51, 52, 206, 249, 251
    freedom 56, 58, 251
    incompetence xxi
    information 102, 192
    needs 52, 57
    rewards 71, 174
    support 33, 53, 173
    women as emotional workers 53, 56, 173
    work 71, 95
emotionality
    as a threat to masculinity 52

vs. rationality 50
emotions 18, 19, 22, 29, 30, 49, 50, 51, 54, 55, 58, 59, 85, 87, 94, 120, 129, 158, 194, 250, 252, 269
empathisers 8
empathy xxi, 29, 40, 63, 71, 75, 95, 97, 130, 197
employee 163
employees 116, 125, 144, 161, 162, 163, 169, 170, 173, 189, 197, 199, 202, 210, 211, 212, 220, 222, 223, 224, 225, 226, 228, 229, 231, 232, 233, 234, 235, 236, 237, 238, 239, 240, 241, 242, 245, 267
employer 2, 68, 171, 219, 223
employment
    a spectacular rise in women's 143
    choices xxv
    female 141, 142, 143, 152, 156, 182, 186
    full time 213
    gap 143, 144
    opportunities 147, 153, 158
    outcomes xxv, 145, 283
    paid 1, 37, 46, 56, 79, 98, 108, 141, 143, 151, 155
    participation rate 153
    part time xv, 7, 125, 144, 145, 150, 154, 156, 176, 188, 212, 213
    rate 141, 142, 143, 144, 186
    temporary 143, 145
empower 20, 196, 197, 225, 228
empowering others 222, 243
empowerment 204, 205, 221, 222, 225, 227, 228, 243, 245
engineering 107, 112, 124, 136, 137, 146, 151, 181, 234
Enlightenment 49, 50, 54, 194
entitlement

beliefs 113
pay 115
women's depressed xvi, 113, 114,
    115, 116, 167, 196
work 170, 171
environment 28, 54, 79, 88, 109, 117,
    129, 131, 133, 160, 223, 234,
    249, 255
brain and 15, 16, 19, 21
changing environment to change
    our mind 216
gene interaction with xxii, 20,
    25, 28
harmoney between behaviour and.
    See behaviour, harmoney
    between environment and
harmoney between mind and 25,
    94, 216
role of emotions in shaping our
    relationship with 22
environmental
conditions 11, 218
events 15, 22
factors 14, 27
influence 16, 24
inputs 255
signals 18, 19, 20, 23, 28, 29, 54,
    94, 120, 203, 218, 249, 255
epigenetic
control mechanisms 24, 28, 29,
    84, 85, 94, 130, 133, 182,
    203, 216, 218, 249, 255
studies 203, 249
epigenetics xxiv, 18, 20, 21, 22, 23,
    29, 216
equal
family leave 219, 220
labour market outcomes 201
sharing of housework 179, 183
status 226, 255
equality

discourses 156
gender 11, 44, 56, 69, 72, 110,
    111, 152, 157, 175, 212, 250
in caring 65, 70
principles 79
sex xvi, xix, xxiii, xxiv, xxv, 1, 11,
    31, 47, 69, 79, 128, 133,
    146, 152, 154, 155, 156, 157,
    202, 203, 208, 209, 213,
    215, 216, 226, 239, 243,
    244, 245
vs. sameness 4
executive xv, xix, 1, 107, 159, 181, 182,
    199, 210, 211, 215, 221, 224
expectations 29, 40, 73, 80, 81, 82, 83,
    84, 85, 87, 89, 91, 96, 100, 104,
    133, 159, 166, 188, 197, 204,
    237, 255
experiment 23, 25, 115, 117, 118, 119,
    122, 180, 241, 256
expressive 52, 97, 100, 105, 180

F

face time 187, 214, 220, 235, 238,
    241, 242
failing to become masculine 90, 179
false
assumptions of the 'ideal
    worker' 6
belief 183, 255
career-life choices xvi, 5, 173,
    182, 191
consciousness 111, 112, 165, 167,
    182, 254, 255. *See* beliefs,
    women's gender beliefs and
    false consciousness
family
care 65, 159, 184, 187, 222, 238
friendly policies 187, 202, 214

life xvi, 6, 33, 73, 95, 141, 177,
179, 184, 185, 186, 187,
191, 215, 242, 260, 262
fatherhood 56, 65, 67, 73
fathering 65, 73, 266
fathers 6, 53, 56, 58, 63, 65, 66, 67,
70, 72, 73, 93, 95, 96, 147, 150,
152, 170, 232, 261
fear 37, 42, 43, 50, 51, 55, 61, 80,
90, 119, 130, 131, 139, 182,
193, 202, 220, 228, 235, 242,
243, 252
femaleness 35, 38, 86
feminine
confusing the gendered for the
real 256
devaluation of the 67, 195
fear and dread of the 41, 42, 56,
59, 62, 90, 202, 243
gendered 258
men's rejection of the 206
mututally exclusive with the
masculine 32, 40, 63
powerful and empowering 196
the awesome 205, 258
the real 195, 205, 262
women's fear of being truly 204
femininity
and masculinity as pillars of
gender 38
associated with 40, 52, 179,
193, 206
conditioned. See conditioned
femininity
confounding with women 90,
190, 191, 195, 203
confusion about masculinity and
37, 256
constructs of masculinity and
xxiv, xxv, 39, 40
de-gendering masculinity and 206

embracing 75, 206, 207, 243, 257,
258, 261
exclusively assigned to women 40,
78, 203, 252
incongruent with leadership
165, 199
masculinity and power 48
mixing with masculinity 198
repressed in men 190, 252
the centrality of mothering to
47, 72
trends in masculinity and 107
feminism xviii, xix, 108, 171, 173
feminists 127, 205, 261
fertility 186, 191, 230
fighting sexism 134, 201, 204
Finland 97, 141, 144, 145, 153, 154,
155, 156, 176
flexibility xv, 87, 126, 129, 151, 213,
229, 231, 232, 233, 234, 235,
237, 238
flexible work. See work, flexible
arrangements
folk wisdom 12, 25, 27, 102, 192, 252
France 142, 145, 149, 155, 176
freedom 33, 131, 160, 189
free will 17, 20, 127, 132, 207
fulfilment xxv, 7, 53, 75, 77, 78, 100,
132, 140, 187, 195, 209, 220,
224, 237, 239, 252, 254, 261
full time xv, 6, 150, 153, 154, 174, 176,
178, 184, 188, 212, 213, 214,
220, 229

G

Geis, Florence 40, 41, 85, 119, 120,
121, 122, 123, 126, 127,
129, 162
gender
as a social construct 74
beliefs 111, 113, 203

lower status 89, 106, 111, 114, 165, 166, 168, 174, 175, 179, 183, 187, 254, 257

M

macrocosm 202, 219

Maitland and Thomson 170, 189, 222, 224, 230, 232, 233, 234, 236

male
   dominance 8, 45, 46, 49, 108
   dominated societies xv, 12, 14, 255, 259
   identity 61, 90
   managers 199
   power and privilege 44, 45, 52
   superiority 17, 31, 190
   supremacy 8, 29, 47, 78, 81, 249

maleness 35, 38, 58, 86, 140

malleable 15, 84, 87

management xv, 6, 147, 149, 157, 161, 165, 168, 189, 197, 201, 214, 219, 222, 226, 229, 233, 237, 240, 243, 245

manager 80, 86, 149, 222, 226, 236, 240, 245

managers' distrust in employees 223, 236

manifest 29, 30, 103, 109, 193, 203, 205, 207, 253

marital satisfaction 177, 178, 180

marriage xvii, 32, 33, 37, 38, 43, 66, 76, 132, 190, 193, 244, 250, 260

masculine
   all things 187, 230
   and feminine are mutually exclusive 32
   boys are raised to be 192
   code 43, 252
   embrace the real 257
   identity 48, 51, 65, 67, 86

project 52, 62, 90, 187, 190, 203, 242, 257
   standards of success 204
   superiority 56, 194
   the real 205, 259

masculinisation
   of contemporary women 5, 204, 206
   of the workplace xvi, 3, 5, 185, 190, 243

masculinity
   and power 45
   a socially viable 57, 62, 72
   as problematic 56
   associated with 40
   breadwinner 73
   caring 65, 66
   configuration of 47
   confounding with men 191, 194, 203
   constructs of xxv
   de-gendering 40
   different and oppositional to femininity 42, 48
   dominant 49, 50, 55, 58, 67, 69, 170, 210, 214, 252, 253
   embracing in women 207
   emotionality as a threat to 52
   exclusively assigned to men xxiii, 40, 41, 65, 102, 203
   gendered xxiv, 37, 78, 200, 205
   hegemonic 45, 64, 65, 213
   socially constructed 38
   tempering with femininity 103
   uncaring 259
   underpinned by men's economic provision 47
   untenable ideals for 74

maternal 48, 60, 66, 142

maternity leave 2, 153, 171, 212, 219, 242

maths 2, 8, 10, 14, 17, 29, 83, 107, 112, 118, 122, 136, 137, 139, 140, 146, 148, 181

microcosm 170, 202, 219

mind 28, 29, 133, 210, 216, 253
  changing our 127
  conscious 127, 129
  intuitive 251
  response to environment 29
  subconscious xxiv, 36, 37, 90, 120, 121, 123, 127, 128, 129, 132, 207
  system 22, 29, 109, 133

misperceptions 30, 123, 158

mission statement 211

mother xiii, xvi, xvii, xix, 3, 34, 41, 43, 47, 56, 60, 66, 67, 70, 72, 76, 80, 86, 87, 92, 93, 95, 96, 98, 131, 142, 147, 148, 150, 152, 170, 171, 174, 179, 181, 232, 240, 251, 261

mothering 38, 47, 66, 67, 69, 87, 131

mutually exclusive 74, 78, 86, 243

myth 47, 48, 54, 89, 128, 192, 193, 235, 247, 248, 252, 253, 260

N

narcissism 105, 195, 205

natural xxiii, 23, 24, 41, 47, 68, 80, 115, 135, 164, 193, 247, 249

negotiations 115, 116, 118, 167, 168, 264

Neo Freudian 38, 41, 48

nervous system 15, 22, 30, 54, 133

neural connections 17, 30

neurobiology 15, 28, 291

neuroplasticity xxiv, 15, 17, 216

neurotransmitters 30, 54

nocebo effect 24

Nordic countries xxiv, xxv, 34, 141, 145, 146, 152, 153, 154, 155, 156, 157, 250

Norway xxiv, 70, 97, 141, 143, 145, 153, 154, 155, 156, 170, 176

Norwegian 65, 70, 72, 98, 155

nurturance xxi, 35, 53, 56, 57, 75, 76, 130, 193, 198, 222, 249

nurturant
  imperative 70, 76

nurturant imperative 180

nurturing 33, 47, 56, 71, 73, 91, 93, 95, 180, 197

O

obscure 43, 76, 98, 106, 132, 256

occupational
  class 175, 176
  mobility 168
  segregation 146, 147, 148
  status 70, 175

OECD countries xxiii, xxiv, 1, 10, 136, 141, 142, 143, 144, 145, 146, 151, 152, 153, 154, 186

organisation xxiii, 6, 46, 116, 134, 155, 158, 169, 197, 198, 201, 203, 212, 215, 221, 228, 239, 241

organisational 5, 222, 240

organisations xxiii, 141, 157, 160, 196, 202, 209, 211, 213, 215, 224, 226, 237, 239, 257

other-focused 130, 132, 190, 193, 198

overarching 41, 43, 76, 114

P

paid work xxiii, 46, 47, 63, 67, 68, 70, 72, 80, 106, 110, 131, 146, 150, 185, 188, 193, 213, 257

paradigm 5, 6, 20, 28, 152, 185, 187, 209

parental leave 153, 170, 171

170, 181, 182, 185, 194, 196,
200, 204, 208, 211, 215, 216,
218, 219, 242, 245, 248, 253,
255, 258
reversing 204, 207, 216, 219, 220
the truth about 261
sexist xxii, 3, 69, 132, 133, 134, 203,
207, 243
assumptions 211
behavioural reality 203
patterns 134
sexual vi, 32, 33, 37, 42, 43, 46, 88,
109, 135, 188, 243, 250
division of labour 46, 135,
194, 243
relations 32, 33
shame 48, 51, 55, 57, 58, 182, 250
slavery xxii, 110, 255
social
conditioning xix, 25, 33, 86, 87,
89, 91, 92, 93, 99, 130, 132,
157, 192, 249, 255, 256,
258, 259
culture 17, 20, 21, 25, 27, 29,
30, 31, 34, 38, 40, 45, 47,
54, 85, 87, 105, 133, 158,
203, 214, 215, 234, 235,
245, 260
discourses. See discourses
entities 32, 78, 91
environment xxv, 28, 30, 84, 88,
130, 134
identity xvi, 8, 35, 43, 157
norms 35, 40, 89, 154
system xix, xxi, 33, 36, 109
socialisation 25, 42, 59, 60, 76, 91, 92,
93, 96
socially constructed xx, 38, 45, 69, 74,
86, 90, 251
society at large xxv, 43, 86, 187, 259
socio-cultural environment 29

status 4, 8, 237, 251, 253, 257,
258, 259
abolishment of 228
as a proxy for competence 165
characteristic 166, 167
father 73
hierarchy xvi, 74, 111, 167, 172,
219, 245
higher. See higher status
loss of when men care 58, 64,
65, 66
lower. See lower status
males distance themselves from
femininity to preserve
higher 42
marker 166
men apprehensive about
losing 226
men overly focused on their 179
only masculine is seen as deserving
of 170
privileged. See higher status
quo xvii, 109, 110, 114, 242
social 110, 115
women's subordinated xx, 8, 81,
108, 135, 179, 182, 205
stay at home 67, 187, 214
Steele and Aronson 117, 139
STEM
careers 138
fields 181, 182
studies 137
stereotypes
agentic leader 164
and conscious beliefs 127
as a system of justification 111
communal female 164, 189
conscious 42, 48, 80, 81, 109,
120, 123, 129, 133, 139,
163, 288
cultural 140

trust 169, 193, 197, 222, 223, 224, 226, 234, 239, 240, 246
truth v, xxii, 3, 10, 34, 74, 120, 157, 204, 206, 211, 223, 248, 253, 260, 262, 271
Twenge, Jean 6, 100, 104, 105, 106, 108, 195, 230

U

uncaring 179, 202
unemotional 63, 93, 250
unhappiness xx, 248, 253, 260
universal principles of justice 103, 201
universe 195, 248
unpaid work 63, 80, 146, 152, 154, 155, 170, 174, 175, 187, 188, 190, 191

V

vertical segregation 148, 151
vulnerability 5, 51, 52, 55, 56, 57, 58, 59, 60, 61, 62, 64, 71, 90, 118, 252, 254, 266

W

wage gap 113, 145, 149, 150, 151, 154
welfare state 153
wellbeing 101, 153, 174, 194
Western societies xviii, xxiii, 49, 105, 230, 250
Wexler, Bruce 16, 79
who we are xx, 8, 33, 34, 74, 84, 85, 89, 157, 205, 253, 260, 261
wife xv, xvi, 34, 48, 95, 96, 148, 178, 179, 181
womanhood 35, 70, 258
women
    and careers 172, 180, 211
    are conditioned to be other-focused 46

are disliked when they are agentic 140, 166, 204
are feminine xxiii, 102, 190, 192, 243, 248, 256
centrality of childcare to 72
concentrated in lower-ranked and lower-paid positions 149
feel entitled to less pay 113
high achieving 195, 206, 258
leaders 6, 164, 189
managers 149, 160, 189
seen as neglectful 43, 76, 98
the nature of 30, 108, 163, 188
what it is to be a 'woman' 181
work 170, 171, 220, 221, 263, 273, 282, 289
    assigning to men xxiii, 254
    continuous history 6
    environment xxv, 99, 133, 159, 163, 211, 218, 245
    flexible arrangements 171, 184, 187, 233
    flexibly 213, 232
    hours 144, 153, 173, 176, 193, 235
    -life 244, 245
    -life and home-life integration 219, 227
    -life balance 5, 212, 231, 239, 267
    -life conflict 155, 178
    -life separation from home-life 220, 239, 244
    men are more suited for xxi
    new 79, 237, 238, 245
    norms xv, 7, 155, 187, 188, 204, 209, 220, 242
    organisation 7, 186
    practices 3, 186, 191, 216, 220, 221, 239, 243
    rigid norms 173
    space 220, 242
    sphere 208